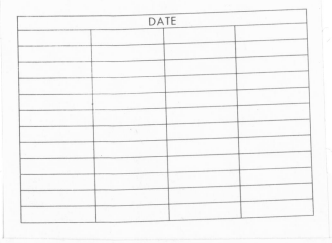

FAIR, SQUARE, AND LEGAL

FAIR, SQUARE, AND LEGAL

SAFE HIRING, MANAGING & FIRING PRACTICES TO KEEP YOU & YOUR COMPANY OUT OF COURT

Donald H. Weiss

amacom

American Management Association

This publication is designed to provide accurate and authoritative
information in regard to the subject matter covered. It is sold with
the understanding that the publisher is not engaged in rendering
legal, accounting, or other professional service. If legal advice or
other expert assistance is required, the services of a competent
professional person should be sought.

Library of Congress Cataloging-in-Publication Data

Weiss, Donald H., 1936–
    Fair, square, and legal : safe hiring, managing & firing practices to keep
you & your company out of court / Donald H. Weiss.
      p.   cm.
    Includes bibliographical references and index.
    ISBN 0-8144-5976-5 (hardcover)
    1. Labor laws and legislation—United States.   2. Personnel
management—United States.   I. Amacom.   II. Title.
    KF3457.W45   1991
    344.73'01—dc20   90-56196
    [347.3041]   CIP

Printing number

10   9   8   7   6   5   4

Table of Contents

Introduction   *vii*

Section I   Safe Hiring Practices   1

1   Safe Recruiting Practices   11
2   Safe Interviewing Practices   25
3   Safe Employment Decisions   44
4   Preventing Sex Discrimination in Hiring   59
5   Preventing Negligent Hiring   79

Section II   Safe Management Practices   89

6   Safe Evaluations and Promotions   93
7   Safe Management, the Right to Privacy, and
    Defamation   112
8   Preventing Sex Discrimination and Sexual
    Harassment on the Job   143
9   Mismanaging Disabled People   178
10 Employee Action Rights and Labor Laws   193

Section III   Safe Firing Practices   205

11 Safe Discipline and Firing Practices   209
12 Public Policy   230
13 Safe Management of Older Employees   246

Epilogue   Personnel Decisions: Where Are We
            Now?   *265*

Appendix   What Civil Rights and Other Personal
            Protection Laws Say   *279*

Index   *311*

Introduction

With Americans suing each other for most any reason, our times have been called the Age of Litigation. Some personnel decisions belong in court because they were intentionally harmful. Others, however, result from ignorance of the law or mistakes in judgment.

This book should help prevent your decisions from being challenged in court, but if they are, the suggestions made here should help you defend them. In short, this book should help make your personnel decisions legally safer than they would have been without it.

Most well-informed managers, once they understand the consequences of some of the decisions others have made, would not make the same mistakes, but the complexity of legal issues sometimes seems too much for a nonlawyer to grasp. That complexity often restrains managers from learning all they can about laws or procedures that could guide their actions. And often, fearing to make the wrong decision, conscientious managers refrain from taking actions that are entirely legal.

I hope to reduce the complexity and fears by simplifying the issues and taking some of the uncertainty out of the decision-making process. Safe management is an informed and proactive management that follows essentially commonsense rules.

A Management Book

Fair, Square, and Legal is written about managers, for managers, by a manager. At the same time, to ensure accuracy, the book has been reviewed by a practicing attorney.

This book should be read by all managers because it addresses managers' concerns and practices in all sectors of economic society—private for-profit, private not-for-profit, and public—and should be useful to policy-making executives and policy-implementing managers alike. References to the "organization" are really to the managers who operate it. They make the decisions that wind up in court. The book is therefore written for general managers as well as for human resources professionals.

The legal picture examined in this book affects three basic aspects of personnel decisions: hiring, management practices, and discharging. For our purposes, all people-management activities fit into one of the three analytic categories laid out in the table below:

MANAGEMENT ACTIVITIES

Hiring	Management Practices	Discharging
Advertising	Training	Discharging
Recruiting	Evaluating	(with or
Interviewing	performance	without
Testing	Promoting	cause)
Selecting	Disciplining	Downsizing
Compensating (pay/benefits)		

Many organizations (especially large companies or agencies) write policy manuals that govern these management activities. Most do not. Still, managers frequently get themselves in trouble with or without policies to guide them. In fact, the policies themselves can produce more problems than they prevent if they are applied incorrectly.

The Management Activities Table reproduced here simplifies the activities of management, although managing is not simple; it is a rose garden only to the extent that you have to watch out for the thorns.

Fair and consistent application of personnel policies defines safe management and also contributes to proactive management, that is, preventing problems or at least preventing them from getting out of hand. Explaining your positions on employment contracts, discrimination, harassment, references, disciplinary action, performance reviews, and personal conduct benefits you and your organization by reducing liabilities *and* by inspiring more commitment from your employees to achieve your business objectives.

Even if they are not explicit, your *business* objectives and the employees' *personal* objectives interact in every employment situation. Sound, therefore safe, management practices capitalize on a blend of those objectives through policies and practices that show a genuine concern for people and their rights, as well as for furthering business objectives. Setting policies where none exist or enforcing those that do can prevent *some* (but not all) legal disasters. Besides, respecting your people and their rights makes good management sense.

When it comes to the legalities that affect management decisions and practices, most people plead ignorance. In many cases the plea is true; in some, it is not. Most of the time, the law comes into play only after someone simply ignores the dictates of sound management thinking. Effective managers usually do not violate the law even if they do not know what the law itself says. Nevertheless, every manager should be aware of the laws that personnel actions could violate.

Few managers consciously decide to breach a contract, or to discriminate, or to violate public policy. Instead, they find themselves in trouble because they did not think at all or because they spoke or acted out of ignorance of the law. Still, ignorance of the law is no defense. Managers should know what the laws say they can and cannot do as managers, and senior managers have a legal obligation to teach middle and first line their rights and duties.

If you are a *policy maker*, you should be able to explain the laws that affect management's personnel decisions. You should use the information in this book to examine and test your existing policies against our models, instead of waiting for warnings of impending disasters. If written policies do not exist, you should be able to devise them. You should then teach your middle- and first-line managers what they can and cannot do under the law. Then, no one can make the futile ignorance plea.

If you are a *middle or first-line manager*, by taking the steps I describe, you should be able to make day-to-day personnel decisions within the limits of the law. At the same time, do not ignore the policy issues. While perhaps only senior managers or key executives *make* policy decisions, *all* managers can *influence* policy. An informed management is akin to an informed electorate, and armed with the information this book provides, you will be in a better position to protect yourself, the organization, and your employees from unpleasant working conditions, violations of the law, or messy, expensive courtroom challenges to your actions. As you read, watch for how policies could be jeopardizing the organization. If you think that you see ways of preventing the organization from becoming embroiled in time wasting, money wasting, or needless courtroom battles, you should notify upper management.

Issues, Answers, and Real-Life Cases

This book addresses many legal issues you could possibly confront when you make personnel decisions: not just civil rights issues *or* contract issues, but both. Key terms are defined whenever needed. I make clear what you as a manager cannot do and outline the steps or procedures you can utilize. Each chapter ends with a Casebook.

The section in each chapter on *what you cannot do* as a manager covers legal or common law prohibitions you should be aware of to avoid violating the law due to ignorance and to avoid errors of omission or errors of judgment. A second section in each chapter then tells you *what you can do* within the law.

The Casebook section is included for these reasons:

1. To illustrate the legal issues underlying my suggestions and document the validity of what I have said with judicial, or EEOC, or NLRB decisions
2. To point out cases in which the courts have defined key terms, e.g., "because of sex," in unusual ways
3. To give you a chance to compare your organization's situation with cases that could affect it
4. To provide materials for improving management safety, e.g., a "safe" employment application

I have framed the cases within both their legal and management contexts. While the *legal* issues are very complex—even judges and attorneys will disagree over them—the management practices that could have prevented these legal hassles are much more straightforward. You do not have to be an attorney to understand the management issues affected by common or statutory law.

To make the cases useful to you, I ask you to think through the issues to conclusions based on your experience. I ask you to question yourself, your opinions, or the way in which your organization operates. And I provide the answers that clarify the issues and also furnish useful tips to help you correct possible problems or prevent them from occurring.

That a particular courtroom scene was played out in some state other than yours or in a specific federal court could be immaterial. Cases from anywhere may be used as precedents on which your case will be decided. These decisions can help you evaluate some of your own words or actions or some of your organization's policies and procedures. Something you read could possibly lead to positive steps to prevent problems from arising.

The cases are real. Names have been changed, but not the essential facts, to protect the identities of the parties involved. Even though all these cases are a matter of public record, many happened a long time ago, and where penalties were imposed, the people involved—many of whom are no longer employed by the organizations implicated—paid them. To drag them through the court of public opinion serves no learning purpose. I follow this practice, which is followed by other publishers as well, only to prevent *needless* embarrassment.

By identifying what you cannot do and what you can do, as well as discussing sample cases, I try to answer these important questions:

1. What are the limits of your rights as an employer?
2. To what extent do the laws grant rights to employees?
3. How are your personnel decisions constrained by legal requirements or procedures?
4. What does having a policy manual do to your freedom of action?
5. What can you or your organization do to protect yourselves from lawsuits (or at least from losing them)?

But the most important question I try to answer is:

6. What can you do to be a more effective manager?

The Limits of This Book

I do not cover every possible management decision or every possible legal issue. I do address equal opportunity and collective action, and most other key personnel and legal issues that affect mainly white-collar, nonunion, industrial- or service-related employments. I deliberately exclude safety problems (under OSHA) and benefits concerns (under ERISA) because they involve too many large technical problems and are too complex to include for this type of book. An organization should have an OSHA officer to monitor safety requirements and a personnel manager to set up the insurance and benefit programs governed by ERISA (and, more recently, COBRA). A sequel about those laws may be in order, but this book already covers more than most single volumes do.

Regarding labor (union) issues, I cover only those aspects of the National Labor Relations Act (NLRA) that concern union organizing and other labor-management issues and stop short of talking about union shops. If a union contract limits your management actions, adapt these discussions to the contracts that bind you.

The book assumes that your organization does not have a set of employment and personnel policies, but if it does, you can check them against our recommendations and, if necessary, make or request revisions. Because of its generic nature, the book does not address your local issues, but it includes ways you and your organization can avoid being hauled into court or win in the event that you are. My recommendations could serve as models for writing policies and procedures, but please note that nothing in this book substitutes for an attorney's advice. If legal advice or other expert assistance is required, *the services of a competent professional person should be sought.**

The Epilogue of this book tries to put it into this perspective: Safe management is an effort to stay afloat in a sea of legal turmoil. I believe I have taken a balanced view that values both employee needs and rights and employer needs and rights. Sometimes I seem to come down heavy on one side or another, and that is probably because I sometimes (but not always) see the issues from within the same framework of values and perceptions as the court or other legal body.

It would not be honest to say that the book does not have a point of view. I take a long view. With history on which to build and the future as a guide, I take a backward- and forward-looking view of what I think is best for managers, their organizations, their employees, and society as a whole.

The New Personnel Climate

A new personnel climate drives the book's point of view. Employees (and former employees) have discovered their rights—not just civil rights, but also contract and tort rights. And most courts encourage them by awarding remedies and damages under contract law as well as civil rights and labor laws. Unless your organization protects itself, it could face claims of breach of contract, wrongful discharge, discrimination, harassment,

---

*Adapted from *Declaration of Principles Jointly Adopted by a Committee of the American Bar Association and a Committee of Publishers.*

or whatever. Almost as many possibilities for taking legal action exist as there are possibilities for making personnel decisions.

What policies govern your organization's hiring and firing decisions? If yours is a nonunion shop, does it exercise its right to employ at will or has it circumscribed its own rights by publishing and distributing a personnel handbook that unwittingly limits how you can manage your employees effectively?

What policies make clear that your organization hires, trains, and promotes people without regard to race, color, creed, national origin, religion, age, sex, or disability?

Does your management refuse to give out information about employees or former employees unless the other person has a need or right to know?

The publication and fair and consistent application of such policies may not *prevent* a hassle in a court or with the Equal Employment Opportunity Commission (EEOC) or with the National Labor Relations Board (NLRB), but it may help you win your day.

Here's a *partial* list, a mere sampling, of possible actions against your organization—and you personally—if you have not phrased your rules properly or if you do not follow those you have:

- ▸ Breach of contract for firing someone without just cause
- ▸ Retaliatory discharge for firing someone after he or she files a workers compensation claim or a harassment complaint or has been involved in a protected action to protest working conditions
- ▸ Violation of public policy because a supervisor denied an employee time off for jury duty
- ▸ Slander or defamation for telling a caller the reason for dismissing an employee for cause
- ▸ Sexual harassment for failure to take immediate action to remedy an ugly situation someone else created
- ▸ Wrongful discharge and breach of contract because your handbook calls for progressive disciplinary action and a manager skipped a step
- ▸ Sex discrimination because one of your managers pro-

moted an employee who granted sexual favors over an employee of the same gender who refused

- Age discrimination because your executive management reorganized a division to reduce costs by laying off the highest-paid managers, who also were the oldest
- Race discrimination because, in the absence of a job posting system, a black person with the proper qualifications did not know of an opening to which he or she could have been promoted

The list neither exhausts all the possibilities nor identifies those that occur most frequently. The situations identified all occur regularly and could occur at any time. Indeed, practically any personnel decision is open to challenge in court or before the EEOC or the NLRB, *or all three at the same time, in the same case.*

The Cost of Management Mistakes

Ignorance of the law, thoughtlessness, and, sometimes, plain stupidity cost U.S. organizations millions of dollars each year, not in production losses, but rather from mistakes in judgment that managers make when they hire, supervise, and discharge employees.

Take the following case, for example. There must be a more profitable way to spend nearly half a million dollars.

Kent Williamson was elated the day Discount Warehouse Sales hired him as a forklift driver. Bill Perry, the supervisor who hired him, had said, "Kent, when you come on board, you've got it made. We want our employees to feel they found a home here. As long as you do your job and meet our standards, you've got a job for life—at least, until you retire."

Much to Kent's dismay, things didn't work out that way. Without knowing why, Kent found himself out on the street, but once there he went straight to an attorney. He was much too young for early retirement.

Kent's attorney argued that not only did firing Kent contradict promises made to him when he was hired but that he was fired contrary to company policy statements that guaranteed him that he would not ever be fired without cause or without following a progression of disciplinary procedures mandated by the employee handbook. The employer, Kent's attorney argued, failed to meet any of these contractual obligations, and the Nevada Supreme Court agreed.

The employer, the court ruled, violated its "covenant of good faith and fair dealing." Williamson's payoff came to $382,120 in compensatory damages and $50,000 in punitive damages.[1]

Can your organization afford to waste that much money, too?

Very frequently, the courts agree with the plaintiff in situations such as the one described above. In fact, more than ever before, state and federal courts now rule in favor of employees who feel wronged—especially when they can pull out the employer's own oral and written statements as incriminating evidence. What better evidence can a victim have than a "smoking gun" in the defendant's hand?

The Future of Lawsuits

The major battles of the day, and for many years to come, take place in two different courtrooms. One involves employment at will (or termination at will), wrongful discharge, labor–management relations, and defamation. Much of Sections II and III concerns legal situations in which you, your organization, and your employees can find yourselves if you say things or take action outside the constraints of common law as well as statutory law. Since the outcomes may differ from court to court and from state to state, the questions raised by these courtroom sagas serve as warnings—that the cost in resources (money and time) may not be worth the struggle.

Civil rights battles are fought in the other courtoom, with many new issues emerging in addition to the familiar race bias cases. The EEOC did not go to sleep during the 1980s, as some people believe. Instead, it actively took up newer avenues: the claims of older employees, women, veterans, and disabled people. The claims come more quietly to the docket than did race discrimination claims in the past, but come they do—in growing numbers.

The Reagan Justice Department shifted administration policy by backing or supporting *employers* in class action and "pattern or practice" cases. Investigators have been required to identify specific instances of discrimination before bringing suit. To this extent, the federal government has reversed its stance on affirmative action, which could affect the way in which cases are handled for many years to come, unless later administrations shift back toward supporting affirmative action. The important impact on civil rights comes from the Supreme Court's sudden turn to the right.

As of the beginning of 1989, we cannot be too confident about what the courts will say about anything, especially about civil rights and equal opportunity. The so-called Reagan Court defends the First Amendment rights of the press and of dissident flag burners, but it takes a much more conservative stand on employment rights than has any Court in the last twenty-five years. The U.S. Supreme Court may have "eased the burden on employers," as one paper headlined, when it reinterpreted the basic theories of discrimination and removed the burden of proof in some bias cases. It did not, however, then say that managers are free to discriminate against minorities or women, older employees, or disabled people. Prudence still rules management decisions.

On the other hand, the opportunities for being damned if you do and damned if you don't as a result of social and legal climates in the United States have greatly increased. For example, make room for minorities and women in your labor force through preferential affirmative action programs, and white males will howl reverse discrimination. Hire white males, and minorities and women will howl bias. What's going on here?

The answer lies in values and perceptions. They play as large a role in legal decisions as they do in management decisions. The activist courts of the 1960s and 1970s valued equal employment rights of all citizens and perceived certain *classes* of people—racial and ethinic minorities, women, disabled people, Vietnam era veterans, and older employees—as receiving less than equal treatment. The activist court of the late 1980s valued equal employment rights of all citizens also, but perceived *individuals,* not classes, as receiving less than equal treatment. *Whole groups* of people do not apply for individual jobs, and that they are denied access to opportunities is a social and economic accident. Denial of opportunity is to be considered only case by case.

Herein lies the apparent paradox of the Reagan Court. A conservative U.S. Supreme Court values the *liberty* inherent in free speech rights for *all* people, as long as the exercise of speech does not present an "imminent danger" to society and the U.S. Government. On the other hand, a conservative Court is not equalitarian and does not value equal economic and employment rights for *groups* of employees.

The denial of equal opportunities in employment to groups of people is not perceived by the justices as an "imminent danger" to society and the United States Government. The injury, in their opinion, is to individuals, not to the groups to which they belong or to society. Here we see the importance of values and perceptions.

Because perceptions play a major role in judicial interpretation of laws, and because many activist groups and members of Congress share perceptions quite divergent from those of the U.S. Supreme Court, the controversy will continue to affect your decisions for a long time to come.

The pressures may seem to be off the employers' legal burden of proof, but the management burden of responsibility becomes more germane. I will also discuss the importance of the legal concept of intent, now that claims against unintentional bias have been weakened. Groups of employees may have lost one of their important accesses into the courts, but they have not been denied all their weapons. Keep in mind, of course, that new decisions and new laws change the rules, and it is important to keep abreast of the latest developments (this book reflects important decisions and legislation through the fall of 1990).

Acknowledgments

A book of this magnitude required the resources and help of many people—friends, colleagues, librarians, and editors. I especially want to thank Sara Morris, whose reading and rereading, questioning and challenging, helped make it all work.

Cases

1. 2 I.E.R. Cases 56 (Nev. Sup. Ct. 1987).

Section I
Safe Hiring Practices

Selecting one candidate from among a large group of potential employees can be a complicated and tedious process that at any point could become unsafe. Anyone who has ever recruited and hired new employees knows how true that is. Management values and perceptions permeate advertisements and other recruiting materials, applications, interview procedures or questions, as well as your actual hiring decisions. Those values and perceptions could draw civil rights fire unless they reflect contemporary social and economic necessities.

The five chapters that follow should help make the hiring process safer for management and you. In this brief introduction, I give reasons why civil rights laws are written and justify their social and economic value; I also define key terms, explain the consequences of not conforming to the laws, and explain what you cannot and can do under the law. The following chapters then deal with specific issues: advertising (Chapter 1), applications and interview questions (Chapter 2), making hiring decisions (Chapter 3), preventing sex discrimination (Chapter 4), and preventing negligence in hiring (Chapter 5).

Safe Management and Equal Opportunity Hiring

Twenty-five years after the Civil Rights Act of 1964 was passed, discrimination as defined in the Act still exists, and it is still illegal. Society can only try to reform itself through legislation, but the main issue underlying civil rights legislation—prejudice—cannot be erased by laws.

Prejudice means forming opinions or having feelings about a group of people on the basis of *special characteristics,* such as race, color, religion, ethnicity, sex, age, or disability, or making a judgment *in advance*—on the basis of stories, implications, or limited experiences—about people from a particular place or with certain characteristics or specific background. Therefore, anyone can be prejudiced toward anyone else. Most often, ignorance underlies the prejudice; what you don't know usually does hurt.

What you do not know about a group of people—ignorance—can lead to prejudice. What you think you know, but really do not—ignorance—almost always leads to prejudice. Broad, general statements about whole groups of people that impute bad traits or a lack of skills usually express prejudices. You have heard the gospel according to Archie Bunker.

On the other hand, broad or general statements that extol the virtues or favorable traits of a whole group of people usually express prejudices also. And too often, hiring decisions are made more on the basis of such prejudices than on applicants' knowledge, skill, availability, or willingness to do or to learn.

Ignorance and prejudice have prevented many productive groups of people—racial minorities, women, disabled people, Vietnam era veterans, and older citizens—from taking full advantage of economic opportunities available to young, healthy, white males. Regardless of intent, managers often close out large segments of our population whom they perceive as not "qualified" to hold skilled or professional positions. So laws are enacted to protect people whose opportunities are limited merely because they do not share in the characteristics considered "right" by the people doing the hiring. The five laws and the executive order I explain in the Appendix—

- The Civil Rights Law of 1866
- Title VII of the Civil Rights Act of 1964
- Executive Order 11,246
- Age Discrimination in Employment Act (ADEA)
- Rehabilitation Act of 1973; the Americans with Disabilities Act of 1990
- Veterans' Readjustment Assistance Act of 1974

—are all designed to do essentially the same thing: create "protected classes," groups of people whom our legislators have identified as having suffered from economic discrimination in the past.

How Civil Rights Legislation Helps You Manage Effectively

Civil rights legislation produces obvious social benefits such as social harmony, equal treatment, and political franchise. It also produces large economic benefits, such as more capital in circulation, lower unemployment rates, and so on. But how about at the microlevel, at the level of managing a specific organization? What are the values of civil rights legislation to you, a manager?

From an effective, as well as safe, management perspective, civil rights legislation makes available to you a pool of human resources you might have otherwise overlooked. It opens the door of your organization to protected classes of people and allows you to select from a larger array of talent. Rather than create barriers to hiring employees, civil rights laws help managers hire the people best suited to performing a job profitably.

Definitions of Key Terms

Equal opportunity cases often turn on a matter of definition. The terms *protected class* and *discrimination* are matters of legal definition as well as perception and experience.

protected class   A group of people distinguished by the special characteristic(s) that has inhibited its progress: race, color, ethnic identification, national origin, religion, sex, age, disability, and veteran status.

As noted in a 1987 decision, the Equal Employment Opportunity Commission (EEOC) and the U.S. Supreme Court accept the nineteenth-century definition of *race* in the Civil Rights Law of 1866, Section 1981: "any ethnic minority."[1]

You cannot, under the law, discriminate on the basis of a characteristic specific to any protected class, unless the characteristic is a bona fide occupational qualification (BFOQ).

BFOQ   A trait that is integral or essential to the job in question.

For example, except in the state of New York (where state law protects all age groups), you can specify a minimum age requirement. You can require a specific sex when hiring male or female models to photo advertise clothing. Organizations representing or doing business for protected groups, e.g., religious or racial organizations such as churches or action groups, can fill positions requiring affiliation or membership in the protected class. The important ingredient in your decision is that the characteristic for which you are looking must be essential for the proper performance of the job.

Still, laws, as we said earlier, cannot prevent or eliminate prejudice or ignorance. If obeyed, they can only prevent prejudice and ignorance from interfering with a worker's economic rights. And laws do not always mean what we think they mean—or they may mean one thing to one court and something else to another as they undergo judicial review. So what *does* the federal government call discrimination? If you do not know, how can you manage without fear of legal retaliation?

discrimination   With respect to *hiring* practices, the decisions and actions that deny *individuals in protected groups* access to employment, advancement, benefits, training, and compensation permitted to other people in the organization.

What You Cannot Do

Equal employment opportunity laws identify—and the enforcement body, the Equal Employment Opportunity Commission (EEOC), spells out—general guidelines for what managers cannot do:

1. Fail or refuse to hire any person or to otherwise discriminate against any person with respect to compensation, terms, conditions, or privileges of employment because he or she is a member of a protected group.
2. Limit, segregate, or classify employees or applicants for employment in any way that would deprive or tend to deprive a person of employment opportunities, or have an adverse affect on the person's status as an employee.

3. Fail to provide training to a person because he or she is a member of a protected group.
4. Retaliate against any employees or applicants for employment because they made a charge, testified, assisted, or participated in any manner in an action protected by this law.
5. Print or publish (or have someone else print or publish) any notice or advertisement relating to employment that may adversely affect members of a protected group.
6. Discharge any person because he or she is a member of a protected group.
7. Fail to post and keep posted in an obvious place a notice concerning the contents of a civil rights law.

Consequences of Intentional Discrimination

1. A court order stopping the company from conducting unlawful employment practices and ordering affirmative action, which may include but not be limited to reinstating, or hiring employees, with or without back pay, or any other fair relief the court rules is appropriate
2. Court action to force an organization to comply (if needed)
3. Reasonable attorney fees and other costs

As a result of a 1989 U.S. Supreme Court decision[2] that made proving an employer's intent to discriminate in employment or management practices a vital issue, many charges of discrimination that before might have been handled administratively may go directly to court, where they could be tried by a jury and where the penalties could be quite severe. While it may appear otherwise, intent is not as difficult to establish as you might think.

Most courts rely on the common traditions of case law in which judges or juries define torts and in which intentional torts (i.e., wrongful acts or breaches of duties) can result in heavy penalties (especially punitive damages). Although the burden of proof is on the plaintiff to show the accused's state of mind, usually all the person has to show is that the defendant intended to produce the outcomes in question.

Often only showing the defendant's willful or reckless disregard for the consequences of an action is sufficient to prove intent. All someone needs to show is that the defendant intended to commit the act and *should have foreseen* the consequences. Falling behind a shield of "good intentions" may not be a sufficient defense.

Few, if any, challenged decisions and policies about hiring, promotion, firing, or compensation can hide from the requirement that the employer produce evidence that it did not discriminate. Employers could be called upon to defend themselves by producing affirmative action plans, consultants' studies and minutes of employee relations committee meetings, past histories of internal discrimination complaints and investigations, and many other diverse events or activities.[3,4,5]

What You Can Do

You personally can take some steps to correct the errors of the past by looking at your own hiring results to see where you can take your own affirmative action measures. You can prevent legal difficulties by doing the following:

1. Take care not to discriminate against potential employees; avoid even the *appearance* of discrimination. It is up to you and the other managers of your organization to whip your publications, interview materials, and interview questions into line. On the other hand, if you think your organization errs on the side of unfair employment practices, you might suggest that management seek the advice of counsel. Here, however, I will deal with those things you, as a manager, can do to prevent discrimination in hiring.

2. Base decisions that take into account a person's protected characteristics, such as sex or race, on BFOQs. Produce well-written job descriptions based on actual performance requirements; set criteria that identify the characteristics you have to consider. Then, if you match qualifications with the requirements of the job, other characteristics become irrelevant. I discuss these issues in Chapter 3.

3. Consider reasonable accommodations for dealing with someone whose personal situation could conflict with usual work patterns: a disability, military obligations, a gender difference, or religious preference. If you find that for sound business reasons the

only accommodations available will create an unrealistic and unacceptable burden on you, the organization, or other employees, you can say no to the applicant. I discuss the whole issue of "reasonable accommodation" in Section II.

4. Ensure that pay distinctions are not pretextual or the result of deliberate discrimination. The Equal Pay Act requires you to offer equal pay for equal work (and some legislators are still attempting to pass laws requiring employers to offer equal pay for comparable work—comparable worth). However, you can apply different standards of compensation, or different terms, conditions, or privileges of employment as part of a legally acceptable seniority or merit system, or a system that pays for piecework or on commission or according to location.

You can set up different compensation packages that affect different job groups if the differences are authorized by the provisions of Section 6(d) of the Fair Labor Standards Act of 1938 (FLSA) as amended. They are allowed on the basis of factors other than the protected characteristics, e.g., a seniority or merit system, piecework, or quality bonuses. Often different types of labor groups are dominated by one sex or one race. Pay disparities created by piecework, for example, could affect one sex and not the other. That kind of disparity has found court support. For more information about equal pay, read the discussion of sex discrimination in Chapter 4.

5. Use pre-employment tests as long as they are job-related and tested for bias. Pre-employment physicals or offers pending physicals are acceptable, but you should not base a rejection on a disability that does not affect a person's potential to do the job in question. This issue is covered in Chapter 9.

6. Finally, watch what you publish, not only the advertisements you write for job opportunities, but your applications. They, too, can create the appearance of discrimination. A detailed sample application appears in Chapter 2 (Figure 2-1).

Inasmuch as this section deals exclusively with avoiding discrimination in hiring, I have not said anything about preventing breach of contract or bad-faith lawsuits during the recruiting and hiring process. For example, making outlandish promises, such as a promise of permanent employment (discussed in Section III)—can often get you in trouble. One preventive step is to include a disclaimer in your application.

Be a positive influence or force for change. Even if you do not make policy decisions, you can influence them if you see something wrong with the way in which your organization goes about making hiring decisions. Communicate your perceptions and thoughts to management.

Consider these issues: A legally acceptable system must be based on objective considerations or standards and cannot be used in a manner to produce either disparate treatment or adverse impact. The system, especially one including subjective criteria, should be based on sound and reasonable business judgments and should not be used as a subterfuge to discriminate, a point extremely crucial to many age discrimination suits.

Discrimination and unfair treatment begin and end with attitudes, values, and perceptions. What you feel or think about other people dictates whether or not you will hire them regardless of race, sex, religion, national origin, disability, age, or veteran's status—and whether you will treat them fairly in the process. You can take an affirmative action if you put aside many of the common excuses people use to explain away their problems. For example:

▸ *"They won't let me. . . ."* (where they means "the bosses"). Managers allow their supervisors to prevent them from hiring in accordance with the law if they do not protest illegal discriminatory, or potentially discriminatory, hiring policies or practices.

▸ *"My peers will be angry if. . . ."* Same story. Managers perpetuate and reinforce other managers' prejudices by acquiescing to peer pressure.

▸ *"My other employees will hassle [them] or quit if. . . ."* Managers should strive to achieve a positive, productive work environment, and they have an obligation to guarantee the opportunity to work in that environment to all qualified (or trainable) applicants for a job. Hiring a less qualified (or trainable) person to satisfy the prejudices of other employees will only diminish the productivity of the group and introduce negative pressures into the work environment anyway. Communication, training, and exposure can reduce or eliminate the initial shock of having "different" people on the job.

Legal procedures or rules of evidence may change, but one principle underlies all equal opportunity laws: to protect people who have, for one reason or another, been denied equal opportunity in the marketplace. Had not ignorance and prejudice controlled that marketplace in the past, these laws would not exist today.

Equal opportunity, you see, begins where prejudice or ignorance leave off. With you.

Cases

1. 483 U.S. 1011 (1987).
2. 110 S. Ct. 38 (1989).
3. 679 F.2d 762 (8th Cir. 1982).
4. 95 F.R.D. 372, 31 F.E.P. Cases (BNA) 1359 (N.D. Ill. 1982).
5. 598 F.R.D. 27, 349, 31 F.E.P. Cases (BNA) 1366 (N.D.N.Y. 1983), *aff'd*, 729 F.2d 85.

Chapter 1

Safe Recruiting Practices

Safe management begins *before* you hire people. How you advertise, what you write about in company publications, the questions you ask on forms, and your interview questions all talk to other people about you and your organization. Sometimes they may tell the truth, perhaps that you *do* illegally or unfairly discriminate or you *do* pry into matters of no concern to you or to the organization. Other times, they say things that you may not want to say or you do not intend to communicate. In this chapter I describe discrimination in advertising and other recruitment materials and how to prevent discriminatory language from infecting them.

Few managers today directly and openly specify discriminatory characteristics in an ad unless these are required by a BFOQ. However, they identify age limits and other traits that do discriminate, and they often indirectly discriminate in subtle ways.*

What You Cannot Say

The list below identifies the sorts of statements you cannot make in print, unless they specify a BFOQ.

Specific age limits: "17–25," "under 40," "recent college grad," "long-

---

*See also John P. Kohl and David B. Stephens, "Wanted: Recruitment Advertising That Doesn't Discriminate," *Personnel*, 66:2 (February 1989), pp. 18–25.

	term career-minded people," "recent retiree"
Sex characteristics:	"men only," "lineman," "waiter," "waitress," "barmaid," "Girl Friday," "gentlemen"
Racial traits or characteristics:	"blacks," "Asians"
National origin:	"American-born," "Hispanic"
Religious preference:	"Christian person"
Physical characteristics:	"good health"
Geographic areas:	if specifying them would isolate specific protected groups (e.g., limiting recruits for menial jobs to inner-city neighborhoods, or limiting recruits to predominantly white suburban areas)

You cannot specify protected group traits *even to fulfill the conditions of an affirmative action program*. The laws prevent hiring people *merely* on the basis of a qualification that is not job-related.

Questionable Ads

Advertising copy need not blatantly discriminate to suggest you or your organization will not hire specific kinds of people. You leave yourself vulnerable if the ads *imply* the possibility of discrimination. The main issue is not whether or not the organization illegally discriminates. Rather, the *appearance* of discrimination can bedevil you more than the act; people go to court on that basis more frequently than on the basis of actual fact. What you publish can damn you more than what you do.

That is particularly true of the way in which you advertise job openings. Even though very few people go to court because of the way an advertisement is written, someone could use your ads as evidence when suing you for discrimination in some other way. The example in the Casebook at the end of this chapter illustrates how what you write could be used against you.

Later in this chapter I discuss and illustrate acceptable ads, but first let's look at several ads taken directly from the classified section of a St. Louis newspaper, July 21, 1989. Watch for subtleties, rather than for the obvious, and compare the way these are written with the way your organization writes its classifieds.

What is questionable about this ad?

Ever since the mid-1970s, the courts have questioned the *high school diploma* criterion for laborer positions. Unfortunately, a diploma no longer guarantees that someone can read and write. If the job requires that applicants read and write English proficiently, you could state the requirements and ask applicants to take aptitude tests—if the tests meet EEO criteria for bona fide, job-related exams.

Another thing about that ad: You might have difficulty justifying specification of ages 17 to 30 as a BFOQ. What special qualification does that age range entail?

Take a look at this less blatant ad.

CATV LINEMAN
EXPERIENCED

for long-term construction project. We
need 6 experienced linemen for a 2-year
500-mile. . . .

Although the ad is not as blatant as the first one, the words *lineman* and *linemen* suggest that women need not apply. The next ad shows you the difference a word makes.

CABLE INSTALLERS
Experienced. Need. . . .

A subtle but important difference: *lineman* versus *installers*.

Not the act but the appearance of the act raises the question. The company advertising for linemen may in fact consider women, and the company advertising for installers may in fact not consider them, but the ads suggest otherwise. That is the point.

Try yourself out on this one.

THE SKY IS THE LIMIT
FOR
"BROWN, INC."
DRIVERS
With our increasing
mileage pay package
SOLO, TEAMS
AND OWNERS WELCOME
Weekly settlements
Conventional tractors
Many benefits
25 years old, 3 yrs. experience
Contact Safety Dept.
314/555-4321

If you have not seen the problem yet, compare this ad with the following ad for drivers.

DRIVERS/OTR
"JONES TRANSPORT, INC."
IS STILL EXPANDING.
OUR DRIVERS ARE HOME
4 OUT OF 5 WEEKENDS.
· · · · ·
DRIVERS WITH 2 YEARS OR
MORE OF OTR EXPERIENCE
START AT $0.23 PER MILE
Min. age 25, 1 yr. verifiable OTR experience, good driving record, D.O.T. cert., able to pass drug screen. . . .

I added the italics. The previous ad writer may have *intended* to say *"min. age* 25," but he or she did *not* say it, whereas the second writer did say it. That is a big difference. A forty-year-old driver might apply for the second position, but probably not for the first. Who loses? "Brown, Inc."

One more ad should make the case for careful ad writing.

Sales
$$$$
RETIRE YOUNG
Opportunity for aggressive,
money-motivated, sales-
oriented people
Unlimited income potential
Established company now interviewing
professional-minded, career-oriented candidates for sales position. Advance from within through our proven training program. Qualified leads provided. Take charge. Control your own future.
CALL NOW
Ask for . . . .

How many people aged 40 or older will apply for this job (setting aside the fact that the ad reads like a come-on)? You do not have to say, "People over age 40 need not apply" when you use words such as "RETIRE YOUNG" and "career-oriented candidates." The ad, although not out loud, asks that only young people apply.

These examples illustrate that intentionally or unintentionally ad writers screen out potential applicants. Very few employers blatantly discriminate in their ads anymore, the way the deckhand ad writer did. In their recent study of 39,311 ads, John P. Kohl and David B. Stephens found that race bias never appeared; national origin bias occurred only twice (.2 percent); bilingual requirements seemed questionable in about 25 percent of the ads; the predominant violations were sex-based (68 percent), with age bringing up a distant third (7 percent); nearly 50 percent of the ads were aimed at "trade" or "hospitality" (restaurant/hotel) workers; and only 16.2 percent of the ads were aimed at professionals and managers— the better-educated workers.* No telling how many obviously discriminatory ads the newspapers turned down!

What is the real problem with subtly worded ads?

Most people read ads two ways: They qualify themselves *in* or they qualify themselves *out*. "Yes. That looks good for me" or "That does not look good for me." A subtle ad does not have to say, "Women, older people, minorities need not apply" to *prompt* people not to apply. And someone could take you to court for suggesting that he or she would not be welcome at your organization.

What You Can Say

One rule establishes what you can say in a recruitment ad:

All qualifications or characteristics must be job-related.

As long as what you specify is in fact a BOFQ, you can identify it in your recruitment materials. Let's take a borderline exam-

---

*"Wanted: Recruitment Advertising That Doesn't Discriminate," *Personnel*, 66:2 (February 1989), pp. 18–25.

ple. Suppose you have an overseas operation in a Spanish-speaking country such as Mexico and you need a Spanish-speaking supervisor to relocate there. "Spanish speaking" (not "Latin extraction") is acceptable in this case, although it might not be if the position were located in North America.

You can avoid writing illegal ads by doing the following:

1. Write a clearly worded description of the job you are trying to fill.
2. Write a list of specific qualifications or characteristics essential for performing the job properly.
3. Word your ad to reflect both the job description and the qualifications or characteristics.

Job Profiles

To ensure that you do not write illegally discriminatory ads, you need to develop what I call a *job profile*, which consists of two worksheets: a job description and a recruiting guide.

The job description requires a clear statement of the job's objectives and the means for achieving them: what the job is and how the employee filling that job is supposed to do the work. The list of job components defines or describes what you need to include.

Position:	The title of the job to be filled. It should describe what the employee is to do, e.g., "drill press operator," "stenographer," "word processor," "cable installer"
Last revision:	The date on which you or the personnel officer (department) made the revision to the job description from which your advertisement will be written
Pay grade level:	The status of the position within your organization's payroll process, e.g., "entry level," "pay grade 8"
Reports to:	The name of the person to whom the employee in this position would report, i.e., the person in charge
Supervises:	The number of people this person would

	supervise, if this is a supervisory or management position
Primary tasks:	A list of results for which this employee will be held accountable, e.g., "produce and ship twenty widgets an hour"
Major activities:	What the employee will have to do to complete the tasks, e.g., "wrap wire around a spindle," "tie off the wire on the spindle with a plastic clip," "pack wound spindle into shipping carton"
Skills needed:	What the employee will have to know or be able to do in order to perform the activities listed above, e.g., "color code specific products," "operate a wire winder"

Under "skills needed," you can list specific *personal* characteristics if the position calls for them, even if they are subjective (not easily measured). For example, in positions dealing with the public, you can list such characteristics as "comfortable talking with other people" or "good listener."

A blank job description that you can copy for your own use appears in Figure 1-1.

Once you have written your job description, you can prepare a recruiting guide. This document will tell you (or anyone else writing the ad) just what you are looking for in an employee and why you need it. Our recruiting guide is divided into two columns ("job description" and "requirements").

The "job description" categories match the job description in Figure 1-1: "tasks," "major activities," "skills needed," and "personal characteristics." The last category is not essential unless the job does require personal characteristics you might not find in the entire work force population available to you. The "requirements" column will then consist of the background, education or training, and skills or personal characteristics you think are necessary for performing this job either with training or with a minimum of orientation.

The sample recruiting guide shown in Figure 1-2 reflects a need for an experienced, skilled, and trained person with specific personal characteristics: minimum *requirements*, not

Figure 1-1. Sample safe job description.

Position: _____ **Last revision:** _____

Pay grade/level: _____ **Reports to:** _____

Supervises: _____

Primary tasks: _____

_____

_____

Major activities: _____

_____

_____

_____

_____

_____

_____

_____

_____

_____

_____

Skills needed: _____

_____

_____

Figure 1-1. *(continued)*

Position: Training Coordinator

JOB DESCRIPTION	REQUIREMENTS

Tasks

To provide technical training

Major Activities

Needs assessment technical
training
    Collect and analyze
    data.
Training design
    Write outlines, manuals,
    aids.
    Prepare, present/dem-
    onstrate, provide
    practice, follow up.
Training evaluation
    Review supervisor's
    feedback, follow up,
    revise

Skills Needed

Operate AV equipment

Work History Skills

Experience in technical
training
Experience evaluating technical training needs in an
organization like this

merely preferences. That means that to do this job, you need
someone with the credentials listed because you do not have
the time or resources available to train someone to do this job.
But that will not always be the case.

If you have the time and the resources to develop someone
in the position, you could list basic requirements, e.g., "B.A. in
psychology," with other requirements, e.g., "training experience *preferred*." The ad would then reflect both requirements
and preferences.

Figure 1-2. Sample recruiting guide.

Position: Training Coordinator

JOB DESCRIPTION	REQUIREMENTS

Task

To provide technical training

Major Activities

Needs assessments/
technical training
  Collect and analyze
  data.
Training design
  Write outlines, manuals,
  aids.
  Prepare, present/
  demonstrate, provide
  practice, follow up.
Training evaluation
  Review trainee
  feedback, revise.
Learning evaluation
  Review supervisor's
  feedback, follow up,
  revise.

Skills Needed

Operate AV equipment.
Analyze/evaluate.
Communicate.
Write, design training
practices.

Personal Characteristics

Outgoing, friendly, open,
creative, team-
oriented

Work History/Skills

Experience in technical
training
Experience evaluating
technical training needs
in an organization like
this
Experience in workshop
design
Experience in workshop
delivery

Education/Training

Minimum of a B.A. in
psychology or related
human resources field
Technical skills training
and three years'
experience

Skills Needed

Knowledge of an experience
with state-of-the art
training equipment
Proven writing and oral
communication skills

Personal Characteristics

The ability to work without
close supervision
The ability to communicate
well with all levels of
employees

Let's look at an ad based on the sample recruiting guide.

TECHNICAL TRAINING COORDINATOR

EXPERIENCED Training Coordinator. B.A. in psychology or related human resources field; 3 years' experience in state-of-the-art design and program delivery in electronics environment required. Outgoing, proven skills in communicating with all levels of employees. Exempt position, salary up to $25,000 commensurate with experience.

Obviously other items could be added—"good benefits," "exciting environment"—to encourage qualified people to apply. These, however, are not relevant to the points we are illustrating.

This ad does not limit the type of people who can apply. Any interested person satisfying the advertised requirements is eligible regardless of race, sex, age, religion, national origin, disability, whatever. That is the issue at hand. Meet the job-relatedness criterion in all your ad writing, and you solve the puzzle of what constitutes safe recruiting practices.

Effectively designed job descriptions include only job-related qualifications and help prevent discrimination before you begin your applicant search. Their appropriate use guarantees advertisements neutral with regard to protected characteristics. Neutrality should permeate any and all of your organization's publications, which may or may not fall into an applicant's hands and could become the basis for a lawsuit against you or your organization.

Recruiting Materials

Everything your organization publishes—marketing copy, employee manuals, procedure manuals, newsletters, in-house magazines—can be (and often are) used as recruiting materials. Especially if you intentionally communicate them, orally or in writing, to "headhunters" or other adjunct recruiters or to applicants, you leave yourself vulnerable if they imply the possibility of discrimination.

Remember, the main issue is not whether an organization illegally discriminates but whether there is the *appearance* of discrimination. That is not only true of the way in which you advertise job openings, but it is also true of the other publications. That is why the Casebook begins with a sample of the problems biased publications can generate.

CASEBOOK

Employers use many different types of materials in addition to advertisements when recruiting future employees, such as brochures and in-house magazines. What they say communicates more about your organization than you may think. Preventing discriminatory language from creeping into these publications is just as important as monitoring your classified ads.

Consider this case concerning an edition of an in-house magazine that extolled the company's practice of recruiting recent college grads. The suit was brought by an employee, not by a job applicant, which underscores the importance of keeping your eye on in-house publications: Anyone who takes exception to language in them can bring suit against you. What is that old saying about "an ounce of prevention"?

Can Your In-House Publications Be Used Against You?

Bauder, Inc., prided itself on its open communication, including the corporatewide distribution of a house organ called *The Bauder Review*. When an article in *The Review* proudly proclaimed that Bauder's sales success could be directly attributed to its recruiting policies, one fifty-two-year-old salesman took issue.

The article, Sam Kowalski charged, lauded the company's

"youth movement" by claiming that its success was due to a policy of recruiting either recent college graduates or inexperienced sales-people who could learn from the company's more experienced sales personnel. The examples—only *younger* superstars—reinforced the company's image of blatant discrimination against older people.

Bauder's attorney asked that the article not be allowed as evidence against the company. It was too well written and could unduly persuade the jury against his client.

With whom do you think the court agreed and why? Does your organization publish a newsletter or magazine? If so, pay heed.

Judicial Discretion

The plaintiff's attorney appealed to the appearance of discrimination, but evidence rulings are usually a matter of judicial discretion. The court decides what can and cannot be admitted as evidence.

In the Bauder case, the trial court refused to accept the implication of discrimination the magazine created, and the First Circuit affirmed the trial court's decision. The courts agreed that the jury might give undue weight to the magazine when trying to decide if the company's recruiting policies were in fact discriminatory, as the article implied.[1] However, a publication making the same assertions could be used in a different case, especially one in which a rejected applicant sued for discrimination.

Use the case as a barometer for measuring the implications that your organization's publications could create. Consider tone and references to age, gender, race, religion, or nationality. Do they focus on job-related factors (skills, talents, aptitudes, achievements) or do they laud irrelevant characteristics such as youth and religious values? Avoiding such possibly incriminating materials in the first place can prevent a costly self-defense later.

Case

1. 687 F.2d 526, 29 F.E.P Cases (BNA) 1253 (1st Cir. 1982).

Chapter 2

Safe Interviewing Practices

Have you taken a close look at your organization's employment application lately? What kind of information does it seek? Are all the items necessary for deciding if someone can do the job for which he or she is applying? How about your interview questions? Do you ever ask questions about age, or child care, or where someone comes from?

If your application asks for unnecessary or non-job-related information, if your interview questions encroach on personal issues, they could be discriminatory. Just how safe are your interview practices?

This chapter can be summed up with the same rule we apply to any aspect of the hiring process. To be safe, *ask for job-related information only.*

What You Cannot Do

Questions regarding protected characteristics are unacceptable, period. You cannot ask them. Regardless of what the case—sex, race, age—an employment application or interview question without a job-related motive for knowing the information may be unlawful per se.

On an Employment Application

If you cannot refer to specific protected characteristics when you advertise, you surely cannot ask about them on an application. Three items, in particular, belong on the list of what you cannot include in an application.

1. *Date of birth.* Some applications continue to ask for date of birth (DOB), which is the same as asking, "How old are you?" Now it is true that logic and simple arithmetic can help you decide approximately how old anyone is. Check the dates an applicant lists for attending or graduating from high school, and you can easily figure it out. However, you should not use this information as a basis for making a hiring decision unless you feel you can waste your own and your organization's resources defending yourselves.

2. *Arrest records.* Never ask applicants *arrest* questions. Arrests without convictions are totally irrelevant and have an adverse impact on minorities (who are often arrested—but not necessarily convicted).

3. *Membership in religious or other groups.* Asking someone what church or synagogue he or she attends would be an obvious no-no, but just as managers sometimes use arrest records to discriminate against racial minorities, they also use membership in social or religious organizations to deny racial and religious minorities access to employment. Membership in the Urban League, for example, usually suggests that a person is black, while members of B'nai B'rith are usually Jewish. Unless the information is pertinent to the job for which a person is applying—as it often is for sales, professional, or executive positions—don't ask for group affiliations of any kind. In Figure 2-1 and the accompanying discussion, you will find out how to get information appropriately.

During an Interview

The best advice repeats what was said at the beginning of this section. *Questions regarding protected characteristics are unac-*

(text continues on page 34)

Figure 2-1. Sample safe application for employment.

APPLICATION FOR EMPLOYMENT

[PLEASE PRINT]

Last name	First name	Middle name	Soc. Security no.

Address	City	State	Zip	Phone no.

Position(s) Applied For: _____

_____

Employment History   Begin with current or last job. Include military service assignments. If you include volunteer activities, you may exclude organizations that indicate race, color, religion, national origin, disability, or other protected status.

1. _____ _____ _____
   Employer   From   To   Duties or responsibilities

   _____
   Address

   Hourly/salary: _____

   Start/final: _____

   _____ _____
   Job title   Supervisor

   Phone no.:   _____

   _____
   Reason for leaving

Figure 2-1. *(continued)*

2. _____ _____ _____ _____
   Employer   From   To   Duties or responsibilities

   _____
   Address

   Hourly/salary: _____

   Start/final: _____

   _____   _____
   Job title   Supervisor

   Phone no.:   _____

   _____
   Reason for leaving

3. _____ _____ _____ _____
   Employer   From   To   Duties or responsibilities

   _____
   Address

   Hourly/salary: _____

   Start/final: _____

   _____   _____
   Job title   Supervisor

   Phone no.:   _____

   _____
   Reason for leaving

4. _____ _____ _____ _____
   Employer   From   To   Duties or responsibilities

   _____
   Address

Hourly/salary: _____

Start/final: _____

Job title   Supervisor

Phone no.: _____

Reason for leaving

IF YOU NEED ADDITIONAL SPACE, PLEASE USE A SEPARATE SHEET OF PAPER.

Education Years Completed: 6 7 8 9 10 11 12 14 16 18 19 20 20+

	School	*Location*	*Diploma/ Degree*	*Studies*
Elementary				
High school				
Trade/professional school				
College/university				
Graduate school				

Specialized Training, Apprenticeship, Extracurricular Activities ____

_____

_____

Figure 2-1. *(continued)*

Honors, awards, copyrights, or patents

Special Job-Related Skills and Qualifications From Employment or Other Experience: _____

_____

Foreign Languages	Fluent	Good	Fair
Speak			
Read	_____	_____	_____
Write	_____	_____	_____
	_____	_____	_____

Professional, Trade, Business, or Civic Organizations/Offices

You may exclude organizations that indicate race, color, religion, national origin, disability, or other protected status.

Military History

When   Release/type

Job-related training

Current status

Personal

Yes _____   No _____   If under 18 years of age, can you provide proof of eligibility to work?

Yes _____   No _____   Have you ever applied to us before?

If yes, when? _____

Yes _____   No _____   Have you ever been employed with us before?

If yes, when? _____

Yes _____   No _____   Do you have a relative or friend employed with us?

If yes, who? _____

Yes _____   No _____   May we contact your present employer?

Yes _____   No _____   Are you physically or otherwise unable to perform the duties of the job for which you are applying?

Yes _____   No _____   Have you ever been convicted of a crime (other than a traffic violation)? Conviction will not necessarily disqualify you from employment.

If yes, please explain _____
_____

Yes _____   No _____   If applying for a position that requires driving, do you have an appropriate license?

Yes _____   No _____   If applying for a position that requires driving, have you ever been ticketed for a moving traffic violation?

Figure 2-1. *(continued)*

If yes, please explain _____

_____

Yes ____   No ____   Are you a citizen of the United States?

Yes ____   No ____   If no, does your immigration status
                         permit you to work?

Proof must be provided: Visa, green card, Social Security card,
and driver's license.

Yes ____   No ____   Are you currently on "layoff" status,
                         subject to recall?

On what date will you be available for work? _____

Availability:
____Full Time ____Part Time ____ Shift Work ____Temporary

Yes ____   No ____   If required, are you available for
                         travel?

Yes ____   No ____   If required, are you available for
                         relocation?

References Other Than Previous Employers or Relatives

Providing this information means that you give this organization
permission to contact the references listed.

1. _____
   Name   Address   Telephone No.

2. _____
   Name   Address   Telephone No.

3. _____
   Name   Address   Telephone No.

4. _____
   Name   Address   Telephone No.

APPLICANT'S ACKNOWLEDGMENT

[This application shall be considered active for no more than 45 days. After that time, applicants will be required to resubmit a completed application. The applicant understands that neither this document nor any offer of employment from this employer constitutes an employment contract unless a specific document is executed in writing by the employer and employee.]

I certify that answers given in this application are true and complete to the best of my knowledge. I authorize investigation into all statements I have made on this application as may be necessary for reaching an employment decision.

In the event I am employed, I understand that any false or misleading information I knowingly provided in my application or interview(s) may result in discharge and/or legal action. I understand also that if employed, I am required to abide by all rules and regulations of the employer and any special agreements reached between the employer and me.

FOR PERSONNEL DEPARTMENT USE ONLY

Arrange Interview: ____Yes ____No Comments:_____

_____

If employed, start date:_____ Hourly/salary: $_____

Department:_____ Title:_____

Notes: _____

_____

_____

_____

Figure 2-1. *(continued)*

_____

_____

_____

_____

_____

_____

_____

_____

_____

By: _____
                    Name and title   Date

ceptable, period. You cannot ask them. Regardless of what the case—sex, race, age—an interview question that is not job-related may be unlawful per se.

What You Can Do: Safe Questions

An application should ask only for information that will help you sift through the possibilities when considering several applicants for the same job and help you make the best or most reasonable hiring decision. It should be divided into three relatively self-explanatory main parts: work history, educational background, and personal information that could affect job performance.

You can solicit specific kinds of information that go beyond routine items such as name and address or previous employment. For example, you can ask questions about convictions, about disabilities, and about organizational membership, but only as long as the questions are appropriate to the job.

Questions about convictions for crimes related to the work the person is expected to perform—e.g., conviction for embezzlement in relation to an accounting job—are relevant, and you can ask them. Hiring a convicted felon can leave you vulnerable to a repeat crime or can lead to a lawsuit if a felon convicted of a violent crime harms or injures another employee, a customer, or a member of your public at large. Circumstances make it difficult for employers to offer felons rehabilitation opportunities.

General health questions or general questions about disabilities will not fly in court. On the other hand, you can ask about disabilities that could possibly interfere with a person's ability to perform the duties of the job for which he or she is applying, but you cannot deny someone an opportunity if his or her disability would not interfere. The question concerning disability in the sample application is not discriminatory because it is specific to the person's abilities to perform the duties of the job for which he or she is applying. The courts do recognize your right to hire people who can in fact do the work for which they are hired.

As for affiliations, a simple disclaimer solves most of your problems. Whatever you are asking for—previous employment, professional or social membership—just add the following statement:

[*In response to any relevant question:*] You may exclude organizations that indicate race, color, religion, national origin, disability, or other protected status.

That statement is incorporated in the sample safe application for employment shown in Figure 2-1. In addition, the sample includes the applicant's acknowledgment, which you can use for comparing your organization's current paperwork for applicants with what I believe are legally safe formats. You may make a copy of the sample format for use in your organization.

Although this is not the place for a detailed discussion, you should note that immigration laws obligate you to ask for detailed proof of an applicant's eligibility to work in the United States. While it is not legal to ask someone where he or she comes from, you can ask for proof of citizenship or other right-to-work papers (e.g., green card, visa). Check with your personnel officer to see if your organization is meeting those federal requirements.

Your personnel officer is also responsible for how your application is written and what it asks for. If you find a questionable item in it, bring that item to his or her attention. That includes asking applicants to acknowledge that they have read and understood the application and the basic terms and conditions of employment in your organization. While not a safeguard against a lawsuit, it can protect you or your organization in some suits for breach of contract, which I describe in Section III.

During an Interview

Although you cannot ask certain questions or solicit specific types of information during an interview, you can ask questions that will allow you to get information you need for choosing among applicants. It is not always the question itself, but the way you ask it that offends or violates the law. Again, appearances often speak louder than words.

For example, although you cannot ask if a person's religion prohibits him or her from working on a Sabbath, if the position requires weekend shifts, you may say, "We work rotating shifts on Saturday. How do you feel about working Saturdays?" If the applicant objects to working on a Sabbath, and if accommodating that belief would create an undue hardship on the organization or other employees, you can reject his or her application.

A rule of thumb for questioning during an interview: *Keep all your questions job-related and ask them of every applicant.* Any qualfications are acceptable as long as they are clearly job-related, are applied equally, and do not have an adverse impact on protected groups in which members are qualified.

The left-hand column in the chart shown in Figure 2-2 lists inappropriate or illegal comments or questions, and the opposite column lists properly phrased questions that refer to a certain job requirement, condition of employment, or business necessity. In some cases, an item as phrased may not apply to your situation. You may have to modify it to make it work for you. Therefore, I offer this table as representative and general suggestions and do not assume responsibility for their use or for the manner in which you use them.

CASEBOOK

It should be clear by now that you should avoid saying or doing anything that can be construed (or misconstrued) as evidence of discrimination, such as requesting a photograph, birth date, or birthplace on résumés or of applicants. What other kinds of requests are unacceptable?

Are Special For-Women-Only Medical Questions Discriminatory?

Frampton and Sons, Inc., a manufacturer of plastic products, considered good health a prerequisite of employment. It would hire disabled people as long as they could perform the duties of the job for which they were hired, but because some jobs presented a health risk in the first place, the company considered it prudent to ask all seriously considered applicants to have pre-employment physicals and have their own doctor complete a medical form.

One section of the form, labeled "Women," requested information about urogenital problems (e.g., menstrual problems, disorders of the ovaries or uterus, and number of pregnancies). No one had ever refused to complete the form until Sally Stevens and her physician objected to completing the for-women-only section. Instead, the physician wrote *Healthy Female* on the form, and Sally returned it signed but incomplete.

The company then sent back the form with a cover letter asking for the omitted data. Rather than submit, Sally filed a sex discrimi-

Figure 2-2. Impermissible and permissible questions to ask during an interview.

DON'T ASK	ASK INSTEAD
[*Of a woman:*] Which do you think is more important to you, a family or a career?	[*If true and asked of all applicants:*] We need people interested in a career. What are your career goals?
[*Of parents, especially of women:*] What arrangements do you have for taking care of your children?	Sometimes we have to work overtime. How do you feel about that?
Jews don't work on Saturdays. You're Jewish, aren't you?	We often work on weekends. How do you feel about that?
Do you have transportation to work?	We begin the workday at 8 A.M. Would you have a problem getting here on time every day?
Are you Hispanic?	Some of our employees speak only Spanish, and the ability to communicate with them is essential to the job. Can you speak Spanish?
Do you have a high school diploma?	[*If true and asked of all applicants:*] Reading instructions and doing arithmetic are important parts of the job. Are you willing to take an aptitude test?
Do you use drugs?	[*If true and asked of all applicants:*] All applicants are required to undergo drug screening as a condition of employment. Have you any objections?

You're very overweight. Can you get around okay?	[*If true and asked of all applicants:*] The job requires a lot of moving around, carrying things, climbing up and down stairs. Do you have any disabilities or other conditions that would prevent your being able to do those things well or safely?
We don't let women do heavy or dangerous work. Okay?	We work around chemicals and radioactive materials. How do you feel about heavy or dangerous work?
[*Of a member of the opposite sex, in particular:*] Will you have dinner with me?	We like to get to know the candidates well, including socially. Would it be possible for you and your spouse or guest of your choice to have dinner with me?

nation complaint charging that the company's application procedure treated women differently from men because it did not ask men to answer questions concerning their urogenital health as well.

The company replied that the difference in treatment was merely apparent, driven by the concern that women usually resist intrusive pelvic examinations. Sensitive to women's concerns, they merely accommodated women's sensibilities.

Do your job applications include separate health questions for women only? How do you think the employer fared in this case?

The Danger of Generalization

According to the Connecticut Supreme Court, the issue is not a matter of health but rather one of making generalizations about the preferences of a whole group of people, in this case women. Even a true generalization, the court said, is not sufficient reason to disqualify someone to whom the generalization does *not* apply. The employer's medical history procedure illegally discriminated because it did not give a woman the option of completing the questions or demonstrating her good health through a physical examination, an option male applicants received.[1]

This ruling does not prevent employers from setting reasonable health screening procedures. Instead, it warns them that health forms or other medical policies should not discriminate on the basis of any bias. It outlaws medical questions that require one gender to supply information not requested of the other, a principle applied to race and age-related questions as well.

Interview Questions

The way in which you treat different kinds of people during an interview, rather than the specific questions you ask, may cause problems.

Can You Ask a Woman About Pregnancy, Childbearing, or Child Care?

During a job interview, major U.S. corporations usually do not make potentially sensitive inquiries about pregnancy, childbearing, or child care. But when a major airline did just that, the applicant, Donna Sales, took the company to court alleging sex discrimination.

"No," the company protested, "we did not discriminate against the woman on the basis of those questions." Although it admitted to not asking them of all applicants, it claimed that Donna's poor references, her close relationship with one of the airline's employees, and her history of excessive absences were the reasons for not hiring her.

What kinds of questions do you ask during an interview? How do you think the Eighth Circuit would rule on your questions?

Equal Treatment for All

A federal court of appeals ruled that the applicant had shown clearly that the airline had discriminated against her in its hiring *process* by conducting her interview differently from the way it conducted others.[2] The employer, on the other hand, could not show that its questions about child care and child-bearing were in any way job-related. The court also decreed that the several lawful and otherwise undisputed criteria for not hiring the plaintiff were irrelevant and possibly pretextual.

The specific questions—

1. What arrangements can you make for taking care of your children?
2. Do you plan to have more children?
3. Will you be able to work when you're pregnant?

—are not as important as the charge the woman leveled at the airline company. It *treated her differently during the interview process from how it would have treated a man*, which is not the same as charging it with illegally refusing to hire her. Those are two different matters: (1) discriminatory treatment during the interview process and (2) making the ultimate hiring decision. If the questions or their answers had played a role in the ultimate hiring decision, then the plaintiff would have been entitled to damages; nevertheless, the company was liable for violating Title VII merely in terms of its hiring process.

As I said at the outset, questions regarding protected characteristics are unacceptable, period. Dwelling on gender- or race- or age-related questions or issues during an employment interview without a job-related reason could be seen as biased or discriminatory (unlawful per se). An employer should not have two interview policies for job applicants, one for men and another for women, or one for whites and one for non-whites, or one for young people and another for older applicants. In 1971 the U.S. Supreme Court outlawed such dual systems when it held that an employer's policy of accepting applications from men with pre-school-age children while rejecting those from women with children of the same age violated Title VII.³ Questions or discussions should be pertinent to the job in question and should form a part of every interview, or they could land you in court.

Our sample case violates the EEOC's Sex Discrimination Guidelines,⁴ which prohibit sex-based pre-employment inquiries unless based on a BFOQ. Questions concerning child care arrangements may in themselves be neutral, but they could have a disparate impact on female applicants and reflect the bias that women have more child care responsibilities than do men.

The sample case not only distinguishes between two forms of hiring discrimination claims (the process and the decision), it also underscores the fact that you must prove that legal considerations led to a decision not to hire. In the event that you cannot prove this, you could be held liable for damages (or relief), as was the airline in the case.

See Figure 2-3 for a sample of the Voluntary Data Record Survey that should be attached to your organization's employment application.

Figure 2-3. Sample Voluntary Data Record Survey.

[*Use this document only if your organization has affirmative action obligations or if it is required to submit the information collected for some other reason. This information should be kept separate from the application.*]

Voluntary Data Record Survey

[PLEASE PRINT]

Date: _____

[Applicants and employees are treated equally, without regard to race, color, religion, sex, national origin, age, marital or veteran status, medical condition or disability, or any other legally protected status. At the same time, as an employer with an affirmative action program, we comply with government regulations, including affirmative action responsibilities and reports where they apply.

Government agencies periodically require reports on the status of protected employees. The purpose of this Voluntary Data Record is to comply with government record keeping, reporting, and other legal requirements. These data are for statistical analysis with respect to the success of the organization's affirmative action program only.

Completing this Voluntary Data Record Survey is optional. All data records are kept in a confidential file and *are not* a part of your Application for Employment or Personnel File.]

NOTE: THE DECISION TO SUBMIT THIS INFORMATION IS VOLUNTARY.

Job Title

Check one: Male: __ Female: __

Age: __ Vietnam Era Veteran: __ Disabled Veteran: __ Disabled __

Check one of the following (ethnic/racial background):

White: __ Hispanic: __

Native American/Alaskan Native: __

Black: __ Asian/Pacific Islander: __ Other: __

Cases

1. 188 Conn. 44, 32 E.P.D. 33 (CCH) 791 (1982).
2. 738 F.2d 255, 35 F.E.P. Cases (BNA) 102 (8th Cir. 1984).
3. 400 U.S. 542 (1971).
4. 29 C.F.R. §1604.11(e) (1983).

Chapter 3

Safe Employment Decisions

Civil rights laws *do not say* you *have to* hire minorities, women, older people, disabled people, or veterans. They *do not say* you *have to* hire them in proportion to their numbers in the community's general population. Rather, they say that *if you do not hire* protected individuals, *you must exercise sound business judgment* and base your decisions on a BFOQ or some other valid business reason.

You have read how to avoid accidental or intentional discrimination by wording your advertisements appropriately, asking only for work- or job-related information on your applications and asking only work- or job-related questions during your interviews. But you are not out of the woods yet.

You still have to make the hiring decision, choosing the one candidate from the many to fill any one job opening. Here, all your safeguards against even the appearance of discrimination can be breached by a decision that seemed safe at the time you made it but was not as safe as you thought. To prevent any such mishap, you should be aware of what you cannot and can do at this point in the hiring process.

What You Cannot Do

Here, the edges between *cannot* and *can* blur. For example:

1. You cannot refuse to hire someone whose personal religious practices conflict with work schedules, unless—

44

2. You cannot refuse to hire a woman in some jobs that could endanger her ability to bear children or would harm an unborn fetus, unless—
3. You cannot apply subjective criteria for judging a person's ability to do the job, unless—
4. You cannot underemploy women or minorities, unless—

You cannot do anything that would exclude protected individuals from certain jobs—*unless you have reasonable business grounds for doing it.*

What You Can Do

You can do anything you have to do to run your business efficiently, effectively, and productively, as long as you can justify your actions on valid, reasonable business grounds. The courts are quick to perceive pretexts and subterfuges that attempt to hide the truth. If you carefully evaluate your hiring criteria and procedures and take a proactive stance toward hiring, you can prevent unnecessary court appearances or at least give yourself a solid defense if you are hauled into court.

Subjective Hiring Criteria

I have said that you should base your job descriptions and other selection aids on objective, measurable criteria. Subjective ("soft") criteria can be too easily used as a subterfuge for discrimination. Yet not all job descriptions fit neatly into an objective and measurable mold.

How do you measure "ability to relate well to other employees and to customers"? "listens well"? "motivates others"? "receptive to new ideas"? "creative"? "innovative"? You may be able to pull together *indirect* measures—low absentee rates, increased customer activity, improved productivity—but you would be hard-pressed to *prove* that any one thing a new employee does would necessarily produce those changes.

Still, some positions, e.g., supervision/management and sales, by their very nature require that you consider the can-

didates' ability to work well with others, to motivate them, or
to relate to them as hiring criteria. You have to judge applicants for these positions (whether moving within the organization or coming to you from the outside) on the basis of soft
standards. Most courts[1] and the EEOC will accept decisions
based on soft criteria if they pass two tests:

1. The same criteria are applied evenhandedly to all applicants for a position.
2. The subjective criteria are job-related, that is, they
   meet the standard of business necessity.

The courts merely ask managers to manage well when
making personnel decisions.

Hiring by Committee

One way to prevent soft criteria from becoming illegally or
unfairly discriminatory is to hire by committee.

Now committees do not always make a camel from the
blueprint of a horse. Especially when making a hiring decision,
a committee can give the kind of input or feedback that
prevents subjective factors from interfering with an appropriate choice. Unless your organization's culture and climate
interfere with good management judgment, more than one
person's opinion undermines blinders—personal biases and
preferences.

An effective committee will function well if its composition
incorporates at least one person from a protected class, especially if at least one candidate is from the same protected
group. There is no need to worry that just because that person
is a member of a protected group, he or she will decide in favor
of a "protected group" candidate, as one of the Casebook
studies shows.

When minorities or women participate in the selection
process, you get the benefit of the perspective they bring to the
situation. You see how well the new employee will fit in with
the other employees with whom he or she will have to work
(an important point in this day of increased interdependence

among workers). And, most importantly, by including minorities or females on hiring or promotion committees, you create a safeguard against errors that also blocks charges of discrimination. In short, participatory hiring makes good management sense by ensuring that you hire the right people into the right jobs and by making a defense against bias charges easier.

Proactive Action

I wrote this book, in part, to provide you with tests, such as the three below, that courts apply to discover if reasons for not hiring someone are pretextual or bona fide.[1,2,3]

Test 1:   Is a given criterion a *requirement* for the productive, proper, and safe performance of the job?

Test 2:   Are criteria evenhandedly applied?

Test 3:   Has every reasonable effort been made to recruit or to accommodate members of protected classes?

From a management perspective, all such tests force managers to give careful thought to their job analyses and criteria for hiring people. Not a bad management practice, really.

You can refuse to hire a member of a protected class, the courts have said, but you must be prepared to defend your decision. Nothing prohibits you from saying no to applicants who cannot perform the duties of the job if in fact you do not have the time or resources for training them. If you need to hire someone competent to perform up to or close to the standards of the job, and you hire someone from a nonprotected group to train to do that job, then your hiring policy falls within civil rights guidelines.

Proactive managers should make business necessity their main concern: e.g., safe and efficient operation. If a situation makes it impossible for a person to perform the job's duties or perform them safely, you are preventing problems and can defend your decisions on the basis of a BFOQ. But you should be able to prove in court that *sound criteria* defining a BFOQ exist, if you deny employment to members of protected groups.

Affirmative Action

Adhering to an acceptable affirmative action plan, something
with which your personnel administrator should be concerned,
remains the most proactive approach to safe hiring practices.
All government agencies, government contractors, and subcontractors are required to have one. Many organizations have
adopted voluntary affirmative action standards also.

If your organization has published a plan, you should ask
to read it, if it has not been disseminated to everyone with
hiring responsibilities. If you do not know what the plan
requires and if you do not know where the organization stands
with respect to its affirmative action goals, you cannot be
expected to abide by the plan.

While affirmative action is a proactive approach to rectifying many years of excluding protected people from the economic advantages enjoyed by white, healthy males, many of
those white healthy males see it as a form of "reverse discrimination." They could challenge you if you hire protected employees rather than them, even if your organization has a court-
approved agreed judgment that specifies numerical goals for
hiring or promoting minorities, women, and other protected
groups. The Casebook contains an example of this sort of
situation.

CASEBOOK

This Casebook highlights problems that could arise when
you hire new employees. Situations such as denying promotions or unemployment benefits may not seem to have a direct
bearing on hiring decisions, but courts apply legal definitions
and conclusions from them to a wide range of cases. Pay as
close attention to them as you do to situations involving
immediate hiring decisions, as in the following case.

Does an Older Employee Have to Accept Your Offer?

Although she knew full well that she would be the oldest person
applying for the job, Sally Johnson applied for an entry-level position

advertised by a printing company because, in spite of her age, she met all the conditions stipulated by the employer, including extensive prior work experience. Imagine her shock when she was told there were no openings. She was even more shocked when the company asked her to come to work for it *in the cafeteria*.

When Sally answered, "No, I have more skills and experience than you need in the cafeteria, and I'm really not interested in that line of work," the interviewer shrugged and thanked her for applying.

Sally, however, could not shrug off her rejection. She took the company before the EEOC, and when the company refused to settle, the EEOC took it to court.

In court, the company argued that it had offered the woman a job that she refused, and therefore they were not guilty of discrimination; Sally was not entitled to a settlement that included back pay. She was the unreasonable party in the affair.

How would you have treated Sally if she had applied to you for an entry-level position? What does your organization say about hiring older employees?

The Right of Refusal

In a similar case, an appeals court, ruling in favor of the applicant, answered that she was not unreasonable in turning down a job that was not substantially equivalent to the one for which she applied. Prior U.S. Supreme Court decisions[4] do not require a person to go into another line of work, accept a demotion, or take a demeaning position just to protect his or her claims or rights. Here, the *printing company acted unreasonably* in assuming that an applicant should accept whatever it wished to offer her just because she was older than the average applicant for an entry-level position.[5]

Several mistakes made the company's managers liable for back pay. In our case, two simple steps could have prevented this:

First, they should have hired the plaintiff at the outset, but failing that, they should have offered her a position that approximated her skills, background, and experience. The Eighth Circuit Court made it clear that the closer the approximation, the less likely the employer will be held liable if the person refuses the offer. An older worker should not be asked to accept less than a younger person would just because he or she is older. The company's hiring criteria could not pass the tests of job requirement and evenhanded application.

Second, the company should have properly conveyed the offer to her. They offered Sally a job and merely shrugged off her rejection. With proper documentation—a written, dated offer and a written, dated acceptance or rejection—they would have demonstrated that they took the application seriously, but that a legitimate business reason prevented them from hiring the applicant into the position for which he or she applied. But courts demand a *"legitimate business reason,"* not a pretextual excuse.

The next case involves judgments that affect hiring decisions insofar as the situation involves definitions on which hiring decisions are made.

Can You Refuse to Hire Someone Whose Personal Religious Beliefs Prevent Him or Her From Working on a Sabbath?

Frank Williams was laid off in 1984. When he turned down an offer of a temporary retail store job that would require him to work Wednesday through Sunday, the manager understood. Explaining the situation to the state's unemployment officer was a different matter. "Why won't you work on Sunday?"

"It's against my faith to work on Sunday," Williams answered.

"What faith is that?"

"I'm a Christian."

"What kind of Christian?"

"Presbyterian."

"But the Presbyterian Church doesn't forbid work on Sunday."

"No, just as a Christian, I feel it's wrong."

The officer studied the man's face for a long, silent moment. "Since you refused to accept a position when it was offered, we have to deny your claim for unemployment insurance."

Supported by the Rutherford Institute, a nonprofit organization that litigates cases involving religious freedom, Williams took the state of Illinois to court. The appellate court upheld the official's decision, ruling that constitutional protections extend only to "a tenet or dogma of an established religious sect." The plaintiff then carried his case to the U.S. Supreme Court.

How do you think the Court ruled, and what difference would that ruling make in your hiring decisions?

"I Believe" and the Law

The Court cited an earlier, 1963, U.S. Supreme Court decision extending the First Amendment clause on the free exercise of religion to cover observants of established minority sects, such as Seventh-Day Adventists and Jehovah's Witnesses, and protecting them from having to choose between practicing their religion and forgoing government benefits. Turning down a job offer requiring work on the Sabbath, said the 1963 Court, clearly conforms to the teachings of such churches.

But this case involved a matter of *personal* conscience or faith. Did the law's protections extend to it as well? The Anti-Defamation League of B'nai B'rith (a Jewish group), in a friend of the court brief, had warned that the Illinois decision to deny the claim threatened the rights of American Jews, more than one-third of whom observe Jewish holy days even though they are not formally affiliated with any of the religion's organized branches.

Justice Byron R. White, writing for the Court, said that the law does not stop at protecting only formal doctrine. "We reject the notion that to claim the protection of the free-exercise clause, one must be responding to the commands of a particular religious organization." The belief need be only "sincere" and of a "religious" rather than of a secular or "bizarre or incredible" nature to qualify for protection.[2]

So what does a case involving unemployment insurance have to do with hiring or not hiring someone who refuses to work on a Sabbath?

The issue of *what constitutes a religious belief* makes a crucial distinction for the First Amendment and for civil rights laws. Although it left ambiguous the meaning of *religious*, the

Supreme Court ruled that personal convictions mean as much to the law as do formal doctrines. A large, diverse group of religious organizations (representing millions of evangelical Christians and many Jews) hailed this decision because it supported the same rights enjoyed by members of recognized churches for devout but nonaffiliated religious people.

This case provides two steps you can take to prevent risking a day (or many years) in court if a person's religious practices present barriers to hiring him or her:

1. Be sure that working on a Saturday or Sunday (a Sabbath day) is a *necessary* condition of the job in question, and, if it is, make that information known either in your recruitment information or early on in the discussion; let the applicant rule him- or herself out of the job.
2. If working on a Sabbath day is not essential, but desirable, and if a person is otherwise qualified, see what you can do to accommodate that person's needs.

These proactive steps could prevent a possible lawsuit.

Here is another, seemingly different question. Since the courts expect you to recognize your employees' needs (such as accommodating religious preferences), how far can you go to protect what you perceive to be their needs?

Can You Discriminate to Protect Women From Toxic Environments?

Because studies of the work environment in a manufacturing plant showed a high level of exposure to lead existed and since medical evidence indicates exposure to lead can produce birth defects, the managers of the plant closed positions in that part of the process to women. "The union is sure to grieve," the CEO cautioned.

And grieve the union did, alleging discrimination against both men and women under Title VII. In federal district court, the union argued that lead poses a reproductive risk to *both* sexes. To exclude only women from those jobs was discriminatory.

The company countered with medical evidence showing that the risk of lead exposure to an unborn fetus was greater than the risks

to fertile men: Damage to the fetus' central nervous system, retarda-
tion or learning disabilities, and possible stillbirth were cited.

On which side do you think the court came down? Which
side would your organization support? Why?

Imminent Danger

The district court used a three-part test to decide if the employer's policy *unfairly* discriminated on the basis of sex.

1. Does substantial risk of harm exist?
2. Is the risk mainly to members of one sex?
3. Is there no acceptable alternative that would produce a
   lesser impact on the gender affected (e.g., protective
   clothing)?

The court agreed that, given the medical testimony, the
managers *appropriately* discriminated against women. In addition, the union did not advance an alternate plan for lessen-
ing the negative effects on women and better protecting fetuses
from lead exposure, which, the court declared, is the union's
responsibility. Case dismissed.[3]

The issue is not a matter of whether or not the company
discriminated, because it did. But it did so on the basis of a
reasonable business necessity, the safe performance of duties,
that made hiring decisions *fair* as opposed to unfair. That is an
important distinction you should apply when making your
own decisions.

Other courts have applied more stringent tests than the
above. The Pregnancy Discrimination Act of 1978 makes it
illegal not to hire an applicant (or to fire someone) merely
because she is pregnant.[6] To treat a pregnant applicant or
employee differently is as discriminatory as it is to treat
someone differently just because she is black or Jewish or
disabled. The court, in the case on which this discussion is
based, required an employer to pass at least one of three tests
similar to the three tests listed earlier:

1. A nondiscriminatory reason exists, such as incompetence.
2. The discrimination results from a bona fide occupational qualification (BFOQ), such as a job as model for maternity clothing.
3. The policy satisfies a business necessity.

In sum, have sufficiently good reasons, such as safe and efficient operation of the employer's business *as well as* imminent danger to the fetus, if you refuse to hire members of protected groups, e.g., pregnant women who are qualified or competent to do or learn how to do the job.

If you proactively apply such legal tests to your job analyses and criteria for hiring people, you will be prepared to defend your decisions in court. As I said before, nothing prohibits you from saying no to applicants who cannot perform the duties of the job, if in fact you do not have the time or resources for training them. If you need to hire someone competent to perform up to or close to the standards of the job, and you hire someone from a nonprotected group to do that job, then your hiring policy falls within civil rights guidelines and administration if qualified protected individuals are not available. If you hire a nonprotected person *to train*, you could be in trouble.

By making business necessity—safe, productive, and efficient operations—your main concern, you can defend your decisions on the basis of a BFOQ. But you should be able to prove in court that *sound criteria* defining a BFOQ exist, if you deny employment to qualified members of protected groups. The issue of what constitutes sound criteria, especially with respect to supervisory or management positions, was settled in the next case.

Can You Use Subjective Hiring Criteria?

Francine, a black woman, worked long and hard at doing her job well and could not understand why, whenever it came time for promotion, she was passed over. Explanations about communication skills, the ability to interact with all levels of employees, appearance, ability to take command made little sense to her. "No one does the job better than me, and I have the evaluations and letters to prove it," she argued when she took her employer to court for racial bias.

"Yes," the employer agreed. "Francine does her job well, but she is talking about technical skills, and we are talking about different, more subjective skills important for supervisors to have. She is just not qualified for a supervisory position; we have told her so and what she can do to improve herself."

Is the use of *subjective* criteria, by itself and in the appropriate situation, per se discriminatory? What do you think?

"Soft" Criteria

That this case involves a promotion rather than a new hire is irrelevant. In the court's perception, promoting someone from within is a hiring procedure because you could have hired someone from the outside to fill the same position. In effect, the promotion is hiring someone to perform new duties.

In this case, the decision not to promote the plaintiff was upheld because it passed the tests of job requirement and evenhanded application. A job function integral to a position is definitely required, even if it is not necessarily measurable by a numerical test.[1]

In the model case, the employer had another defense. Blacks and women participated in the selection process. Including minorities and women on the committee served as a safeguard against errors and blocked charges of discrimination. Francine was a black woman, but blacks and women turned her down for the job. Their decision, in the court's view, was fair and proper.

Hiring decisions often appear biased in spite of safeguards because social history has created situations for today's managers over which they may not have any control. It may seem from this discussion that the courts presume your guilt until you prove yourself innocent of wrongdoing. But consider this case before you come to a final conclusion.

On Whom Is the Burden of Proof?

Minorities find it tough enough to get a job unless they can get training. Most companies do not have the resources to train all their entry-level employees. Where unions control the work force of an industry, employers often depend on them to provide worker training.

One labor union offered training at its hiring hall. But rarely could anyone find a minority person in the program, a legal aid group charged, filing on behalf of minorities under Section 1981 of the Civil Rights Act of 1866.

Union officials responded that, although it is true that few minorities had been included, they did not *intentionally* discriminate. The lack of minorities resulted from nondiscriminatory, skill-related criteria.

If you had to, could you prove that your organization selected people for training on strictly skill-related criteria? In this case, which occurred in 1982, on whom do you think the burden of proof fell?

Plaintiffs, Make Your Case

The burden of proof fell on the plaintiff, and seven years later, in a different case, the Supreme Court ruled the same way: Under the Civil Rights Act of 1866, an employer cannot be held liable for race discrimination in the absence of proof of *intent* to discriminate. In the present case, the evidence of intent was missing.[7] But intent is not always difficult to prove, especially if your own or your organization's words or deeds can be used against you.

To prevent the appearance of discrimination, many organizations have voluntarily adopted affirmative action programs, recruiting minorities or other protected individuals and giving them opportunities they might not otherwise have had. Other organizations, attempting to head off unnecessary and wasteful litigation, have entered into court-approved agreements with representatives of protected groups that would provide the essential ingredients of affirmative action. How valid are such agreements?

Will an Affirmative Action Program Through an Agreed Judgment Prevent Litigation?

In 1981 a federal court agreed to a settlement between a major southern city and the National Association for the Advancement of Colored People to increase the number of blacks hired and promoted in the fire department. This was a *consent decree*, which means the court supported a mutually agreed upon alternative to the city's hiring practices that satisfied the city and the NAACP, in spite of the predominantly white firefighter union's protests.

Several months later, a group of white firefighters challenged the agreement, arguing that it discriminated against them. The district court dismissed the suit; the city, it said, was following the dictates of a consent decree and could not be guilty of discrimination against anyone. In 1987 the Eleventh Circuit Court, persuaded by the Reagan Administration's arguments, overturned the district court's dismissal and agreed to reinstate the white firefighter's suit. The city and the black firefighters appealed to the U.S. Supreme Court.

What do you think? Is your organization in safe waters if it enters into a court-approved voluntary affirmative action program?

The Rights of Strangers

The accepted opinion of "the great majority of the federal courts of appeals" has been that if parties choose not to intervene in a lawsuit that could affect them in the end, "they should not be permitted to later litigate the issues in a new action. . . ." The U.S. Supreme Court overruled that opinion.

Chief Justice William H. Rehnquist, writing for the majority, took "the contrary view [that] a judgement or decree among parties to a lawsuit resolves issues as among them, but it does not conclude the rights of strangers to those proceedings." Anyone with a justifiable interest has the right to contest a consent decree.[8]

This decision complements one rendered in January 1989 that struck down a minority set-aside program for contractors. Here, Justice Sandra Day O'Connor expressed the majority view that race-based preference programs may be scrutinized for the violations of equal protection under the Fourteenth Amendment that the plan purports to remedy. Careful studies of past discrimination must precede any legislative action. In the absence of clear-cut evidence of past discrimination, set-aside programs may be nothing more than a "product of unthinking stereotypes or a form of racial politics."[9]

Safe management is not easy. You can be hoisted by your own petard if you try to do what seems right to you at the time. This is one of those damned-if-you-do and damned-if-you-don't cases that could happen in many other situations as well, especially since some U.S. Supreme Court rulings in 1989 confused the issues surrounding civil rights. Regardless, no one should suppose that those decisions render discrimination-in-employment laws null and void. The laws still stand, and as a manager you must act within the laws (outlined for you in the Appendix). However, just as the law creates limits that constrain your hiring decisions, it also allows you to take action to satisfy reasonable business demands.

Cases

1. 757 F.2d 1504, 37 F.E.P. Cases (BNA) 633 (4th Cir. 1985).
2. No. 87-1945 (1989).
3. No. 84-C-472 (D. Wisc. 1988).
4. 458 U.S. 219, 29 F.E.P. Cases (BNA) 121 (1982).
5. 703 F.2d 276, 31 F.E.P. Cases 621 (8th Cir. 1983).
6. No. 82-7296 (11th Cir. March 16, 1984).
7. 458 U.S. 375, 102 S. Ct. 3141 (1982).
8. 467 U.S. 561 (1984).
9. 110 S. Ct. 11 (1989).

Chapter 4

Preventing Sex Discrimination in Hiring

Economic necessity has driven traditional homemakers into the work force. Today, more working women are divorced or never married; the number of single working mothers has doubled since the late 1950s and early 1960s. According to the U.S. Census Bureau, they will dominate the work force by the turn of the century; 85 percent of all new workers will be women and minorities. Women will have fewer children on the whole, but they will also have fewer dollars with which to take care of them, mainly because the shift to a service economy will keep incomes lower.

Whereas equal opportunity for blacks dominated the 1960s, equal opportunity for women dominates our times. That domination will probably continue, fueled by both economic necessity and personal aspirations.

The complexity and subtlety that mark sex discrimination issues necessitate this separate chapter and Chapter 8 (on sexual harassment). Legal confrontations ebb and flow in a seething whirlpool created when fast-moving change surges against a sluggish but forceful stream of long-held values, attitudes, and practices, forcing women as well as men to flounder and cast about for some lifesaving set of rules to grab on to. But, with the rules changing daily, no one has a secure lifeline to throw as yet.

Our "lifeline" comes down to the overriding theme of this

book. Safe management is effective management: data-driven, objectively administered, constituency-oriented. Let's look at specific barriers that have blocked women from pursuing opportunities available to men, or that have placed women in inferior positions, or that have made sex a part of the hiring process.

What You Cannot Do

It does not take much effort to prevent sex discrimination in the workplace. Mostly it requires not doing many of the things that male employers have done for many years. In other words:

1. *Don't apply irrelevant criteria.* You cannot evaluate a woman's skills or abilities differently from the way you do a man's solely on the basis of gender differences unless a BFOQ or other sound business reason is involved. But then, criteria you might suppose are bona fide could turn out, upon careful examination, not to be so important, e.g., height requirements or strength tests. You should examine job criteria for anything that might be construed as a subterfuge to prohibit women from filling specific jobs.

2. *Don't give unequal treatment.* During interviews, you cannot treat women differently from the way you do men by asking questions you would not ask men or by dwelling on sex-oriented or sexually loaded subjects. An example is a woman's physical appearance. Childbearing or child care questions, such as those discussed in Chapter 2, are irrelevant unless they are asked of men as well as of women.

Predicating the hiring of an applicant on his or her willingness to be your bed partner should be obviously taboo. Yet women (more often than men) still find "jobs for sex" a part of the marketplace. We discuss this in more detail in Chapter 8 on sexual harassment.

3. *Don't publish sexist recruitment materials.* You cannot communicate with or recruit only from a male-dominated segment of society. "Good old boy" networks, male social

clubs, male friends, or male relatives of male employees have often been a means for maintaining an all-male elite clique, barriers that the courts break down. Organizations now have begun to resort to "mixed message" communications, such as brochures with photographs of men in professional positions and women in secretarial or other line positions.

Brochures with only men in top management or in the sales force tell women, "No future for you here, sister." Conveying the mixed message, whether directly or indirectly, is as illegal as the blatant recruiting methods of the past, and it can be used against you in court. So, whereas in Chapter 1 I talk about nondiscriminatory publications and illustrate the topic with an allegedly "ageist" magazine article, here I point out the dangers inherent in sexist materials, which I illustrate with the first case in this chapter's Casebook.

4. *Don't provide disinformation or misleading information.* You cannot use scare tactics to discourage women from applying for male-dominated jobs. Exaggerating the importance of being a man in order to do the job, exaggerating the importance of women in certain roles rather than others, or making success appear impossible for women are tactics managers have used to keep women from seeing themselves in professional, management, or sales roles. Tell people the truth, and let them judge whether or not they can succeed in a given job.

5. *Don't create an intimidating climate or environment.* You cannot decorate your facilities in a manner offensive to most women—nude centerfolds, obscene jokes, sexually oriented graffiti on the walls—or permit male employees to greet female applicants with catcalls or wolf whistles, or invite them to dinner or to bed, or make other suggestions that would make women fearful of working in your organization. Likewise, in a female-dominated environment, male applicants should not be treated in a discriminatory manner.

6. *Don't restrict convenience.* You cannot restrict a lavatory or dressing room to men only, even if you have only one. Schedules or other accommodations (e.g., "occupied" posters to signal use) can easily circumvent limited resources.

7. *Don't interfere with a person's right to apply.* You cannot

prevent someone from applying for a job just because his or her spouse works for the organization. Such policies usually have a disparate impact on women, but men can be affected as well. The courts allow antinepotism policies to prevent spouses from working for the same supervisor, as long as the policy is applied evenhandedly (i.e., either the man or the woman could be required to transfer or leave the company), but they do not allow you to close the door on spouses altogether.

8. *Don't offer unequal pay for equal work.* You cannot offer lower pay to women with skills and experience equal to those of men doing the same job. Everyone is entitled to earn the same pay for doing the same work under the same conditions.

Do not confuse equal pay for equal work with equal pay for "comparable worth," which has become a popular topic for debate in Congress. The argument for "comparable worth" attempts to remove the disparity in wages between traditional women's jobs and traditional men's jobs when such jobs require similar or equal knowledge and skills, make similar or the same mental demands, require similar or the same levels of accountability, are performed under similar or equal working conditions, and provide the employer with similar or equal value. The jobs are not equal, but they have comparable worth.

To date the courts have not accepted this theory and have said that it is an accident of history that men and women frequently do not earn equal pay for jobs that fall in the categories just described. Women find ready access only to some jobs or professions, e.g., secretarial work, in which wages are usually lower than wages paid in jobs open mostly to men. Historically, employers have measured the pay in the jobs open to women not in terms of what their job performance is worth to the company, but rather in terms of what women have been willing to accept.

Until recently, women accepted lower wages on the basis of the same fallacious theory employers use: Women in the work force tend to be married and are not the sole or equal support of the family. Most women have acquiesced and accepted those market rates for their jobs, and they now battle low wages regardless of their family status.

Whereas the courts have accepted the validity of equal pay for equal work, they still rule that requiring an employer to remedy the equalities in a marketplace it did not create is asking too much of the individual employer.[1] But the ebb and flow of legal decisions could turn that position around, especially if Congress legislates equal pay for comparable worth.

What You Can Do

Before any of that happens, you can balance compensation between men and women, which leads us into what you can do to avoid sex discrimination in the workplace.

1. *Publish policies, standards, or guidelines.* You can prevent accidental or apparent discrimination by following your organization's written procedures. If your organization has not published standards, ask that your personnel people produce the appropriate documents and disseminate them. Proactive management reduces the risk of needless time in court.

Policies, standards, or guidelines should identify what managers cannot do and can do when recruiting, interviewing, and hiring employees. Obviously, such policies should not be restricted only to the "how to"s with respect to women, but they are our immediate concern. The sample antiharassment policy statement shown in Chapter 8 (Figure 8-1) will provide you with a model for writing any policy statement.

Policies and procedures should also include instructions on how to design nonsexist job descriptions, such as the examples in Chapter 1. The criteria for hiring should be objective and measurable, unless "soft" functions and performance criteria are inherent in the job. Then subjective criteria should be well defined.

2. *Publish inviting, accurate recruitment materials.* You can describe your organization in terms that will invite *anyone* to apply. That requires that managers and other employees have an open mind to gender and sexual preferences (as well as to racial and other differences). Women and minorities in high

places in your organization should become visible to the public not only for recruiting purposes but also to improve your image among customers and the community at large.

Open traditionally male jobs to female employees. Few positions have BFOQs that make them inaccessible to women. The barriers are mostly social, not physical or mental. Social barriers can even play havoc with organizational policies on hiring husbands and wives, as described in the Casebook.

3. *Treat a promotion as a new hire.* You can treat all employees fairly. Just because someone already works for you is not sufficient reason for treating him or her differently from the way you would a new hire. That difference in treatment has often retarded the advancement of women.

The courts recognize the mutual advantage of employees' learning and developing new skills on the job and of not expecting an employer to reclassify these employees immediately. An employer needs a reasonable amount of time to evaluate a new hire's potential in a job; the employer also needs time to evaluate a promotable person's potential before reclassifying that person by placing the candidate in a temporary ("acting") capacity. The employer could also reserve the right to decide if organizational needs require filling the higher-paid position after all.

However, once you are satisfied that the employee can perform the new duties and you become aware that a woman employee is performing work equivalent to that of a higher-paid man but with lower pay, you have two options:

a. Require the employee to restrict his or her activities to the lower-paid job.
b. If you let the person continue in the higher-graded job, pay the employee the higher salary plus any retroactive pay or seniority.

Delay or failure to give equal pay or to maintain an employee's seniority could both be considered unreasonable by the courts.[2]

4. *Guard against a dual compensation system.* If your orga-

nization pays men and women differently for the same jobs, encourage your personnel administrator to produce a single compensation system or call in a consultant who can do it for the organization.

To *correct* inequities in pay requires a detailed analysis of your compensation system, but if you follow the simple steps below, you will be able to *identify* whether or not discriminatory wage variations exist. In most settings where several men and one woman perform substantially the same work, you can judge the woman's wages against those paid to men employee*s* (the plural is used in the Equal Pay Act itself) by:

a. Holding all factors, such as seniority and skill levels, equal,
b. Taking an average of the wages paid to the men, and
c. Comparing the woman's salaries against the *average*.

If the woman's salary is lower than the average, you *may have to* raise it.

If this simple formula suggests that a discriminatory pay disparity exists, your organization should have a statistician do a *thorough* analysis. Then call upon an attorney for advice before taking any action. Without legal counsel, you could take the wrong action.

The courts have declared that unless you have a compelling reason to raise it higher, you need raise a lower salary only by the *difference* between it and the *average*. That is how the court might award damages, should you lose in court to a woman who believes her pay is inequitable.[3] In the Casebook I discuss several variations on the equal pay theme.

Reducing disparities between men's and women's wages is just good management. The labor market operates on principles of competition just as any other free market does. Offer good wages and you will attract good people. Good employees work efficiently and effectively, reducing costs of operations and balancing the increased cost of labor.

5. *Manage effectively.* As in other cases of civil rights legislation, you are free to manage your operation on the basis of sound judgments. Why would a manager do less?

Only ignorance and prejudice prevent fair and equal treatment in the hiring of women. Especially as more women enter the work force at all levels and in all professions, the old social barriers will have to crumble. You can smash a hammer against those barriers by providing women with equal opportunities in your own hiring practices. In other words:

a. Use effective management practices to establish acceptable criteria for your actions,
b. Become aware of cultural attitudes and values that interfere with rational decision making, and
c. Avoid irrelevant or extraneous comments related to sex or sex-related differences during interviews.

There is only one rule to follow for safe management: the rule of sound management.

CASEBOOK

Have you or your organization done what you can to prevent illegal discrimination, especially against women? In addition to applying the lessons of this chapter to the cases that follow, compare your organization's practices and policies against the decisions involved, and see how you might fare in similar circumstances.

Is the Number of Women in Your Work Force Sufficient to Prevent a Charge of Deliberate Discrimination?

Sylvia Posner, a secretary, tried for many years to get at the big money earned by the sales force of Rural National Insurance of California, a subsidiary of a major property and casualty carrier. But every time she applied she was turned down.

Supported by a national organization, Sylvia filed a class action suit under Title VII. The plaintiffs testified as follows:

The company applies no objective criteria or qualifications for Agent Trainees, an entry level position. No minimal education, specific work experience, or net worth. In fact, they prefer prospective trainees not have prior insurance experience. Yet, in 1981, only 3.5% of the agents were females and only one held the position of agency manager. No woman had ever held a VP, RVP, or Director title.

With between 35 percent and 45 percent availability and a recruitment goal of 50 percent, the company still had not extended many agent openings to women. Compare the 3.5 percent figure for sales against 46.8 percent women in operation divisions. With so many secretaries, office managers, and solicitors in agent offices, as well as in various operations areas, it seems deliberate that few women hold the coveted agent roles.

The company countered that whatever discrimination existed was not deliberate. "Females are either unqualified or do not apply for these jobs."

Look around your own organization. Are there women in the high-income or professional ranks? Do you think your own organization's personnel distribution would hold up in court?

All But the Smoking Gun

The Northern District Court of California decided that the company did not issue a policy or guideline saying "Don't hire women to be agents" but that it might as well have.[3]

In this case, as in most, traditional conditions and informal policies block women from access to important positions. Compare the outline of Rural National's hiring guidelines or policies with your own or those of your organization.

► *Word-of-mouth/nepotism.* Instead of issuing written policies, standards, or guidelines, the company allowed its managers' uncontrolled discretion and "talking network" to do the hiring from a pool of personal contacts, social/professional groups, business associates, and clients. Between 1965 and 1977, company policy favored "sons and sons-in-law, brothers, brothers-in-law, and other close relatives of agents." The use of the network and nepotism, well known to everyone, discouraged women from applying.

▸ *Advertising image.* Recruitment brochures depicted only men agents (thirty-one men-only pictures on one brochure), used the male pronouns only, and stated that an agent "must also serve as 'the friendly guy' who lives nearby." Noting that this condition discouraged women from applying, corporate management ordered changes in the brochures; "[P]ictures of females and minorities, appropriate to today's environment," were to be included.

▸ *Reputation.* The company's managers were notorious for not hiring women trainees. Women office employees testified that they believed the company would not hire women because they saw only men agents and heard male managers say they would not hire women.

▸ *Active efforts to discourage.* Testimony was heard that secretaries were given misleading information (e.g., incorrect educational qualifications) when they applied. Their prospects were minimized. Their value as clerks or office managers were inflated. They were also told, "Just think of how lucky you are to be part of a successful agency."

▸ *Undefined, subjective criteria.* Subjective criteria are acceptable as long as they are inherent in the job and are well defined. However, Rural National applied these undefined criteria:

1. The desire and motivation to establish and manage an independent insurance business
2. The stability to maintain such a business
3. A pattern of success in past activities and employments
4. The ability to make sensitive and subtle judgments
5. The ability to cope with the demands of a career, with a drive to work hard
6. The ability to meet and relate well to people
7. An interest in having a high income and security as a private businessperson
8. Competitiveness
9. An active social life

These criteria, the court noted, were highly subjective and arbitrarily applied with no thought to fairness or consistency. No specific guidelines or policies ruled the process of the decision-making group, which until 1981 (when a woman agency manager was hired) was all male. They were undefined and subjective, tradition-bound, uncontrolled, and unmanaged. The obvious moral to this story: Although actively recruiting women is a sound management practice, ensuring that you do not actively discourage them is just as important.

Compare your organization's hiring criteria and procedures against the list above and decide how well yours stacks up. An effective, useful system should be well-defined and objective. The criteria should be based on work-related skill requirements or observable personal characterisitcs, appropriate to the work force available, and appropriate to the jobs being filled.

Natural male-female distinctions dominate gender-based cases, but a new side to sex discrimination based on sex preferences now emerges that has implications for society as a whole as well as for business.

What Does a Case of Firing Someone for Having a Sex Change Operation Mean to Your Hiring Practices?

Joelyn Cassidy, né Joel Cassidy, took her former employer to court under Title VII when the airline fired her after she underwent a sex change operation. "They discriminated on the basis of sex because they hired me as a man, and when I had the operation they treated my former maleness as a condition of employment."

The company answered only, "Title VII does not form a basis of the plaintiff's cause of action" and asked for a summary dismissal.

Give this situation some serious thought. What do you think would happen in your organization if an employee had a sex change operation? How would you handle such a situation? And finally, what do you think this case means to the issue of sex discrimination?

Because of Sex

The judge in the Northern District of Illinois applied Title VII while admitting that Congress probably never considered the term *sex* to include a person who had a sex change operation. He concluded that the plaintiff was fired because, in effect, the employer demanded that she remain male as a condition of employment. That established a causal connection between the discharge and the alleged discrimination "because of sex."[4] The hiring standards changed, but only with regard to sex, when he became she.

So what does this case mean to you? After all, sex change operations are not common, and they pose few everyday problems.

This case broadens the definition of "because of sex" under Title VII to include sexual preference with respect to one's own gender. While it may seem difficult to imagine, an attorney might just use this case as a precedent to argue that sexual preference with regard to sex partners is also covered under Titel VII. Although the law today does not extend to sexual preference in this sense, you may at some time have to broaden your definition of sex discrimination to include homosexuality. Besides, what legitimate business reason *could* you have for not hiring a gay person?

No law says you must hire women or homosexuals, but both groups must be given equal opportunities to compete on the basis of their qualifications or their trainability. It is wise to consider only the kind of work the applicant or employee is required to perform and the ability of that person to do the job and do it well, and fairly reward him or her for doing it.

When Does a Wage Scheme Discriminate Illegally?

In a professional job setting such as a college, some people are employed in the same job classification and perform substantially equal work although paid different wages. So it was at a state college on the West Coast, where a woman employee checked her salary against the highest pay in the classification and discovered that the recipient was a man. That another man also received lower pay than the highest-paid person made no difference. The woman took the school administration to court under the Equal Pay Act.

Could this happen in your organization? How come?

The Difference

The Equal Pay Act does *not* prohibit variations in wages, the court declared. It prohibits only *discriminatory* variations in wages *because of sex*. If a woman employee earns more (or no less) than men doing substantially the same work, even if a man is at the top of the salary bracket, the employer has not automatically violated the Equal Pay Act.

If you manage several men and one woman in a professional setting in which they perform substantially the same work, you can determine if wage variations among them are discriminatory by comparing the woman's wages against those paid to men in the manner just described. If your analysis suggests that a discriminatory pay disparity exists, ask for a more thorough statistical analysis.

The court in this case was the one that declared that unless you have a compelling reason to raise it higher, you need raise a lower salary only by the *difference* between it and the *average*.[3]

These rules usually work for claims brought under the Equal Pay Act. Should a person bring a "but for" claim under Title VII, the situation could be quite different. Let's say the woman brings a Title VII sex discrimination case instead of an Equal Pay claim. In this new scenario, she could say:

> I'm doing essentially the same work as the highest-paid person, who is a man. I am as qualified, I have as much experience, and I have performed as well as he. Therefore, I merit or deserve equal pay for equal work, and if I weren't a woman, I would receive it.

The court in our previous case would have ruled that even if the woman employee were earning more than the average wage for the male employees, but for her sex was not receiving the higher wage paid to the comparable male employees, she should receive the higher wage. If she also marshaled the proper evidence of intent to discriminate, she would receive the pay raise, plus back pay as damages.

Wage variations can exist as long as they reflect the "factors other than sex" exception of both Title VII and the Equal Pay Act. The nonsex justification must account for the *entire* wage difference between male and female employees, not just form a partial basis.

One such basis is called "red circle" wage rates, which are unusual, higher than normal wage rates maintained for legitimate business purposes such as paying a higher rate to a temporarily reassigned employee or to an employee whose previous job was eliminated.

In one case in point, a man employee was temporarily transferred from a higher-paying position in a hospital to a lower one, where he then performed the same work as did the woman employee who had been employed there before him. During the period they worked together, performing the same duties, the man's pay scale ranged from $472 to $671 while the woman's ranged from $268 to $430. The hospital justified the differential by saying that the man was only temporarily reassigned and was therefore paid a red circle rate.

The courts agreed with both the woman and the employer. The man employee had been temporarily reassigned and paid a red circle rate; but that accounted for *only part* of the wage differential. Because to fall within the "factor other than sex" exception, red circling must account for the entire differential and cannot form a partial basis for the differential, the woman employee received a pay award equal to the difference between her wage rate and the *un*explained discrepancy not covered by red circling.[6]

Contrast that decision with the red circling that occurred when a transferred man's job was eliminated. The position into which he transferred involved the same duties a lower-paid woman had also been performing, yet he was allowed to keep his higher salary. The court accepted the *sex-neutral* justification the employer offered: to enhance the desirability of the position and to provide job security to a valued employee.[7]

Let's look at what happens when you reassign to a woman tasks that would reasonably place her in a higher pay category but do not raise her pay.

How Long Is Reasonably Long Before You
Raise a Woman's Pay After a "Promotion"?

At a southwestern college, Doris Lake accepted additional responsibilities partly because she saw the need for it and partly because her supervisor requested that she learn the new skills the tasks required. After a year at the new job, she said that her pay grade should be advanced to the next level because she had been doing the work identified in that classification, and noted that a man had been doing it for higher wages.

Two years of haggling and disputing the nature of the classification ended with the salary increase, but only after Doris filed an EEOC claim. When she was not given back pay or retroactive seniority in the pay grade, Doris let her EEOC petition stand.

The school officials argued that because it was to Doris' advantage that she develop more skills and get on-the-job training in the new responsibilities, they held her at her original pay grade until she was sufficiently skilled. A study had shown that she was properly classified, but because she was so unhappy they changed the study's conclusion. That proved, the officials concluded, that they did not discriminate against Doris on the basis of her sex, but the EEOC did not agree and ultimately the case came before the 9th Circuit Court of Appeals.

How do you manage employee training and development? Does your organization have a career development plan? Or do you require the kind of on-the-job training given to Doris Lake?

Reasonableness Standard

This is the case where the court declared the mutual advantage of employees' learning and developing new skills on the job, and of not expecting an employer to reclassify the employee immediately. The employer needs a reasonable amount of time for evaluating the person's potential in the new job before reclassifying him or her. The employer could also reserve the right to decide if it is necessary to fill the higher-paid position after all.

However, the court added, once the employer becomes

aware that a woman employee is performing work equivalent to that of a higher-paid man employee, but with lower pay, it is required to act to raise the pay within a reasonable time. Two years is not a reasonable amount of time. The delay and the failure to give the plaintiff retroactive pay and seniority were both unreasonable.[2]

Can Dual Compensation for Unequal Work Be Equal?

U.S. Ironworks, Inc., when modernizing its operations, set up a systematic approach to its job and pay analyses that compensated jobs in the manufacturing division on the basis of new objective criteria—detailed job descriptions, standardized performance evaluations, publicly known job classifications, pay scale adjustments based on periodic job reviews—the latest human resources technology to match its upgraded manufacturing process.

On the other hand, the company used subjective criteria for determining compensation for nonmanufacturing jobs, with none of the objective standards found in the manufacturing sections. Traditionally, no women were in manufacturing divisions either, and few men were in nonmanufacturing. Therefore, the women plaintiffs contended, compensation was based on two different *and discriminatory* systems.

How does your organization set compensation? One system? Two?

Different Strokes

A lower court saw the contention as a backdoor attempt to use Title VII to litigate a comparable worth claim, an attempt to increase compensation on the basis of a comparison of the intrinsic worth or difficulty of two different kinds of work—one performed by men, the other performed by women.

The Eleventh Circuit court, on appeal, saw the situation differently, identifying the issue as the company's attempt to maintain separate pay schemes for positions traditionally occupied by men, on the one hand, and positions traditionally occupied by women, on the other. That sort of duality, the court said, regardless of what protected class is affected, could be by itself discriminatory.

Yes, the appellate court said, a dual system can be discriminatory if the basis on which traditionally male and female jobs are evaluated results in different evaluations. If that basis does form the grounds for a Title VII compensation claim, the plaintiffs would be entitled to back pay.[8]

The Equal Pay Act requires employers to distribute compensation appropriately for work or services performed, but you need not use *identical* methods for determining pay in all cases. The ruling in this case means:

> *The greater the dissimilarity between pay systems for jobs in the same organization, the greater the risk the differences can form a factual basis for a compensation discrimination claim.*

When any protected group, e.g., blacks or older employees, predominates in any particular job or group of jobs, similar methods should be used to determine compensation of identical or similar job classifications occupied by white males or other nonminorities.

If you are ever involved in contract negotiations, be aware that the same principle also applies to allowing employees outside the protected groups, but not protected groups, to negotiate contracts or contract changes. You could be charged with discrimination if you treat similarly situated employees differently.[9] You must have legitimate, nondiscriminatory reasons for permitting men employees better contract terms than you do women, which reasons would be hard to find in most cases.

BFOQs or legitimate business reasons for differences in compensation packages can and do affect your decisions. Just make sure that your business reasons have a sound factual basis, such as a legal seniority system or significant variation in experience or skills.

Open traditionally male jobs to female employees. Few positions have BFOQs that make them inaccessible to women. The barriers are mostly social, not physical or mental. Social barriers can even play havoc with organizational policies pertaining to hiring husbands and wives.

Can You Ban Spouses From Reporting to the Same Supervisor?

Alice and Martin, sitting side by side in the same department and reporting to the same supervisor, began dating and not long after got married. Upon hearing of the marriage, management gave either one of them thirty days to transfer to a different position; otherwise the less senior employee, Alice, would be removed from her position.

Feeling imposed on, neither transferred in the time allowed, and Alice was reassigned to a lower-level, lower-paying job, whereupon she filed suit under Title VII.

What does your organization say about nepotism? Who do you think won this case involving an antinepotism rule?

Neutrality and Evenhandedness

The employer won. This antinepotism rule treated *individual* cases fairly without adverse impact on a given sex. The court said that the rule, although unwritten, was itself facially neutral and evenhandedly applied. If the husband had been the junior employee, he would have had to accept the transfer.[11] Not separating husbands and wives working in the same department, especially if one is senior to the other, could result in a conflict of interest, and as such antinepotism policies serve a legitimate business interest.[12]

Additionally, close personal relationships on the job could produce conflicts unrelated to business or generate unwarranted favoritism. Awkward situations can develop between members of the same family working closely together, and it makes good management sense to prevent problems proactively (before they occur).[13]

Yet, as the *National Business Employment Weekly* reported* (without identifying the case), a federal judge in a government agency antinepotism case has ruled that "no law, regardless of

*February 11, 1990, page 14.

intent, should have a 'chilling effect' upon marriage. . . . which is a fundamental right" protected by the Constitution. The article concluded that this case may require employers to reconsider policies that forbid marriage among co-workers.

Can You Ban Spouses From the Company as a Whole?

When the meat-packing plant in town opened, it established an antinepotism rule that said spouses cannot work there even if they work in separate departments and report to different supervisors. The company soon found itself in court, charged with sex discrimination because the rule excluded a disproportionate number of women. Although their husbands could work there, they themselves could not.

How does your organization spell out its antinepotism rules?

Adverse Impacts

Here is a case where the theory of adverse impact on a whole group could stand up to legal tests. Spouses working together in the same department could adversely affect production or productivity, but no business necessity justifies an exclusive rule that has an adverse impact on women, such as the defendant's. The Eighth Circuit Court said nay to the rule.[10] Other remedies for potential problems must be found.

Cases

1. 783 F.2d 716, 40 F.E.P. Cases (BNA) 244 (7th Cir. 1986); 770 F.2d 1401, 38 F.E.P. Cases (BNA) 1353 (9th Cir. 1985); *review denied*, 813 F.2d 1034 (1987).
2. 736 F.2d 126, 35 F.E.P. Cases (BNA) 234 (9th Cir. 1984).
3. 38 F.E.P. Cases (BNA) 197 (N.D. Cal. 1985).
4. 581 F. Supp. 821, 28 F.E.P. Cases (BNA) 1488 (N.D. Ill. 1982), *rev'd*, 742 F.2d 1081, CCA 7 (1984); *cert. denied*, 105 S. Ct. 2023 (1985).
5. 718 F.2d 910, 33 F.E.P. Cases (BNA) 1538 (9th Cir. 1983).

6. 780 F.2d 917, 39 E.P.D. (CCH) ¶35,910 (11th Cir. 1986).
7. 866 F. Supp. 209, 45 F.E.P. Cases (BNA) 330 (M.D. Fla. 1987).
8. 784 F.2d 1546, 40 F.E.P. Cases (BNA) 678 (11th Cir. 1986), *cert. denied,* 107 S. Ct. 274 (1986).
9. 120 L.R.R.M. (BNA) 3203 (D.D.C. 1985).
10. 787 F.2d 318, 40 F.E.P. Cases (BNA) ¶580 (8th Cir. 1986).
11. 601 F. Supp. 160, 37 F.E.P. Cases (BNA) 843 (W.D. Pa. 1985); *aff'd,* 779 F.2d 42 (1985).
12. 462 F. Supp. 289 (S.D.W. Va., 1978).
13. 19 E.P.D. ¶91.3 (D.D.C. 1978).

Chapter 5

Preventing Negligent Hiring

"Is there anyone I *shouldn't* hire?" It may seem that you have little choice in your hiring decisions, that you must hire anyone coming through your door, but that is not true. You only need to give everyone applying for a job fair and equal opportunities to compete for it on the basis of the same work-related criteria. As an employer you have the *right* to say no to anyone who does not satisfy bona fide occupational qualifications (BFOQs) or business necessities, or who cannot be trained to meet them.

You also have an *obligation* to say no to some people. After thoroughly screening all applicants, you have a duty to your organization, other employees, and the public to screen *out* anyone whose record raises a red flag or whose past leads you to suspect that he or she could pose a potential threat to the constituencies that depend on your good judgment. To do less could open you to a charge of negligence.

You must exercise due care in prehire screening, in training new employees, in assigning people to jobs, and in supervising them, especially if the job can expose the public to a potentially dangerous or dishonest person. Without the exercise of reasonable care, you can be held liable to parties injured (theft is a legal injury or tort) by a dishonest, unfit, or incompetent employee.[1] To comply, you should know what some of the terms in this legal context mean.

Definitions of Key Terms

negligence   The failure to exercise due care under circumstances where the legal duty to care is owed another person or other people. By not conducting adequate and proper reference or background checks, you could unknowingly hire someone whose past history indicates the possibility of endangering the property or lives of other people. You could be cited for negligence in that case. Negligence seems to be clear-cut in cases where an employer hires violent employees.

due care   All reasonable and legal steps to protect the organization, other employees, customers, and the general public. The Rhode Island Supreme Court, for example, asserts that the exercise of "reasonable care" means more than accepting the absence of complaints about dishonesty as evidence that the person is honest. Especially in service industries, in which honesty, trustworthiness, and reliability are the hallmarks of business, an employer is expected to include in its records affirmations of the applicant's qualifications.

the doctrine of respondeat superior   When an employee acts within the scope of his or her job as agent for the employer, any wrongful act the employee commits can be attributed to the employer vicariously. But, under this doctrine, if an employee commits a wrongful act *outside the scope* of the employment or *not in furtherance* of the employer's business, the employer cannot be held liable by a third party.

Now, under the doctrine of negligent hiring, the employer can be held liable in such a case.

What You Cannot Do

The courts expect employers to take all *reasonable* and *legal* steps to protect the organization, other employees, customers, and the general public. However, "all *reasonable* and *legal* steps" exclude the use of polygraph (lie detector) tests except in a very limited number of cases, which I will discuss in Chapter 7. You must use other means to protect yourself from the possibility of hiring someone who might get you into serious trouble.

What You Can Do

What follows are reasonable and lawful steps that you can take.

1. *Request conviction information.* On applications and during interviews, you cannot ask applicants if they have ever been arrested, but you can ask for conviction records. You can question an applicant about a report that he or she received a dishonorable or bad conduct discharge from military service.

You should ask the person convicted of a crime what the crime was. The nature of the crime could disqualify the applicant for a given position, not only because of the potential for repeating a crime but also because the conditions of a person's parole or probation may exclude him or her from holding certain jobs.

2. *Check out gaps in the record; probe.* If an applicant's job history includes a significant time gap between school and work, between military service and a civilian job, or between jobs, you may ask, "What did you do from this date to that one?"

3. *Check out unclear statements or answers.* If you have any reason to suspect an answer, later in the interview or during a second one ask the same question in a different way; see if the answers jibe. Ask the applicant's references or previous employers what they know about the answer you find troublesome.

For example, you can ask, "What did [John/Joan] do from September 5 to January 1 that year?" The person may not know or may not be able to answer, but no law says you cannot ask.

And have an attorney check public records about convictions for crimes if you suspect that a criminal record exists.

4. *Document all inquiries (including reference checks) in writing.* Enter your own notes into the interview record. Send preprinted forms for references to complete. If appropriate, ask for a credit record from a credit bureau. If the budget

allows, hire a professional company to check references of applicants you are seriously considering.

5. *If an applicant volunteers that he or she was hospitalized for mental or emotional problems, pursue the matter.* Yes, it is personal, but it is not private. However, take care *not to initiate this conversation.* If you seriously want to hire the applicant but have reason to believe that the person's problem, e.g., violent behavior, could be a detriment, ask for a release of information or for the right to contact the attending physician; get the permission in writing and get the information you need in writing, as well.

On the other hand, not hiring an applicant merely because he or she has a *history* of mental or emotional problems can lead to a lawsuit charging discrimination against a disabled person. The reason for not hiring someone must be that his or her mental or emotional problems would *continue* to pose a threat to the organization or to other people.

6. *Turn down applicants convicted of a crime or those with a history of injuring other people when they could possibly repeat their offense in a new job situation.* An accountant convicted of embezzlement should not handle other people's money, although he or she may become a fine (and honest) office administrator where direct access to cash or the books is not involved.

Hiring people with a history of violence can be risky business. Many employers refuse to hire them, which in itself becomes a social problem because the inability of convicted felons to get meaningful employment contributes to the repeat of criminal behavior. You could turn someone with the skills and abilities you need (but with a record) into a favorable employee, but you must also take care to protect your organization and other employees (while not overpolicing the individual).

7. *If a person is on probation or on parole, talk with his or her probation or parole officer.* The officer can alert you to whether or not the job you have in mind falls within the terms of the applicant's probation or parole. It may not.

If it does, a person's rehabilitation often depends upon his or her ability to find and keep a meaningful job with a decent wage. You and the officer can make a difference, if you work as a team to help the applicant succeed.

Safe hiring practices are as subtle and complex as the human and social issues that influence them. Still, proactive management practices can prevent hiring problems from becoming legal crises.

CASEBOOK

Just how far and deep does your responsibility as employer run? A review of the following cases should help you answer that question.

How Much Background Checking Is an Employer Supposed to Do?

Wright Security had provided guard service for Ellerton Manufacturing for thirty years. In all that time, nothing untoward had happened to Ellerton's facility in which gold sunglass frames were produced. Suddenly, within a forty-five-day period, the company experienced three separate losses in excess of $200,000 at that plant, which they traced back to the new security guard assigned to it.

On two occasions, Ellerton claimed, the guard admitted the thieves into the plant. On the third occasion, after he had already quit Wright Security, the guard helped plan the break-in and "cleaned out" Ellerton's gold inventory. The company took Wright Security to court, suing for negligence in hiring, training, assigning, and supervising someone suspected of "having sticky fingers."

Wright Security argued that its applications required listing the names of former employers and three references from among people who had known the applicant for more than five years. In this case, Wright contacted the man's current employer and one former employer and also sent a reference form to his high school principal. None of these people said that the applicant was dishonest or criminally inclined, so Wright hired him.

Wright also claimed that all its employees received on-the-job training. Furthermore, low-level employees received supervision from trained, experienced officers. Ellerton's suit was misguided.

Does your organization hire people into positions of public or customer trust? What sort of background checks do you run, especially for positions involving sensitive commodities or information? What do you think the court thought of Wright Security's defense?

Negligence

Often, because employers run into policies of silence or of "name, rank, and serial number," they simply do not bother themselves or other people with reference or background checks. Or, if they do, as in this case, they do not dig sufficiently.

The Rhode Island Supreme Court ruled against the security company. An employer must exercise "reasonable care" in prehire screening, in training new employees, in assigning people to jobs, and in supervising them, especially if the job can expose the public to a potentially dangerous or dishonest person. Without the exercise of reasonable care, the employer can be held liable to parties injured (theft is a legal injury or tort) by a dishonest, unfit, or incompetent employee. Reasonable care was absent in this case.[1]

That the security company had a duty to make a more thorough check than it did, that it had a duty to train, assign, and supervise more carefully than it did constituted only the factual context of the case. What the court ruled has far greater implications than that context.

This case provided us with the expanded "doctrine of respondeat superior" defined in the Definition of Key Terms earlier in this chapter. The court extended liability beyond the hiring of potentially violent employees and declared that the mere absence of specific evidence or claims of dishonesty is insufficient.

As I have said, negligence seems to be clear-cut in cases where an employer hires violent employees. In a case in Texas in 1987, in which the jury awarded the victim $5 million in damages, a Fort Worth cab company hired a driver whose twenty years of crime included convictions for forgery, robbery, thefts, and other crimes. The company hired him without a background check while he was still under indictment for attempted murder in the mistaken belief that the police department would not issue a taxi permit to anyone not qualified.

Wrong. The police never refuse a taxi permit. One month later, the driver raped a woman passenger. Although the Texas Supreme Court thought the damages might be excessive, it agreed that the cab company was clearly liable.[2]

The same verdict was handed down when a trucking company was sued for negligently hiring an over-the-road driver with a history of convictions of violent sex-related crimes, including an arrest only the year before for aggravated sodomy on two teenagers he picked up while on the road for another trucker. This time he picked up a teenage hitchhiker he repeatedly raped and beat, for which crime he received a fifty-year sentence without parole.[3]

The Rhode Island case is different from cases in which the potential for violence exists, yet the principle is the same: The employer has a duty to its other employees, to the public, and to its customers to inquire into the employee's background. The court, applying the doctrine of negligent hiring, held the employer liable when it asserted that the exercise of "reasonable care" means more than accepting the absence of complaints about dishonesty as evidence that the person is honest. But, as you can see, the court's demand for detailed background checks runs up against reference policies of silence or "name, rank, and serial number" (about which I will have more to say in Chapter 7).

An employer can be found liable for acts of violence its employees commit against the public. But can it be held liable for violence against another employee committed outside of the workplace? That is the question underlying the next case.

How Far Does Your Liability Extend If an Employee Commits a Violent Crime?

Craig Millon raped and murdered Cheri West, a co-worker, in her apartment—a capital crime for which he was convicted. When it was brought out in court that Millon had been previously convicted of rape and robbery, West's family brought a charge against the company of wrongful death with prejudice in their daughter's murder.

The family charged the company with negligent hiring or retaining of an employee that it had known, or should have known, was previously convicted of charges of rape and robbery. It assigned him duties (mail-room clerk) that required him to circulate among the company's women employees, where he came into contact with West; those duties also afforded him the opportunity to learn her name and home address. The family also claimed that the company knew, or should have known, that Millon had dangerous proclivities, but that it had not established policies or practices to find out if such proclivities existed; that he had made advances upon and otherwise sexually harassed female employees, including West. The employer's acts or omissions were, therefore, "the proximate cause" of the young woman's death.

The trial court dismissed the case on the grounds that it had failed to state a cause of action. The family appealed, and the trial trail ends with the appellate court's ruling (two motions to transfer to the Supreme Court were denied, July 15 and September 20, 1983), and therefore I do not know if the family received damages.

Where does your organization stand with regard to background checks, especially of people whose records seem shaky?

Cause of Action

The Missouri Court of Appeals thought the family brought a clear-cut cause of action: negligent hiring. It did not decide the factual issue of whether the company was in fact guilty, but it did say that the plaintiffs should be allowed their day in court, their chance to prove the allegations they outlined.[4]

The court recognized the implications of the decision when it ordered the lower courts to hear the evidence in the case. The negligent hiring theory could dampen employers' enthusiasm for hiring mentally disabled people or ex-convicts when charges of negligence can be brought if an employer hires or retains a person it knew, or should have known, was potentially dangerous to other employees, regardless of whether that danger lurked on or off the job.

Cases

1. 474 A.2d 436 (R.I. Sup. Ct. 1984).
2. 725 S.W.2d, 701 (Tex. Sup. Ct. 1987), *rev'd on remand,* 735 S.W.2d 303.
3. 146 Ill. App. 3d 265, 100 Ill. Dec. 21, 496 N.E.2d 1086 (1st Dist. 1986).
4. 655 S.W.2d 568 (Mo. Ct. App. 1983).

Section II

Safe Management Practices

"Scrap the procedures manual," personnel managers have been known to lament. "If someone doesn't follow them to the letter, we wind up in court 'cause the rules form a contract."

A case of damned if you do (have a manual), damned if you don't (have one)? That depends upon (1) how policies are worded, (2) how well managers are trained in implementing the policies, and (3) how well managers apply the policies in which they are trained.

The policies themselves are often successfully challenged for disparate treatment or for having adverse impact; fail to publish rules, and you expose yourself and other managers to lawsuits arising from subjective decision making, from mistreatment of employees, and from employees taking advantage of the absence of rules. Fail to follow published rules when evaluating an employee's performance, and you can produce the same results. Finally, not fulfilling your obligations to protect employees' privacy and reputation, or to accommodate women employees or disabled people can cause lawsuits against you as well. These are some of the management practices on which I dwell.

An Overview of Safe Management

When I talk about specific management practices, I have to use a fine-tipped brush for painting a portrait of personnel decisions man-

89

agers legally cannot make, decisions they should not make, and decisions they can make at the risk of winding up in court. Few universal rules govern the demands employees can legally make on employers, and they only loosely apply to specific practices. The courts usually take each case separately and often disagree with each other on the meanings of legal terminology and coverage. Definitions and perceptions, in the vast majority of cases, determine how the courts interpret words or phrases such as *employee, because of sex, handicap.*

Management Practices

This section covers those management practices, often governed by organizational policy statements, that most frequently come before the courts:

- Performance evaluation and corrective action
- Invasion of employees' privacy
- Abuse of privileged information
- Defamation
- Sexual discrimination and harassment
- Mismanaging disabled people
- Interference with employee rights for collective action

A manager is exposed to possible legal action on each of those counts unless he or she follows the handful of safe management guidelines spelled out in each chapter. While few universal legal rules apply, several general management rules do fit most cases:

1. Respect each employee as an individual having the same rights and privileges to which you believe you are entitled.
2. Treat each employee as a colleague; the organization functions well only to the extent each person contributes to its success.
3. Recognize that "we" are all in this together; the only "they" are competitors who would prefer that your "we" did not exist.

Golden rules such as those above distinguish safe from unsafe management, but one more rule makes your personnel decisions just a little bit safer:

4. Document all important interactions with employees because not all employees will follow the first three rules, even if you do.

Employee?

It is helpful to first know who "an employee" is. In some cases you have obligations to employees you do not have to other people; in some cases you have obligations to all those you engage to work for you, whether or not they are employees.

Under common law, a person is an employee if he or she "performs services subject to the will and control of an employer, as to both *what* must be done and *how* it must be done"; "the employer has the *legal right* to control both the method and the result of the services." According to the Treasury Department,* an "individual is an independent contractor if . . . the employer [has] the right to control or direct only the result of the work and the means and methods of accomplishing the result" (unless specific agreements dictate special terms). However, a "specific agreement" does not make an employee out of a contractor because it affects only the basic contractual relationship itself. To be an employee means to contradict most of the features that characterize a contractor relationship. The chart shown here, extrapolated from an Indiana case,[1] helps distinguish between employees and independent contractors.

CHARACTERISTICS OF EMPLOYEES AND CONTRACTORS

Characteristic	Employee	Contractor
Other employment restricted	Usually	Not usually
Competition restricted	Always	Not usually unless by agreement
Salespeople/marketing reps assigned geographically	Often	Not usually

(continued)

*Internal Revenue Service No. 937, *Business Reporting: Employment Taxes, Information Returns*, 1989.

Hours/schedules assigned	Almost always	Not usually
Daily activity reports required	Almost always	Not usually unless by agreement
Sick leave, vacation, retirement, and other benefits	Usually	Not usually
Reimbursement for travel and other expenses	Usually	Not usually unless by agreement
Taxes withheld	Usually	Almost never

Those distinctions make a difference to a variety of contractual relationships even though they make little or no difference with respect to civil rights legislation, including Title VII of the Civil Rights Act of 1964. These laws blur the distinction between employee and independent contractor; Title VII, for example, uses the phrase *aggrieved person* rather than *employee*. Whether we are talking about race, sex, age, or disability, Title VII is not limited to a situation in which an employee or job applicant is directly tied to the employer.

Until 1983 employers had generally been free under Title VII to choose with whom they contracted, as long as a true independent contractor relationship existed. Now, interfering *in any way* with someone's employment opportunity, whether the person works for the defendant organization *or for anyone else,* violates Title VII.[2]

Fuzzy edges to definitions and distinctions permeate all the cases I cover, which proves that you can take nothing for granted. If you have the mildest doubt about the legality of a personnel decision or if you are under threat of a suit for discrimination, breach of contract, or anything else, consult an attorney.

Cases

1. 593 F. Supp. 6, 32 F.E.P. Cases (BNA) 1107 (N.D. Ind. 1983), *aff'd,* 742 F.2d 1459 (1984).
2. No. 80-431 (9th Cir. Feb. 9, 1983).

Chapter 6

Safe Evaluations and Promotions

No law says you have to give employees performance evaluations. If you do not publish a promise of performance evaluations, you do not have a contractual obligation. In the absence of a contract, you may or may not evaluate employee performance at your own discretion. In the words of more than one court, an employee does not have an inherent right to a performance appraisal.[1,2]

On the other hand, if you do not have officially sanctioned and written procedures, your appraisal and promotion systems are open to challenge because they will probably be subjectively administered. Your organization's published policies and procedures with regard to performance appraisal and the execution of a system based on those policies can, in some cases, constitute an implied contract. Because a court could narrowly construe that the policy manual contains a promise to conduct performance appraisals in a prescribed manner and at prescribed times, the organization could be held accountable should you or some other manager not follow the prescriptions or not follow them properly; and they, in and of themselves, could have a disparate impact. Therefore, you should assess your organization's published evaluation procedures or promotion-from-within policy on the basis of what I say about those procedures.

In the sections that follow, I will concentrate on four ways performance evaluations can be used to discriminate against employees and on ways to prevent a court challenge or to defend yourself if challenged.

What You Cannot Do

Among the many managerial abuses of performance evaluations, four have important legal implications: (1) using subjective criteria to produce a disparate impact on minorities and other protected groups; (2) using a promotion-from-within policy to discriminate against minorities and other protected groups; (3) misusing objective records to discriminate; and (4) "building a file," i.e., writing up your documentation after the fact.

Using Subjective Criteria

Subjective rating systems in themselves are not illegal. The EEOC and the courts recognize subjective job standards (such as communication and leadership skills) and that the words *good, satisfactory, poor,* and *unsatisfactory* carry within themselves subjective elements. So where do they draw the line?

1. When standards are unequally applied or do not exist at all; and
2. When someone shows that the standards or their absence produce disparate treatment in promotion and compensation policies and practices, as, for example:
   - When sex stereotyping tainted the process in which a woman was denied a partnership in a Big Eight accounting firm[3,4]
   - When subjective decision making torpedoed promotion policies that have disparate impact on minorities[5]

EEOC and court rulings encourage objective performance appraisals, but they discourage using them as a subterfuge for discrimination.

Supervisors should not have sole discretion over rating decisions. Failing to set objective rating standards and to provide adequate training on how to interpret those standards can diminish the fairness of the appraisal system. Inadequate application of evaluations can produce a system that is in and of itself discriminatory and has disparate impact on minorities and other groups.[6-8,*]

Promotion From Within

Internal promotions systems, not necessarily in themselves discriminatory, can be misapplied, as in the case of "tracking" employees by hiring minorities or women into certain jobs, e.g., janitorial or secretarial, that prevent them from succeeding into higher-level positions. Safeguards built into a system, such as open posting and career planning, can prevent it from being used to discriminate.

You can help your organization assess the health of its promotion policies by suggesting that a statistician check the organization's *internal* labor market; by yourself, you can do little to identify situations such as these we are describing. Even if the number of minorities or other protected group members in your work force matches the available and qualified people in the population at large, if your internal market exhibits a disproportionate number of white males in high-level positions or in promotable roles relative to nonmajority employees, the system could be blocking protected group members from advancing. That blockage is in itself inherently discriminatory.[8]

Misusing Objective Records

The EEOC and the courts approve the proper use of objective records. Conversely they frown upon the misuse or selective use of those records.

Attendance records, wasted materials reports, and disci-

---

*See also Donald H. Weiss, "The Legal Side of Performance Appraisals," *Management Solutions* (May 1988), p. 27.

plinary action reports make for good documentation in an appraisal system. If those records document unacceptable behavior or performance on the part of both white and minority groups, then tolerating it from one group of employees but not accepting the same or similar behavior or performance from the other could constitute discrimination, especially if you rate down or discharge protected group members and not majority group employees with equally abhorrent records.[9]

Retroactive Documentation

Producing documentation *after* making the decision to demote or to fire someone is in itself illegal. Additionally, entering into a file every trivial thing that happens after a charge of discrimination has been brought against you can be seen as retaliation and harassment.[10] Documentation of poor performance or misconduct must be filed at the time the alleged events occurred, and the employee should be notified of that action, or you face the potential of being charged with "building a file."

What You Can Do

Insofar as performance appraisals are essential management tools, steps should be taken to protect them from court challenges.

Utilizing Legally Defensible Performance Appraisal Systems

Performance appraisal systems make good management sense, and a well-designed and judiciously implemented system does not impose a hardship on employees; it is often seen by employees as a tool that helps them succeed. Courts have ruled that criticizing an employee's job performance does not constitute the infliction of emotional distress as long as the criticism meets these four legal standards:

1. The criticism is not extreme and outrageous.
2. The criticism is not intentionally reckless.

3. The criticism is not intended to cause emotional distress.
4. The distress the criticized employee feels is not severe.

"Extreme and outrageous conduct" refers to conduct any reasonable person would say exceeds the limits of socially acceptable employer practices. The complaint of severe mental and emotional harm often accompanies this charge and, in some cases, actually defines the outrageous conduct.[11]

Because any system, no matter how well designed or implemented, is always open to challenge, you should consider whether or not your organization's approach is legally defensible. AMACOM has published a number of good books, including my own cassette/workbook program *Getting Results: The Performance Appraisal Process,** which you can use as research materials. Here I only look at characteristics of a good system in order to help you evaluate your system.

Defining Performance Appraisal

The goal or purpose of the appraisal determines the system's value:

1. Evaluate an employee's performance at a given moment, e.g., at this time.
2. Evaluate an employee's performance over a given and identifiable period of time, e.g., during the past year.

A performance evaluation at a given moment should correct a performance problem or commend the employee for an accomplishment. The appraisal, usually unwritten and informal, consists of the kinds of judgments supervisors most frequently make on a daily basis. It is also the kind of evaluation that can get a supervisor into the greatest amount of trouble because it is often undocumented.

An employee's performance should be well-documented throughout the rating period. The lack of documentation weak-

*New York: American Management Association, 1985.

ens a system because formal appraisals, the annual kind that many companies require, live or die on the basis of the documentation that supports them. Subjective judgments infiltrate the system when supervisors rely on their memory for rating a performance or writing the narrative about the employee's behavior on the job, frequently producing one of two possible scenarios that can make a shambles of the evaluation process: the "halo effect" (responding to the best employee behavior or performance, which often shows up just before evaluation time), or "demon's jaws" (being bitten by the worst employee behavior or performance, which might only occur once in a while or shortly before evaluation time but which leaves a lasting negative impression).

The annual appraisal is sometimes used to correct shortcomings, but by then it is too late and probably should not be used that way. It should be used, first of all, to point out how well employees met their job standards during the rating period. Second, it should be used to help employees identify the areas still in need of correction. In all, it should be used to further employees' career opportunities. To do that, the evaluation should be based on objective or measurable, achievable goals and standards.

Measuring Against Goals and Standards

A job description should drive the appraisal process or you have nothing against which to measure performance. A meaningful job description should begin by identifying the purpose for the job's existence, e.g., "to generate so much income," "to process so many applications," or "to make this many pieces." If an activity's goal does not contribute to the organization's business goals, it should not exist.

The job's criteria—experience or skills needed to do the job—should be related to the goal. The job's standards should be the measures by which an employee's performance relative to the goals is judged. Written, clearly stated, job-related standards, communicated to the employee at the start of the rating period, should be the *only* basis on which performance is judged. If an employee does not know and understand what the goals and standards of the job are, he or she cannot be held accountable for the job's outcomes.

Most project-oriented or management positions are described by objectives, making Management by Objectives more or less a necessity. In a project-oriented job, the employee performs a series of tasks that have a clear beginning and a clear end. A computer programmer, for example, works on a series of projects, often several different projects at the same time. The job standards usually include something like "Completes Assigned Projects On Time" rather than "Quantity of Work." Completing assigned projects is the objective by which performance is judged.

Managers are often responsible for their work group's success, for example, at meeting production goals, as well as for a quantity of work they personally produce. If the group meets its production goals, we say the manager did well. If it exceeds the goals, we say the manager did very well, unless, of course, the group met or exceeded its goals in spite of the manager's lack of leadership or some other downgrading factor.

One value of a written job description that includes performance standards as well as duties and responsibilities is that it prevents hidden (implicit), often subjective standards that infect evaluations. Companies *successfully* defending themselves against charges of illegal performance appraisal systems or abuse of those systems have had, among other things, clearly stated, job-related performance standards on which appraisals were based, and performance problems related to those standards were clearly *documented* on appraisal forms.* Standards and documentation are the two legal protections of appraisal systems.

Documentation

No one style of appraisal works in all cases. Whatever the style, there should be a direct link between the job's criteria and

*See David C. Martin, et al., "The Legal Ramifications of Performance Appraisal," *Employee Relations Law Journal*, Vol. 12, cited in Edmund J. Metz, "Designing Legally Defensible Performance Appraisal Systems," *Training and Development Journal*, July 1988, p. 48.

standards and the tools used to measure performance. The items evaluated should contribute to successful performance or should not be included; for example, the category "quantity of work" applies to a production-oriented job but not well to a job that is project-oriented. And how do you evaluate a computer operator working alone on the night shift in the category "works well with others?"

Several methods of evaluation contribute to the documentation of a person's job performance:

▸ *Rating scales.* The most familiar and widely used system rates factors such as quality and quantity of work, attendance, leadership abilities, and so forth on the basis of a scoring system, usually 1 to 5 (where 5 is the highest score possible). Some systems weight production activities by 2 in order to fairly evaluate job-related factors (e.g., quantity of work) against behavior (e.g., attendance). Some employees can be absent for one valid reason or another more frequently than others can and still produce better than employees who never miss a day.

Rating scales, by themselves no more than report cards fraught with subjective considerations and personal biases, have little merit. A short narrative based on critical or significant incidents that you record in a performance file strengthens a rating scale system.

▸ *Narratives.* Describe what a person did and how well or poorly he or she did it and explain the reason why he or she received the rating. As long as the narrative is not on its face pretextual, it will almost always hold up in court.

Under "quantity," for example, you could write:

The standard for this job is fifty widgets a year, with less than 5 percent waste. Josephine produced forty-eight widgets with 4.5 percent waste. That is why I rated her performance 3.5.

▸ *Performance files.* One way to guarantee that your narrative is objective, unbiased, accurate, and comprehensive is to keep a file of critical or significant incidents, a file into which you enter records or memos that reflect important events during the whole of the rating period. These reports describe positive or commendable incidents as well as incidents involving corrective measures.

A short memo may be all you need.

> Yesterday Josephine realized that she was wasting time and effort by moving from her workstation to the supply closet every time she began making a new widget. Therefore, when she arrived this morning, she decided to move all the supplies she needed for the day to her workstation.

You might need a longer memo for something more important.

> Today Josephine broke the third bit on her machine since beginning her new job. She has been shown repeatedly how to apply the proper amount of pressure, but she has not gotten it right yet. Since one important criterion of the job is the ability to use that equipment properly, she is not showing that she can do the job. I told her that unless she stops breaking the bit on the machine, she will have to return to her old job if it is still available. Otherwise, we may have to find another, lower-paying job for her or discharge her.

The incident in the example was serious enough to warrant a warning. Any incident that serious should be recognized not only with the supervisor's signature but with the employee's as well.

> I acknowledge reading this warning and understanding the consequences of not meeting the standards of the job.

That signed acknowledgment, as important as the documentation itself, could save you grief later because an employee cannot say he or she never had the problem brought to his or her attention.

The performance file ensures that you rate the employee's performance for the entire period, not just for the last few days of it. The accuracy and completeness of the appraisal depend on your ability to recall what the person did in the beginning of the period, how well he or she performed in the middle of it, and what happened as the period neared its end. Improvements in performance can affect a rating. Deterioration can be spotted early and corrective measures taken before things get out of hand. There should be no surprises during a year-end evaluation interview, and the performance file prevents surprises from happening.

Your organization has to keep other employee personnel files also, but they can be used against you even if they are put together by other supervisors and several years prior to the present circumstances. Federal courts have found that supervisors can deliberately place an inaccurate, discriminatory evaluation in an employee's file with the intent to harm the employee. That record then follows the employee and adversely affects his or her future opportunities or conditions of employment or compensation.[10]

Therefore, you should give employees the opportunity to review their evaluation files and rebut them, if they believe rebuttal is necessary. They then should be required to sign a statement indicating they have reviewed their file, a procedure that by itself can prevent many frivolous lawsuits.

▸ *Performance evaluation interview.* You should have a written appraisal to share with your employees, but you should set aside ample time to discuss appraisals with the employees as well. It will not do to give an employee a document and say, "Read this and if you have any questions or complaints, come see me." The employee may go see an attorney instead.

▸ *Audit systems.* A defensible appraisal program should have a built-in method of checking out an evaluation's validity. Working closely with your boss when evaluating another person's performance and having him or her review your appraisals to prevent your personal biases or some unusually bad or good feelings from coloring your appraisals could save you a great deal of embarrassment later. However, only you and other people who have worked closely with the employee being appraised can accurately assess the employee's performance; do not let your boss push you into decisions you cannot support or that could land you in court.

Some companies use other forms of checks and balances: peer reviews, reciprocal reviews, or a grievance system.

In a peer review, employees contribute to each other's assessments. This could give you insights into employee performance to which you may not have access.

A reciprocal review provides employees with an opportunity to give feedback to their supervisors about how *they* perform *their* jobs, thereby balancing the review process. It is very difficult for an employee to charge an employer with discrimination or unfair business practices when he or she is given a chance to answer any complaints you make with complaints about you. On the other hand, you must be on guard against resenting an employee's review and retaliating.

None of these alternatives is required, especially not a grievance procedure, but check the law in your state. Some states' courts construe a published procedure as an enforceable employment contract (e.g., Nebraska),[12] while others do not (e.g., Florida).[13]

Personnel Decisions Based on Evaluations

You should make your personnel decisions—pay raises, bonuses, job assignments, and promotions—on the basis of your evaluations. Any other method could cause you to wind up in court for bias or discrimination or for breach of contract. In fact, if your organization permits it, major decisions such as pay raises, bonuses, and promotions should be made by a review board that uses your performance evaluations as one of several tools by which the decisions are made. If your organization does not have such a system, you might suggest it take a look at one.

One way to protect your promotion-from-within policy is to adopt a work measurement system that you can demonstrate is unbiased: standards that any well-trained, experienced employee can meet without undue fatigue. Promotion policies based on the same objective standards that govern evaluation and appraisal procedures protect against disparate treatment or adverse impact. The Eleventh Circuit Court, in 1985, accepted a process similar to the one below that can help prevent subjectivity from tainting your promotion process.[14]

1. Establish objective or measurable job criteria (minimum experience or skill requirements) for each position available.
2. Decide which applicants for a promotion satisfy the job criteria by reviewing the applicants' files, e.g., written applications, performance appraisals. Set aside as "unqualified" applications that do not meet those minimum requirements.
3. Under the supervision of a personnel officer, have a panel of employees familiar with the job's technical criteria examine "qualified" files, interview each applicant, and rate each one on a numerical scale of 1 to 4, with a 4 denoting the best qualified and 1 the least.
4. Ask the panel to reconcile the differences in the ratings until a consensus is reached.
5. Have the panel issue a written report on why they rated the applicants the way they did.
6. Have the personnel officer identify applicants with ratings of 3.0 or better for further consideration.
7. Have the manager who has to make the final decision or his or her advisory committee interview the "certified" applicants (who do not know, yet, how they were ranked).
8. Make and implement the final decision.

This process may seem complicated or cumbersome (especially for a small organization), but it or some variation of it could prevent a more complicated or cumbersome and expensive day in court.

Any management procedure is open to challenge, even the evaluation process I just outlined. However, some systems, or the manner in which they are applied, are more defensible than others.

Conclusion

Every organization should satisfy a minimum level of sophistication in its performance system. It should have:

1. Up-to-date, written, clear job or position descriptions that have been given to each employee at the start of the employee's tenure in a given job or position.
2. Job standards communicated clearly to each employee at the start of each rating period.
3. Training for supervisors on how to evaluate employee performance and how to administer the organization's appraisal system.
4. Performance feedback, both informally on a daily basis and during a formal appraisal interview at least once a year.
5. A review audit system to prevent bias or feelings from infiltrating the system.
6. Performance coaching and counseling systems administered by managers trained to give effective feedback and coaching or counseling.
7. Documentation through performance files, job-related testing, rating systems, appraisal forms, signed memoranda, and so on.
8. Written policy statements approving only a specified procedure for conducting appraisals.

If any of these components is missing from your organization's performance appraisal system, you and the organization could be asking for trouble.

CASEBOOK

The recommendations in this chapter follow from numerous actual cases, only a few of which can be covered in this Casebook. Use these cases to test your ability to recognize the legal problems in them and to compare the situations with possible problems in your own workplace.

Can Your Performance Evaluation System Be Illegal?

Jorge Gonzales, an installer, had worked for Independent Electric for four years, during which time he had never received a reprimand or complaint about his work. Yet, in several performance reviews, one or another factor was rated "needs improvement," which was defined as "peformance somewhat below the supervisor's expectations." The ratings were given without comment.

Because the promotion system hinged on the performance appraisal, which in this case meant that an employee's promotion depended on the supervisor's personal evaluation of the installer's work, Jorge felt that his Anglo supervisor was intentionally discriminating against him, holding Jorge back from promotion by his evaluations. An attorney for Jorge and several other Hispanic and black employees argued that the company's promotion system, in and of itself, had disparate impact on minorities.

The company's attorney, in turn, defended Independent Electric's affirmative action program and minority representation. The company had hired and trained minorities in proportion to the work force available in the community.

What is the principal method of evaluating employees in your organization? Objective standards based on goals and objectives, a rating scale, a supervisor's narrative? Judge your system with an eye to the district court's decision in this case.

Supervisor's Discretion Not Enough

The district court in Texas found that the supervisors had sole discretion over rating decisions. The company failed to set objective rating standards, and the criteria varied from supervisor to supervisor, none of whom had sufficient training for setting standards. In effect, the court concluded, supervisor evaluations were based entirely on subjective perceptions of skills. Those inadequacies made the utility's promotion system, in and of itself, discriminatory because it had a disparate impact on minorities.[6,7] The U.S. Supreme Court, in 1988, reinforced the disparate impact analysis of subjective criteria.[5] As I cautioned earlier, take care to protect your own system or the appraisals you produce by creating a set of objective standards by which anyone performing a specific job can be evaluated.

Can Your Promotion-From-Within Policy Be Discriminatory?

When First National Bank defended itself against a class action suit challenging its promotion policies, it argued that it had hired blacks in proportion to their representation in the general population within the particular geographic area. Blacks, the bank showed, were hired at all levels within its organization on balance with their representation in similar skill levels in the community.

The challengers showed, on the other hand, that over 75 percent of the above-entry-level positions and 50 percent of the highest-level managerial and technical positions were filled through a promotion-from-within policy. Even though the bank hired some minorities into higher-level positions, they did not promote them from entry-level positions with the same or similar frequency that they promoted white males.

How does your organization operate with respect to promotions? Do you hire from without, promote from within, or use a different procedure? Are minorities or women hired into positions that block them from the promotion-from-within system itself? For example, hiring blacks into only maintenance positions is tantamount to blocking them from the succession process into technical, professional, or management positions.

Legitimate Business Interests

A promotion-from-within policy can foster legitimate business interests by creating a stable work force, the Eighth Circuit Court declared. The policy usually encourages loyalty and productivity when employees can expect to move up within an organization and not constantly have to compete against outside hires. Therefore, the policy is not in itself discriminatory.

However, an examination of this organization's *internal* labor market and the statistical evidence indicated that black employees had not been promoted sufficiently in comparison to whites; the evidence created an inference of discrimination. The relationship between employees and external populations, the bank's defense, was misleading.[8]

This case demonstrates that the best defense is to ensure that minorities and women have equal access to the system and are well-distributed throughout the technical, professional, and management ranks of the organization via both the external and the internal promotion processes.

How Can Objective Records Be the Source of Discrimination?

Fred Jackson had an abysmal attendance record: 101 unexcused absences and one suspension in 1977, 114 unexcused absences and 3 suspensions in 1978, and 32 additional unexcused absences in the year he was fired (1979). The brewery management was therefore dumbstruck when they had to defend themselves in court against a charge of discrimination, under Section 1981 of the Civil Rights Act of 1866, for firing the black man on account of his race.

Jackson argued that he was fired even though white employees with comparably bad absentee records at the time of his termination were not. For example, one white employee had 98 unexcused absences and one suspension in 1977, 44 unexcused absences and one suspension in 1978, 43 unexcused absences in 1979 (the year Jackson was fired), and 51 unexcused absences in 1980, after which the white employee was suspended and subsequently fired. The evidence, Jackson claimed, pointed to discrimination on the basis of race.

For how long would you or your organization tolerate unexcused absences or tardiness? Among several delinquent employees, whom would you fire first and why?

Sheer Numbers

Excessive absenteeism and tardiness create scheduling problems, damage employee morale, and affect productivity. No court would challenge that claim. What the Eighth Circuit

Court in this 1984 case did challenge was the lack of evenhand-edness in the manner the firing decisions were made.

Although the black employee had the worst possible record and more total unexcused absences than did the most compa-rable white employee, the court, in a two-to-one decision, held that the plaintiff was indeed fired because of his race. The jury's award of $125,000 in damages (including damages for mental and emotional distress) was affirmed against the em-ployer.[9]

Why? Because firing the worst offender may not necessar-ily be the best course of action. Tolerating flagrantly bad behavior (the unexcused absences) was in itself poor manage-ment. Firing the black employee but not firing white employees with comparably bad records *at the same time* indicated that management was more tolerant of white employees with bad attendance records than it was of black employees: evidence of disparate treatment.

To avoid or to be prepared for litigation, your organization should publish written standards of conduct and procedures for taking disciplinary action. Supervisors should be trained on how to apply disciplinary procedures equally. All com-plaints of misconduct should be handled the same way for anyone against whom a complaint is raised. Incidents and any corrective or disciplinary actions should be documented *at the time they occur,* and the employees should acknowledge by their signature that they understand the action taken.

When Is Documentation Not Legal?

Cynthia Katz believed that the only reason she had not been promoted during the years she worked for the company was that she was a woman. Less qualified male employees received all the great assignments and subsequently all the great promotions, too, she believed. So she filed a sex discrimination suit with the EEOC, after which a manager ordered her supervisor to document in her person-nel file all unusual incidents involving Cynthia.

Before she brought the unlawful sex discrimination charge against the company, Cynthia's file contained only a few complimen-tary letters. Within two years after she brought the charge, the file contained approximately 100 discipline slips, including reports of trivial, petty, and insignificant incidents that were never written up against other employees. For this, Cynthia filed suit in federal court for unlawful sexual harassment.

How do you document employee misdeeds? Do you wait until you have reason to discharge him or her before writing up your case? Or do you keep an ongoing record of all reports, good or bad? Would you build a file after an employee registered a complaint with the EEOC?

"Building a File"

Whether discrimination charges are brought against you or not, "building a file" after a decision to take corrective action or to fire someone has been made is in itself an illegal act. When discrimination charges are involved, building a file, such as the one built against Cynthia, can be judged retaliatory and harassing.[14] This case should underscore the need for giving careful thought to writing up an employee's misdeeds.

Whether the issue is performance deficiencies or behavior problems, an employee evaluation should be based on the employee's actual performance or behavioral history, which is the only fair and evenhanded basis on which an evaluation system can work to your and your employees' benefit. The courts will also probably rule on your behalf if the files you keep are current rather than after the fact.

Cases

1. 502 F. Supp. 876, 116 L.R.R.M. (BNA) 2047 (N.D. Ill. 1984), *aff'd*, 795 F.2d 39 (1986).
2. 65 N.Y. 2d 724, 492 N.Y.S.2d 9, 119 L.R.R.M. (BNA) 3415 (N.Y. Ct. App. 1985).
3. 825 F.2d 458, 263, 44 F.E.P. Cases 825 (D.C. Cir. 1987).
4. No. 87-1167 (1989).
5. 56 U.S.L.W. 4922 (1988).
6. 30 E.P.D. (CCH) ¶33,078 (D.C. Tex. 1982).

7. 694 F.2d 1146, 30 F.E.P. Cases (BNA) 703 (9th Cir. 1982).
8. 688 F.2d 552, 29 F.E.P. Cases (BNA) 1233 (8th Cir. 1982), *cert. denied,* 103 S. Ct. 1772 (1983).
9. 728 F.2d 989, 34 F.E.P. Cases (BNA) 93 (8th Cir. 1984).
10. 682 F.2d 971, 20 F.E.P. Cases (BNA) 85 (D.C. Cir. 1982), *cert. denied,* 103 S. Ct. 1427 (1983).
11. 330 N.W.2d 428, 31 F.E.P. Cases (BNA) 139 (Minn. Sup. Ct., 1983), superseded by statute, 392 N.W.2d 670 (Minn. Ct. App. 1986).
12. 215 Neb. 677, 340 N.W.2d 388 (1983).
13. 727 F.2d 1075, 115 L.R.R.M. (BNA) 3452 (11th Cir. 1984).
14. 764 F.2d 1539, 38 F.E.P. Cases (BNA) (11th Cir. 1985).

Chapter 7

Safe Management, the Right to Privacy, and Defamation

The U.S. Constitution clearly protects everyone's right to privacy. Additionally, various statutes and case laws regarding defamation protect a person's right to defend his or her personal and professional reputations as well as his or her right to privacy. Let's look at some relevant laws and key definitions before considering what you can and cannot do.

Privacy and Constitutional Guarantees

Because privacy cases involve mainly constitutional issues, and the Constitution is written to limit the powers of government, our examples deal largely with government agencies that have appeared in federal courts. Nevertheless, these cases help identify what *any* manager should consider with respect to employees' privacy, especially because several federal and state laws limit the rights of all employers, as in the cases of polygraph and drug testing. Such laws could become forerunners of statutes that protect employee rights against private employer invasion of privacy.

What the Laws Say

First, let's look at brief summaries of the five amendments to the Constitution that form the basis for most privacy claims.

First Amendment:	Governments are prohibited from interfering with the free exercise of religion or speech.
Fourth Amendment:	Governments are prohibited from unreasonable search and seizure of a person, or of his or her home, papers, and effects; prohibitions against illegal search and seizure include prying into a person's personal and intimate life.
Fifth Amendment:	The due process of law shall be applied to any attempt to deprive a person of life, liberty, or property, and no person may be required to incriminate or to be a witness against him- or herself.
Ninth Amendment:	Listing only specific rights in the Constitution is not to be construed as denying other rights reserved to the people.
Fourteenth Amendment:	Section 1 of the amendment gives equal rights to all natural or naturalized citizens.

The First, Fourth, and the Fifth Amendments are most frequently invoked in privacy cases. First Amendment rights have been extended to cover the off-duty sexual activities of a police department clerk who was turned down as a cadet in the police academy.[1] Fifth and Fourteenth Amendment rights were used to prevent a city in Michigan from "arbitrarily and capriciously" discharging a married male police officer who was having relations with a married woman other than his wife.[2] The Ninth and Fourteenth Amendments sometimes show up in privacy cases, but they are invoked more frequently in civil rights cases than in privacy cases.

The safe management questions raised here concern balancing an employer's *right to know* against the employees' *right to privacy*. For example:

- Can you test for the HIV antibody associated with AIDS?
- Can you test for drugs?
- Can you test for honesty with a polygraph test?

The answers? Well, it depends. It depends on the circumstances or on the conditions dictated by law or by court decisions.

Privileged Information and Defamation

Most people consider their personnel files (including credit or background checks), medical records, and performance evaluations to be private and confidential. Employer rights and employee rights often clash over how that information is used or how it is published. And, at times, in the effort to protect certain employee information, an employer's obligation to preserve employee privacy clashes with the public's right to know, or other employee's or employers' right or duty to know. Reference checks, reports to a workers compensation commission, performance evaluations, medical records, explaining to other employees why someone was fired, all can give rise to allegations of defamation. So managers are confronted with another legal maze through which they must find their way. Here are more definitions of key terms and a brief review of other relevant laws:

privilege The right or need to know certain types of information. That right is usually qualified or conditional, limited to the immediate and legitimate concerns or interests of the parties involved. Not everyone has a right or need to know everything about anyone.

However, some government agencies, such as the Internal Revenue Service, possess *absolute* privilege. They cannot be sued for publishing or soliciting information about people. This application of privilege, coupled with the Freedom of Information Act (discussed later in this list), could possibly make a person's financial life an open book.

defamation · Communicating to anyone who does *not* have the right or need to know private information that *could* cause injury to the person's personal or professional reputation. A person could feel injured, slandered or libeled, even if what you say or write is true.

slander   Oral publication of a defamatory statement.

libel   Written publication of a defamatory statement.

with malice   Deliberately publishing information that you know will harm the person some way, especially if the information is false or if you recklessly disregard the truth.

access laws   State statutes that require employers to allow employees access to their personnel files. Connecticut, for example, requires access at least twice a year and allows employees to copy the files.

 Some states' courts have construed published policies regarding access to personnel records as contracts; employers with published policies are obligated to allow employees access to their files. In states without right of access laws, employers may deny employees the right to inspect their own personnel records.

the Privacy Act of 1983   The law requiring federal employers everywhere to maintain a system of records and permit employees access to their own files on request, regardless of the legal status of records in the agency's locale. On the other hand, the Act restricts disclosure of information to anyone without the employee's consent.

the Freedom of Information Act   This law, its privacy provisions notwithstanding, allows third parties access to federal government information that might otherwise be considered confidential, which includes employee job performance.[3]

 The issue here comes down to how to maintain and safeguard private personnel information. Your perception of what you need to know from within a personnel file can come into conflict with the right of employees to maintain the privacy of personal information.

What You Cannot Do

Let's look at invasion of privacy before discussing defamation.

Invasion of Privacy

Especially if you manage a government agency or government-funded agency or a work unit within one such agency, you cannot take your perceived perogatives for granted. Testing for the HIV virus associated with AIDS or testing for drug use, searching the office of an employee you suspect of *on-the-job* misconduct or disciplining an employee for what you think is misconduct outside the workplace, or using a lie detector for screening applicants for their honesty would seem to be legal. But in each of these matters, the courts have expressed serious reservations about employers' rights relative to the Fourth Amendment's protections against unreasonable search.

What a person does in his or her home is a private matter; when it comes to medical or drug screening, a person's body and body fluids are at least as private as his or her home. How you investigate a wrongdoing is governed by laws protecting due process and privacy, and lie detector testing, in most cases, is just flat illegal. Let's take the issues one at a time.

▸ *Mandatory medical screenings.* The federal and some state courts have accepted the available medical evidence that the risk of transmitting the AIDS virus through casual contact in a workplace is, statistically, hardly possible. *Fear* of trans-mission is insufficient grounds for violating the Constitution. They have rejected *mandatory* medical screenings unless strong business reasons exist to require them (e.g., testing restaurant employees who authorities suspect may have been the source of typhoid).[4]

▸ *Testing for drugs.* Unless an employee is involved in an accident or has given someone sufficient cause to suspect him or her of wrongdoing, you have slim grounds for testing. The U.S. Department of Transportation and the courts, although restricting legal mandatory, random testing to jobs involving public safety, such as air traffic control or driving a train, or involving great hazards or government secrets, have widened the scope of permissible testing.[5] As a general rule, sufficient and reasonable suspicion of wrongdoing is the legal standard recognized by the courts. The same principle supports prohibitions against firing someone for failing a drug test. Overzealousness in applying a law is not uncommon in society.[6]

▸ *Office searches.* Unless your organization has published a broad policy that authorizes blanket surveillance or searches of offices, that the employees have acknowledged and to which they willingly submit, chances are the courts will say you cannot violate the Fourth Amendment by searching an employee's office or locker. Precedents for applying this principle to the private as well as to the public sector already exist.[7]

▸ *"Off duty" privacy.* If your organization has a published policy ensuring employees the right to privacy outside the workplace, as long as their activities do not interfere with doing their jobs, you can expect to face, and probably lose, a court challenge if you meddle in their private lives.[8] Even in the absence of such a policy, you could be challenged in court, but you would stand a better chance of winning if in some way the person's conduct created a burden in your ability to conduct business.[9]

▸ *Polygraph tests.* You cannot use lie detector tests to prescreen applicants for employment except under circumstances spelled out by law. (See below, "What You Can Do.")

▸ *Defamation.* You cannot always tell the truth about someone, unless the person to whom you are telling it has a right to know it. In fact, speculating in public without facts to back up your opinions could be safer, although not wise, than talking about actual facts.[10] You do not have to lie; you can just refuse to discuss the matter with anyone. In short, you cannot divulge private information that *could* cause injury to the person's personal or professional reputation to anyone who does *not* have the right or need to know that information. If you communicate the information with the *intent* to harm the person, even if the information is true, you could easily lose in court.

You should not offer explanations for why an employee was fired without carefully considering why anyone else has a right or need to know. You should not offer more information to a former employee's prospective employer than is absolutely necessary. You cannot discuss any information in an employee's personnel file without making yourself vulnerable, and this is especially true of an employee's medical or psychiatric reports, reports to the workers compensation commission, performance evaluations, or salaries.

Tuck this away as a rule of thumb: Only people with a right or need to know have at least conditional (qualified or partial) privilege to that kind of information. Identify for yourself who in your organization, in any specific situation, should have information about your employees. Check to see if you are right.

Here is another wrinkle in the things you cannot do: You cannot expect a person to communicate reasons why you discharged him or her to a third party, especially if you could have or should have reasonably foreseen that the defamed person would be *required* to disclose the statement.[11] That statement could turn out to be defamatory. Indeed, the key to understanding what you cannot do is the idea that if you, as the former employer, can predict that the employee will be under a strong compulsion to disclose the defamatory statement to someone else, as in the case of applying to a new employer, then you are making yourself vulnerable.[12-14] Self-publication under these circumstances can cause a person professional injury or harm, especially if the alleged defamatory statement is not true. If a court decides that the statement, that is, the reason for being discharged, is false, the organization can be held liable for making the statement with actual malice for the purpose of injuring the plaintiff.

Other employers adopt the policy of silence. Statements such as "Did not perform up to standards," or, safer, "Not eligible for rehire," offer some protection. However, termination for cause provisions of union contracts or of personnel policy manuals can clash with this policy of silence. Yet silence is difficult to enforce under the rules of unemployment compensation procedures, the 180- or 300-day filing period rules of Title VII, and other federal or state civil rights statutes. Such agencies have absolute privilege.

The self-publication rule requires that the employer guarantee the truth of the stated reason for termination. Juries can now be called upon to decide on the truth or falsity of the statement and on the intent to defame with or without malice. Again, simply refusing to discuss a situation with someone could turn out to be the safest management policy.

Consider the implications of what I just described. Candid, forthright reference letters and letters of service have lost the war in court often.[15,16] Even saying that an employee was discharged "for cause" could cost employers great sums.[17] So many employers, to reduce the possibility of being sued for defamation, will not give references for former employees. Others have adopted "name, rank, and serial number only" policies. Now comes this self-publication rule.

If you feel a need to talk about an employee's physical or mental health, or about his or her job performance, or anything at all that is truly of no concern to anyone else, you should question your motives. Do you bear ill feelings toward the person for some reason—because of an argument? Do you dislike the person for some reason—for the person's life-style or work habits or race or religion? Do you *want* to injure the person's personal and professional reputation? If you do, be extra careful. Defamation with malice can be very costly.

What You Can Do

Difficult as it may be to see them, employers do have rights, too. How you execute them marks the difference between unsafe and safe management. Let's take the same issues in the same order that I just discussed.

Mandatory Medical Screening

Government employees have the constitutional protections of the Fourth Amendment, and some states (e.g., California) have made such tests illegal in the private sector as well, unless strong or compelling business reasons exist to require them. Where good physical health is a prerequisite for successful performance of a job, as in certain physically taxing or hazardous jobs, requiring a medical exam as a precondition of employment is usually acceptable, as long as you ask it of everyone (male and female alike) to whom you have a job offer "pending passing a physical examination." Some insurance policies require such screenings also, where a previously existing condition could make a person uninsurable under your group plan. Mandatory testing of current employees is much more difficult to justify, unless, as in the case of airline pilots, in the public interest, physical fitness on the job must be recertified regularly.

Drug Testing

Mandatory, random screening of *current* employees for drug use is legal under some circumstances:

- ► Where the suspicion exists that the employee has been using drugs or was under the influence of them while on the job
- ► When an employee has been involved in an accident or had given someone sufficient cause to suspect him or her of wrongdoing
- ► For members of the armed forces or for government personnel in top-secret or other sensitive jobs
- ► For prisoners
- ► For persons engaged in a hazardous occupation, or one involving public safety, such as air traffic control, or for other employees falling under the public safety mandates imposed under the U.S. Department of Transportation's regulation (53 Federal Register 47,002) requiring public or private-sector employers to conduct random urine tests.

In other circumstances, you would struggle to justify such screenings in the absence of some *reasonable suspicion* that widespread drug (including alcohol) abuse exists that could interfere with your organization's ability to conduct its business.[18] Then you must be careful to administer the tests properly. (See the Casebook, this chapter.)

Careful administration of drug tests can support your decision to fire someone for drug abuse, if one of the conditions cited earlier also exists, e.g., to ensure the "safe operation and maintenance of a railroad."[19] On the other hand, random testing of current employees may be a costly waste of time and resources. As reported in *Resource*,* a Bureau of Labor Statistics survey of 7,500 businesses, involving 950,000 employees (excluding applicants and new hires) tested within a twelve-month period, shows that only 9 percent were found positive for drug use.

If you think drug testing serves your organization's or the public's best interests, test *all* applicants for initial hire or for promotion. The courts will probably uphold this testing, as did the U.S. Supreme Court in 1989.[20]†

Search Policies

If your organization has not published a broad surveillance and search policy, encourage it to do so, *if you think such a policy would serve the organization's, its employees', or its customers' best interests.* Publishing one just to have it on the books could alienate your employees beyond the value of the policy; therefore, be sure that a compelling business reason, combined with due process, protects you. At the same time, you should also look at other published policies with which this search mandate could clash.

For example, if the employee works with confidential infor-

---

*The January 1989 publication of the American Society of Personnel Administrators.

†Drug testing occurs in about 20 percent of the private work force. Cited in David O. Steward, "Slouching Toward Orwell" (Supreme Court Report), *ABA Journal* (June 1989), p. 48; see also Eric Rolfe Greenberg, "Workplace Testing: Who's Testing Whom?" *Personnel* (May 1989), pp. 39–45.

mation concerning other employees, as would a human resources director, or if he or she works with sensitive information that investigators have not been cleared to see or hear, an invasion of the employee's privacy could lead to serious consequences. Finally, check to see if your organization reserves the right to inventory, in the employee's presence, an office when an employee voluntarily or involuntarily leaves your employ. Such a reserved right could preclude a lawsuit.

"Off Duty" Privacy

An organization need not publish a right to privacy policy that incorporates conduct outside the workplace. However, if yours has published one, you should observe and uphold it. Still, you can hold a person accountable for "off duty" conduct if it interferes with his or her work or is sufficiently outrageous as to interfere with your organization's ability to conduct its business—as long as you handle these situations under the umbrella of "a compelling business necessity."

Lie Detector Testing

Yes, you can use polygraph tests, *but only under special circumstances.*

The federal government, in 1988, legislated a limited ban on the use of polygraphs as pre-employment screening devices, the Federal Employee Polygraph Protection Act (December 27, 1988), which prohibits *private*-sector employers from using polygraph tests on applicants and employees, except:

- For national defense or security reasons
- When applicants or employees have direct access to controlled substances
- If applicants or employees are security guards
- In connection with investigations into theft or other incidents causing work-related losses, as long as there exists a "reasonable suspicion" that a current employee (or employees) has access to the property in question and if the employer gives the employee (or employees) a written statement outlining the reasons for testing

This law does *not* apply to federal, state, or local governments—a good reason for not letting the public-agency issue blind you to legal realities. The federal law and statutes in forty-two of the fifty states restrict or prohibit polygraph examinations of applicants and employees. Many courts have extended contract laws to cover constitutional rights of private-sector employees as well as of government employees, especially where the employer's action constitutes "outrageous conduct" in the absence or violation of a policy respecting an employee's right to privacy.

Defamation

It seems as if you cannot say anything to anyone about anything, but you do have more rights than that. In fact, in some cases, you have an obligation to disclose information in situations where other people have a right or a need to know all the facts.[21] The key issue hangs on the definition of defamation: the communication, disclosure, or publication of private information with malice or to someone who does not have the right to know.

You can express your personal opinion, judiciously (you have First Amendment rights, too), but when it comes to matters of fact, you should restrict your talk to these circumstances:

1. *When the third party has qualified or conditional privilege.* For example, supervisors considering employees for transfer to their work units have the right to review employee personnel records, including performance evaluations, as long as the reviewer intends no harm and limits the review to the immediate and legitimate contents.

2. *When the third party has absolute privilege.* For example, if the IRS requests financial information about an employee being audited.

3. *When you do not abuse privileged information.* You should base your decision to disclose information on reasonable grounds and make a reasonable effort to verify or corroborate the information on which you base the decision; an

anonymous letter alleging misconduct, for example, would not provide you with reasonable grounds.

Discuss the situation with the person about whom you will disclose the information before taking action, especially if evidence contradicts an accusation of misconduct.

Be selective about what you publish and to whom you publish any potential defamatory information about a personnel decision. Not every employee needs to know every detail of a situation. Limit the size of your audience to support the claim that people in your organization had a right or need to know whatever you decide to disclose.[22]

Conclusion

Employees sue if they believe their right to privacy has been violated in some way. The concept of privacy extends to employees' desks or lockers; these are places where they keep their personal things. It covers activities away from work on their own time ("It's my life, isn't it?"). Constitutional guarantees in the First, Fourth, Fifth, Ninth, and Fourteenth Amendments, and federal or state statues make most of the issues pretty clear. A person's life belongs to him or her, and only under special conditions can anyone intrude on that life.

Now, what about the matter of privacy rights that pertain to information about an employee, including freedom of information, access to medical records, and other business-related issues? Here we turn back to the concept of defamation.

Privacy rights extend beyond the constitutional guarantees against unreasonable search and seizure, self-incrimination, and so on. They include such mundane matters as the reason for firing someone or the nature of an illness. Disclosure of that kind of information to the wrong person at the wrong time or with the wrong motive could land you and your organization on the wrong side of the court. Care must be taken to avoid making defamatory statements.

Defamation arises from intentionally and maliciously publishing in writing or orally information harmful to a person and could include such things as honestly reporting a person's misconduct in a reference when that information could prevent the person from finding employment. Defamation also arises from giving out confidential information to parties who have neither privilege nor qualified privilege to receive that information.

Fear of becoming a party to a defamation lawsuit has led many employers to avoid asking for or giving references. But, then, policies of silence or of "name, rank, and serial number," are not necessarily protection, either. Sometimes, the *failure* to ask for or give references also causes an employer to wind up in court, as when an employer is sued for negligently putting someone with a suspect history into a position where he or she can injure or otherwise endanger other people. That employer could then turn around to sue you for failing to notify him or her that your former employee had been found guilty of a work-related or violent crime that he or she could or did repeat.

CASEBOOK

All of the information you just read comes from a large collection of actual cases. Here is a small sampling of them. Test your knowledge of what you have read, and use the cases as a basis for deciding how vulnerable you or your organization might be to charges of invasion of privacy or of defamation.

How Far Is Too Far in Trying to Keep the Workplace Safe?

Employers have a responsibility to their employees to maintain a safe and healthy work environment. At the same time, the Fourth Amendment protects Americans from unreasonable search and seizure and assures them the right to privacy. The spread of AIDS has frightened some managers into believing that the disease threatens the safety of their employees, and they have therefore instituted mandatory AIDS testing. These managers sometimes also threaten employees with disciplinary action, including discharge, if they refuse to be tested.

When that happened at the State Office of Mental Health in a midcontinent state, the government employees went to court. Their attorney argued that the testing policy violated Fourth Amendment rights guaranteed all government employees, to have a reasonable expectation of privacy in the personal data their blood and other body fluids carry. Mandatory testing amounts to an involuntary intrusion into their bodies: an unreasonable, warrantless search and seizure. The attorney concluded that this invasion of privacy was not counterbalanced by any significant government interest.

The issue here is, does a government employer have a right, in the interest of the larger group's health, as the Office of Mental Health countered, to force employees to test for AIDS? Does your organization require, or is it contemplating requiring, employees to be so tested? If so, check out the court's answer in this case.

My Blood

The court agreed with the employees and their attorney, that government employees have the constitutional protections of the Fourth Amendment. The government, the court declared, has an interest in providing safe working conditions for all its employees, but, given the medical evidence available, risk of transmitting the AIDS virus through casual contact in a workplace is statistically hardly possible. Additionally, the agency produced no evidence that its clients were at any more risk than were its employees. Only the *fear* of transmission dictated the agency's decisions.[4] You *can* go too far in trying to keep the workplace safe.

Because several states have antitesting statutes also, it is to your advantage to find out what the legal constraints in your state are. Do you or your personnel manager know?

Can You Fire Someone for Having a Positive Urine Test?

"Wait a minute," Karen Martin protested when her supervisor told her that the random drug test she took came back positive. "I don't do drugs." To make her case, the school bus driver submitted voluntarily to two additional tests, both of which came back negative.

"Too bad," she was then informed. "You're fired anyway."

So Karen went to court, where she argued that her Fourth Amendment Rights were violated. Unreasonable search and seizure, an invasion of privacy, she protested. The bus company under contract to the school district had no basis for testing her urine by taking a random sample of it and testing it for drugs *in the absence* of any suspicion that she had ever used drugs or was under the influence of them while on the job. Had she been involved in an accident or given someone sufficient cause to suspect her of wrong-doing, the court could possibly uphold testing in this case, other courts have ruled.

Because Karen was not in the armed forces, she was not a secret service agent, she was not in prison, and she was not engaged in a hazardous occupation or one involving the safety of the general public—cases in which the courts have upheld random testing—she was not required to submit to testing.

The employer argued that random testing falls under the public safety mandate it carries under a regulation of the Department of Transportation (DOT) requiring public- or private-sector employers to conduct random urine tests on nearly 4 million transportation employees whose jobs have safety or security implications; the testing is legal because school bus drivers are responsible for the safety of the children on the bus. Although the decision does not factor into this case, in 1989 the Supreme Court sustained the DOT's regulation.

How do you feel about this case? Whose rights should the courts protect, the employee's or the employer's?

Not Without Reason

Although not an easy case to decide, the court agreed with the plaintiff's entire case, defending the employee's right to protection from unreasonable search. Although the safety of the children on the bus was a legitimate issue, some standard of *reasonable suspicion* must protect employees to prevent many abuses of drug testing in both the public and private sector.[6]

Additionally, a federal court in California enjoined random testing among employees of a federal agency on the grounds that the agency did not demonstrate that it suffered a drug problem significant enough to warrant an invasion of privacy. The random testing seemed more like a "pretext" for uncovering off-duty illegal drug use. The "reasonable suspicion" test did not exist.[18]

Can You Fire Someone for Refusing to Submit to Drug Testing?

In California, as in other states, random testing of railroad employees for drugs is lawful, serving a compelling interest in protecting public safety. However, when a West Coast railroad company announced random drug testing for all employees, a computer programmer refused to provide a urine sample, asserting, "I sit at a computer terminal all day, and my job does not affect public safety in any way." The company fired her.

In court, charging wrongful discharge that intentionally inflicted emotional distress and the invasion of privacy, the programmer claimed that she was the only one who objected to the testing program on the basis of personal principle. She was therefore singled out for retaliation. She then sought both compensatory and punitive damages.

The employer, on the other hand, felt justified in requiring her to submit to the same drug tests other employees agreed to take because she worked for an organization responsible for public safety and covered by DOT regulations. The company had just cause to fire her.

Do you think they did? Or do you think the programmer was justified in refusing?

Drawing Lines

If you agreed with the programmer, you would have awarded her the same $485,000 the jury awarded her in both compensatory and punitive damages.[19] The company, the jury said, failed to show that a computer programmer is involved in the "safe operation and maintenance of the railroad." Therefore, it did indeed violate the woman's right to privacy.

Let's linger on this case a while because it helps make an essential distinction. That the woman was awarded punitive damages indicates that *tort law* was applied in this situation.

A *tort* is a civil wrong, a breach of duty other than a breach of contract under which compensatory damages are awarded. The victim of a tort action is entitled to a remedy from the person or group responsible for the wrongdoing. Some states, e.g., California, have codified various torts, but most states rely on the common traditions of case law in which judges or juries define torts. All tort cases fall into two categories: intentional and unintentional.

Intentional torts can result in heavy penalties, especially punitive damages. Although the burden of proof is on the plaintiff to show the defendant's state of mind, usually he or she only has to show that the defendant intended to commit the act and *should have foreseen* the consequences or intended to produce the outcome in question. In some states, the willful or reckless disregard for the consequences of an action is sufficient to show intentional torts. These versions of "intent" are not all that difficult to prove.

Because unintentional torts, such as simple negligence, usually do not result in punitive damages, the plaintiff is usually not required to show intent. Often, the only criterion on which the tort is judged is the exercise of *reasonable care* under the circumstances, as implied in the notion of reasonable suspicion.

When punitive damages are available, they are almost always sought, especially if aggravating circumstances (e.g., sexual harassment or wrongful discharge) exist. Punitive damages could then be very costly if you lose the case. And some states also recognize "negligently inflicting emotional distress" as a tort, but workers compensation laws usually protect employers from liability in such cases.

These definitions explain the jury's decision in the case we cited. When the railroad discharged the programmer in retaliation for refusing to submit to the drug testing, it thereby *intentionally* inflicted emotional distress. That intent was the measure of the jury's award of punitive damages.

Where Does Privacy Leave Off? Where Do Employer Rights Begin?

Several complaints of sexual harassment and a charge of misuse of a hospital-owned computer led the state hospital's chief administrator to thoroughly investigate the conduct of the chief of staff of training. One part of the probe, after suspending the physician, included entering Bharat Gupta's locked office, where the investigators pored over his personal belongings and papers, as well as official documents. They tied some items to the investigation; others they stored for Gupta to pick up. They also changed the lock on his office door.

Eventually the hospital terminated the doctor, who thereupon petitioned the court. In his lawsuit Gupta charged the state hospital with violating the Fourth Amendment, which guarantees citizens protection against the government's unreasonable search and seizure. He also claimed that the state had wrongfully invaded his privacy and breached a covenant of good faith and fair dealing.

The hospital countered with its right to conduct an investigation into serious allegations against the physician, which required that investigators enter the physician's office on its property. It also asserted the right to fire him when it was convinced that the allegations were true. It had just cause for its action.

Who do you think ultimately won this case, and why?

Keep Out

The decision in this case is a landmark that I suppose will be used to extend the "expectation of privacy" concept, especially where confidential records are involved, to all employment sectors. So set aside the charge of *governmental* misconduct as you think about its implications for you.

The actual case went all the way to the U.S. Supreme Court, which agreed that the chief of staff of training's desk housed personal papers, correspondence, mementos, financial records, and files. Given his medical roles, he also maintained sensitive, confidential information about patients and the medical residents and professionals with whom he routinely dealt. All of these factors would constrain even a private hospital's investigation.

In addition, although hospital policy reserved to employees voluntarily leaving or involuntarily terminating the right

to inventory their offices, Gupta was neither leaving nor terminating. Nor was he granted his right to inventory his office
at the time of the search. An employer's published policies can,
as in this case, form an agreement that cannot be unilaterally
broken.

Given these facts, the physician had a reasonable expectation of privacy in his office.[23]

The hospital's own policies worked against its countervailing interests. It had no policies authorizing blanket surveillance or searches of offices, and at the time it searched Gupta's
office, it did not authorize a general inspection of all offices.
Therefore, the court decided, the only purpose in invading the
office was to collect evidence for the hospital's investigation.
The state hospital violated the Fourth Amendment and wrongfully invaded the employee's privacy, while breaching its covenant of good faith and fair dealing.

Even though this case arises in the context of public
employment, the Supreme Court's backing could, more than
likely, encourage many state legislatures to apply the same
principles to private employments as well. And because those
applications in both the public and private sectors will go
beyond merely entering locked offices, we can expect them to
crop up in drug testing cases as well. Precedents for expanded
applications already exist.

One court has said that a union official (in a shared office)
whose papers were taken without his permission had the right
to expect privacy of his area.[7] Another court ruled that a school
guidance counselor's desk was private.[24] Finally, a police officer could expect privacy even though the department owned
his locker, supplied it primarily for storing police gear, and
secured it by a department lock in addition to his personal
one.[25] Several other courts have agreed that the employer can
support its right to inspect premises, furniture, or equipment
only if it publishes and enforces a general inspection policy,
but the search must be covered by statute and must meet legal
standards for search and seizure.[26, 27]

Let's turn now to another form of privacy. Does your
organization require polygraph tests? Thinking about ordering
them? First consider this situation.

Can You Use Lie Detector Tests to Screen Applicants?

A city in California thought it prudent to test employees for honesty. The city's employees, on the other hand, argued that the pretest and the control questions included invasive probes into arrests, heart trouble or epilepsy, present medical care, and experimentation with drugs such as LSD, heroin, or cocaine. One control question asked, "Did you ever steal anything?" The alleged purpose of that sort of question was to set a baseline for judging the subject's answers to other questions. The employees claimed, however, that the questions invaded their right to privacy under California law.

"No," the city countered. "The tests are essential for protecting the citizens of the community from emotionally disturbed employees, from liars, thieves, or physically impaired public servants."

What do you think? Did the employer have the right to require the polygraph test and to ask those questions? Would your organization ever require them? For what reasons?

Lie Detector Tests Undone

The California Supreme Court said that the pretest and control questions intrude into private matters of no consequence to the job.[28] The testers probed a person's emotions, repressed beliefs and feelings, guilts, and fantasies. Additionally, many questions coerced the subjects into self-incrimination, a violation of the U.S. Constitution's Fifth Amendment. Nothing, the court concluded, justified the city's unfortunate intrusion.

California courts are often ahead of others when it comes to employee rights. In this case, it was ahead of the federal legislation described earlier in this chapter that limits the use of polygraphs (the Federal Employee Polygraph Protection Act).

Can You Discipline or Fire Someone for Conduct Outside the Workplace?

A Fortune 100 company found itself in court in 1984, sued by a management employee claiming the company's own policies protected her private life. The employee sued after she was fired for refusing to stop seeing a competitor's employee socially. When, in court, the company argued that the liaison compromised its ability to conduct business, she stated the following grounds for reinstatement and compensatory damages:

1. The Fourth Amendment guaranteed her the right to privacy with respect to her personal life.
2. The company's privacy policy ensured her the right to privacy as long as her activities did not interfere with her work.
3. Her private relationship did not interfere with her work because nothing she did related to the other person's work.

Does your organization restrict after-hours conduct? How and why? Does it publish a privacy policy? If so, how is it enforced?

Off Duty: My Time

The size and power of the employer not withstanding, the court sided with the plaintiff. Said the California Appeals Court, even though Fourth Amendment rights do not apply here, the company's own privacy policies set a standard by which its contractual obligations under California's covenant of good faith and fair dealing can be judged; the company's failure to follow its own policies therefore provided sufficient evidence that the good-faith covenant had been violated.[8]

Not having a published policy does not protect you either. In a different case, in which a public policy violation was cited when a manager was fired for dating a co-worker, the court ruled *against* the plaintiff but added that *had* he charged the company with "outrageous conduct" in violation of good faith, he might have made his case.[29]

Can You Tell Someone's Co-Workers About His Psychiatric Treatment?

Eddy Brown suffered a series of emotional crises for which he sought psychiatric treatment before he did himself or others harm. He told his supervisor about it, and the supervisor in turn told Eddy's co-workers, with the good intent of enlisting everyone's aid in helping the man. Eddy did not see the situation in the same light, and he took the supervisor and the company to court.

"My medical history is confidential," Eddy charged. "My supervisor invaded my privacy by telling my co-workers about my problems. They had no legitimate interest in this information."

"But," the employer countered, "what would have happened if Eddy became violent and harmed someone, as he himself worried? Wouldn't we have been guilty of negligence?"

How would you have handled this situation? Would you have discussed the employee's problems with his co-workers? Why or why not?

A Need or Right to Know

The Oklahoma Supreme Court said the disclosure was *not* unreasonable, even though other courts will not always agree with it.[21] The court did not answer the question of possible negligence for failing to communicate the information, but it did say that the absence of "disclosure to the public" determined the absence of defamation. *Disclosure "to the public,"* to a person or persons *without a right or a need to know*, is the criterion upon which this privacy judgment hung for the Oklahoma Supreme Court.

This controversial decision helps spell out various aspects of the privacy of information issue and the whole matter of defamation. Because defamation occurs only if private information that *could* cause injury to the person's personal or professional reputation is communicated with malice or to anyone who does *not* have the right or need to know that information, the court disagreed with the plaintiff. It held that the supervisor used reasonable discretion to give the information about the psychiatric treatment to the plaintiff's co-workers, to people who have the right or need to know. If the story had been told to anyone else, that would have been unreasonable, and the plaintiff would have had a case.

Or if the supervisor had communicated the information with the *intent* to harm the plaintiff, that clearly would have constituted defamation, even though the information was true.

When Do Your Statements About Someone Become Slander?

Coastal Airlines defended itself against a pilot's complaint that it slandered him by saying that any statements made about him were merely opinions, not fact, and therefore not defamatory. "Anyone is entitled to an opinion." That is not how Bob Gillette saw it.

He argued that calling him paranoid during an interview with a reporter impugned his mental state and his ability to do his job responsibly. Oral remarks to a third party, said with malice, fell short of calling him insane, but implied he was not fit to exercise his job duties properly and were therefore libel per se.

> Gillette had been complaining for years. I think you ought to know he wrote some very odd letters to the FBI. . . . He said Coastal was out to get him, that we tried to crash a plane in order to kill him. He's paranoid.

In other cases, the argument continued, remarks similar to the airline's agent's statements to a reporter—"some mental problems," "mean, demented old man," and "decided complex"—have been held defamatory per se. Further, when the reporter asked why Gillette was allowed to fly, the airline representative said:

> It's awfully hard to fire anyone these days. Anyway, we have three of them in the cockpit. Know what I mean?

What would stop a spokesperson for your organization from saying something possibly defamatory to a reporter? How would he or she be empowered to do that? Why? Or why would your organization not so empower someone?

With Malice

The Florida Court of Appeals agreed that the statements appeared to be a matter of opinion, but appearances in this case are not deceiving. If the remarks had been nothing more than conjecture on the part of the spokesperson, they would not have formed the basis of a lawsuit. But, the court said, the statements implied undisclosed defamatory facts and therefore could form a cause of action.

The last statement, that if it were not "awfully hard to fire anyone these days" the airline would fire him, clinched the issue by making the pilot's sanity a question of fact, not a matter of opinion, that could be confirmed (or not). That statement contained the "smoking gun." The airline was guilty of defamation with malice.[10]

Can an Employee Sue If a Performance Evaluation Contains Potentially Defamatory Statements?

"The written performance appraisal," Harry Prince complained to the court, "contains statements about my competence with which I take issue. I feel the appraisal impugns my competence and is therefore defamatory. The situation is made worse insofar as my performance appraisal has been placed in my personnel file, to which any manager has access. Therefore, defamatory statements are being published. I want my employer enjoined from publishing that information."

The company responded that everyone's performance appraisal has comments about performance in need of improvement; that is part of the appraisal process. It is in the interests of both the employer and employee that evaluations be completed and used to make promotion and other personnel decisions.

Do you think the court should order the company to remove the defamatory information from the file? Does your company remove less than complimentary reviews from personnel files? Why or why not?

The Importance of Privilege

The court agreed with the plaintiff that the evaluation contained statements impugning his competence; therefore, in that regard, the evaluation was defamatory. On the other hand, the court also agreed with the company that because it intended no malice it had a right, in its interests and those of the employee, to place the evaluation in the personnel file. Unlike the airline company in the previous case, the company and its managers in this case have "qualified privilege" that they had not abused with the intent to harm the employee.[30]

What Are the Limits of Privilege?

During the more than one year that Doris Petrie had worked for Dr. Franklin and several other physicians sharing the practice, no one, including Dr. Franklin, had said anything negative about her. She was called a good, hardworking nurse: honest, generous, and well-liked by everyone, including Dr. Franklin.

In fact Dr. Franklin liked her more than did the other doctors and made his interest in Nurse Petrie well known—asking her out, sending her flowers, calling her at home, and writing notes to her—but to no avail. She did not want an office romance, and she made her wishes equally well known. That angered the doctor, and he assigned her extra and more difficult duties.

One afternoon Nurse Petrie mistakenly asked a patient to take a blood test, and when Dr. Franklin heard about it he accused her of changing laboratory slip orders on the patient's chart. Although she admitted making the mistake, the nurse denied altering the orders.

Not satisfied, the doctor demanded that Petrie name the person who altered the orders, and later, when she still had not found out who changed them, he threatened her: "If you decide to stay, I'm going to ride your ass like you have never been ridden before. I'm going to watch over you, and I'm going to make it difficult for you, if you decide to stay."

The next day, when the nurse was still unable to explain how the orders came to be changed, Dr. Franklin fired her and assembled the five-person staff to explain the events. During the meeting he referred to Nurse Petrie and said that he could not work with a liar, with someone who is not trustworthy.

Although the nurse might have sued the doctor for sexual harassment and retaliatory discharge, she instead took him to court for defamation. Speaking as he did impugned her character and opened up her life to people who had no need or right to know these things.

Nonsense, the doctor retorted. The so-called defamation took place in the course of employer-employee relations. He and the office staff had qualified privilege.

What do you think? Did Petrie's co-workers have privilege?

The Presence of Malice

The doctor paid full price for his indiscretion: a total of $125,000 in various kinds of damages. Why? Even if the office staff shared in qualified privilege, the alleged defamatory statements were motivated by what the court called "actual malice."[31] Here are the important sources of evidence that guided this decision:

1. Until the nurse spurned the doctor's advances, she had been considered an exemplary, trustworthy employee.
2. The doctor had let it be known that he was angry about being rejected.
3. Whatever the mix-up in the laboratory orders, the situation was too insignificant to be anything other than a ruse for retaliating against the nurse for denying him.

Given those three conditions, the court concluded, the doctor had called the nurse a liar and untrustworthy either because *he knew the charges were false or because he recklessly disregarded the truth*. In either case his intent was malicious. Such malice overcomes any claim to privilege.

Can the Absence of Malice Protect an Employer From a Lawsuit?

Bob Pershing, a general manager for Cross Country Transportation, never shrank from an invitation to have a "nightcap" with "the boys" when he went out of town on business. This trip was no exception. Several days later his employer received an anonymous letter complaining that Bob had become drunk, argumentative, and profanely abusive, making "nasty" remarks about the company.

In spite of eyewitness testimony that Bob had not become drunk or made such remarks about his employer, the company fired him without talking it over with him. The anonymous letter was the only justification.

What really angered Bob the most, however, was that the man who replaced him called a meeting of 120 employees and declared:

I gathered you all here to tell you why Mr. Pershing is no longer with the company. The man was drunk and misbehaving in a bar. The man has a drinking problem. Cross Country Transportation looks unkindly on this kind of conduct. It was not the first time. He had been warned.

As soon as he heard about the speech, Bob sued for defamation. In response, the company argued that both Bob's successor and the employees had qualified privilege; the company had the right to inform the employees and the employees had a right to know.

What do you think? What takes priority, Bob's right to privacy or the company's and employee's rights?

The Abuse of Privilege Even in the Absence of Malice

Pay the complainant $350,000 in damages, said both the trial and the appeals courts. Yes, the employer had a qualified privilege to make statements about why someone was fired, but Cross Country Transportation crossed the line by doing two things:

1. It based its decision to disclose information about Pershing on unreasonable grounds, the anonymous letter.
2. It engaged too large an audience to support the claim that people in the company had a right or need to know.[22]

Although malice was absent, those two considerations gave rise to the judgment against the company.

This is the case that provided us with the guidelines listed earlier. Before making a personnel decision that you may publish, take care to base that decision on evidence stronger than an anonymous letter or some equally unreliable source. Make a reasonable effort to verify or corroborate the information on which you base the decision, and confront the accused before taking action, especially if evidence contradicts the accusation.

And be selective about what you publish and to whom you publish any potentially defamatory information about a personnel decision. Not every employee needs to know every detail of a situation. In the case cited, "rank-and-file employees" two levels below Pershing heard the gruesome allegations. That dissemination, the courts ruled, abused the privilege the company would otherwise have enjoyed.

But what about people outside your organization? What are the limits here?

Could You Be Held Liable for What Former Employees Say About Themselves?

Worldwide Life and Health Insurance, as a matter of corporate policy, gives only the dates of employment and the final job title of a former employee, unless specifically authorized in writing to release additional information in response to reference checks. The company adhered to that policy after it discharged four claims representatives for "gross insubordination," a charge stemming from their refusal to revise expense reports they had submitted. Yet several years later Worldwide found itself defending itself before the Minnesota Supreme Court against charges of defamation.

According to the plaintiffs, when they sought out new jobs, they were compelled to explain why they left their last place of employment. To avoid being charged with fraud, they all had to say they had been "terminated" for "gross insubordination," which left them still unemployed. Thus began the long journey through the courts.

What do you think? Did the fact that Worldwide had not published the defamatory information—that, indeed, the plaintiffs themselves had—get the company off the hook? What are your organization's policies with respect to terminating someone, showing cause, and providing reference information? How, if at all, would these results apply locally? Why or why not?

Implicit Defamation in Self-Publication

Ordinarily, Worldwide, because it did not give out reasons for terminating employees, might not have been liable. In general, the employer does not publish information when it gives the information to the employee, who, in turn, discloses it to someone else, e.g., a prospective employer. But, in matters of law, the exception frequently becomes the rule.

The Minnesota Supreme Court declared an exception to the publication rule when it said that if a defamed person is *in some way compelled* to communicate the defamatory statement to a third party, and if the defendant could reasonably foresee that the defamed person would be required to disclose the statement, then the defendant could be held liable for the publication.[11] Self-publication under these circumstances can cause a person professional injury or harm. The question then becomes whether or not the alleged defamatory statement is true; if the statement turns out to be false, then the company loses any privilege in telling the employees the reason for their discharge.

The Minnesota Supreme Court supported the trial jury's decision that evidence indicated that the fired employees had not engaged in gross insubordination. The statement was false, and therefore Worldwide made the statement with actual malice for the purpose of injuring the plaintiffs.

The court did hold out in favor of the employer in one phase of the case, however: damages. Punitive damages, awarded by the trial jury ($600,000), are not available in defamation suits involving compelled self-publication. That denial of punitive damages, the court reasoned, should deter people from *wanton* self-publication. Compensatory damages, on the other hand, are available (in this case, $300,000), and this could lead more and more employers to adopt the policy of silence.

Cases

1. 726 F.2d 459 (9th Cir. 1983), *cert. denied*, 469 U.S. 979 (1984).
2. 563 F. Supp. 585 (W.D. Mich. 1983), *aff'd*, 746 F.2d 1475 (6th Cir. 1984).
3. 788 F.2d 1223 (6th Cir. 1986).
4. No. 87-0-830 (D. Neb. Mar. 29, 1988).
5. S. Ct. No. 87-1555.
6. 628 F. Supp. 1500, 121 L.R.R.M. (BNA) 2901 (D.D.C. 1986).
7. 392 U.S. 364, 368–369 (1968).

8. 162 Cal. App. 3d 241 (1984).
9. 426 F. Supp. (W.D. Pa.) 1328.
10. 438 So. 2d 923 (Fla. Dist. Ct. App. 1983).
11. 389 N.W.2d 876 (Minn. Sup. Ct. 1986).
12. 73 Ga. App. 839, 38 S.E.2d 306 (1946).
13. 16 Mich. App. 452, 168 N.W.2d 289 (1969).
14. 110 Cal. App. 3d 787, 168 Cal. Rptr. 89 (1980).
15. 506 A.2d 901 (Pa. Super. Ct. 1986).
16. 694 S.W. 822 (Mo. Ct. App. 1985).
17. 64 N.Y.2d 770, 475 N.E.2d 451 (1985).
18. No. 6-88-20729-WAI (N.D. Cal. Jan. 6, 1989).
19. No. 843,230 (S.F. Sup. Ct. 1987).
20. 816 F.2d 170 (5th Cir. 1987).
21. No. 62,086 (1986).
22. 662 P.2d 760 (Or. Ct. App. 1983).
23. 817 F.2d 1408, 1 I.E.R. Cases 831 (9th Cir. 1985), *aff'd*, 1 I.E.R. Cases 1617 (March 31, 1987).
24. 579 F.2d 825, 829 (3d Cir. 1978).
25. 557 F.2d 362, 363 (3d Cir. 1977).
26. 521 F.2d 1217 (9th Cir. 1975).
27. 479 F. Supp. 207 (S.D.N.Y. 1979).
28. 227 Cal. Rptr. 90 (Cal. Sup. Ct. 1986) (en banc).
29. 75 Or. App. 638, 708 P.2d 1256 (1985).
30. 748 P.2d 349 (Colo. Ct. App. 1987).
31. 671 S.W.2d 559 (Tex. Ct. App. 1984).

Chapter 8

Preventing Sex Discrimination and Sexual Harassment on the Job

Discrimination and harassment on the basis of race, color, religion, national origin, age, disability, or military status, as well as on the basis of gender, are still extremely pervasive, and just as socially and economically pernicious as ever. We pay considerable attention to the sex issue not because such cases come to court most often but rather because women make up over 50 percent of the population and are entering the work force in numbers that far exceed those of any other group. As a result, sex discrimination and sexual harassment have become the dominant *management* issues of our times. Unless we practice safe management with respect to gender, sex-related lawsuits could overwhelm the legal system.

Because discrimination and harassment still affect all protected groups, you can *use* this chapter as a model of how to prevent unsafe management practices of all kinds, or as a guide to what to do about them when they happen. Mistreating protected groups is illegal, no matter how you look at it, and the definitions and prescriptions I provide apply in the main to any illegal action on the part of management. Safe management comes down to the recognition of the rights and dignity of all people regardless of race, color, religion, national origin, age, disability, or military status as well as gender.

143

The definitions of *sexism, sex discrimination,* and *sexual harassment* describe behaviors that affect women employees more frequently than they do men, but they do affect men and, in their broadest sense, apply to race and age as well as to sex.

Definitions of Key Terms

sexism A value system that holds that one person is inferior to another, for example, "Women are too emotional, especially during their period." Sexism takes several subtle forms found in every form of *-ism.*
   1. *Condescension.* Refusing to take someone seriously, e.g., "Leave the difficult decisions to men."
   2. *Verbal abuse.* Making negative or derogatory comments, e.g., "I like watching your hips sway when you walk."
   3. *Exclusion.* Overlooking or denying someone access to places, people, or information, especially when opportunities for advancement are involved, e.g., excluding women from community organizations.
   4. *Tokenism.* Including a selected one or few members of a group for very visible positions;* also called "window dressing."

sex discrimination Employment decisions based on gender rather than on gender-neutral considerations, or different treatment of one employee merely on the basis of his or her gender.

sexual harassment Unwelcome behavior of a sexual nature or with sexual overtones; sexual harassment takes two legal shapes:
   1. *Quid pro quo.* (a) Where submitting to sexual demands becomes an implicit or explicit term or condition of employment; e.g., "You can have a promotion but only if you have sex with me." (b) Making decisions affecting someone's employment or compensation on the basis of whether the person submits to or rejects sexual demands.
   2. *Hostile environment.* Sexual conduct that has the purpose or effect of unreasonably interfering with a person's job performance or that creates an intimidating or offensive work

---

*See Jane Gordon Chapman, "Sexual Harassment of Women in Employment, Part II: Promising Solutions," *Response* (Fall 1984).

environment.* Whereas *quid pro quo,* above, has a uniquely sexual context, *hostile environment* does not; it can exist for minorities, older people, disabled people, and veterans as well.

unwelcome behavior Conduct "the employee did not solicit or incite . . . and . . . [regards] as undesirable or offensive."[1]

agency and employer liability Any employee acting or speaking on behalf of the employer and relying on his or her apparent authority at the time he or she sexually harasses an employee. An employer need not know about a manager's sexual harassment of an employee to be held liable for that harassment.[2] For Title VII purposes, "the employer" need not be the "person engaged in an industry affecting commerce," but rather "any agent of such a person" as well. As long as the supervisor or manager is an "agent" of the organization when he or she sexually harasses an employee, the employer can be held directly liable for his or her actions.

An employer may be liable for wrongs committed by its personnel even if they act outside the scope of their authority, as long as they *purport* "to act or to speak on behalf of the principal and [they rely] upon apparent authority, or [they are] aided in accomplishing [their wrongdoing by having] an agency relationship." Although a supervisor might act only to satisfy him- or herself, and not for the benefit of the employer, the liability stems from the following key points:

1. The alleged harasser manages some aspect of the principal's business.
2. He or she threatens the person's employment status and has both actual and apparent authority to carry out the threat.
3. He or she uses that authority to harass the person.

Given those factors, the company need not have knowledge of the situation to be held responsible.

*Common experiences that usually get dismissed as just "horseplay" can create a hostile environment; see "Cops: Miami Beach Is Talking," *Newsweek* (August 21, 1989), p. 4.

EEOC guidelines (Section 1604.11e) say that Title VII also protects employees from sexual harassment by nonemployees because employers should maintain and enforce antiharassment policies.[3] While you cannot guarantee that sexual harassment in the workplace will not occur, once an incident is brought to your attention you should be prompt and thorough in your investigation and take reasonable corrective action when such is indicated. You should make it clear to customers or to vendors calling on you that you do not condone any form of harassment—sexual, racial, or what have you.

Gender-based issues take many forms: compensation discrimination, maternity, discipline, promotion, insurance policies, and many others. So let's look at some things you, as a manager, cannot do.

What You Cannot Do

The following accounting* forms only a partial list of possible forms of sex discrimination and harassment.

The Obvious

- Hire or promote a man less qualified than the women available or interviewed.
- Fire a woman when a man might be merely disciplined.
- Lay off qualified women before or in lieu of men.
- Compensate and reward women at a lower rate than men.
- Make employment or promotion contingent upon meeting sexual demands, even if the other person appears to consent.[4,5]

Less Obvious

- Give preferential treatment to a consenting sex partner in a way that discriminates against other female employees.[6,7]

*Drawn from EEOC guidelines of 1988 as well as from a variety of cases.

- Call a woman "girl," "doll," "babe" or "baby," "honey."
- Ogle; block a person's way; stare at, for example, a woman's breasts; wink; blow kisses; whistle.[8]
- Comment on the appearance of a person's body or the sexiness of his or her clothing.[8]
- Make sexually oriented jokes, comments, or innuendoes.[9]
- Ask questions, e.g., about one's sex life or fantasies.[9]
- "Put the make" on someone, e.g., push someone to go out who has refused.
- Tell defamatory stories about a person's sex life.
- Touch, massage, rub against, hug, kiss, stroke, or just "hang around" those to whom these actions are unwelcome.
- Treat maternity-disabled employees differently from the way you treat other people returning from disability leave.[10–12]
- Provide health insurance coverage for one gender but not for the other, e.g., pregnancy-related benefits for women employees but none for spouses of men employees.[7,13,14]
- Discharge a pregnant employee because she plans leave to have a baby as a cost-saving device.[15]
- In any way treat an employee differently from others because she is pregnant, unless the pregnancy interferes with a BFOQ or makes it impossible for the employee to perform the duties of the work available.[15]
- Transfer or discharge a woman whose spouse works for the same supervisor without giving her husband the same options.[16,17]
- Respond differently to a woman's requests, e.g., for a particular travel associate, than you would to a man's similar request.[18]
- Use subjective criteria in promoting people or considering them for partnership (e.g., in a law firm) unless the criteria are clearly inherent in the job.[19–21]
- Impose personal or social values on a person's private life unless the person's conduct clearly interferes with your organization's ability to conduct its business.[22]
- Ignore or plead ignorance of sexual harassment occur-

ring in your organization; managers are liable for actions of their employees.[2,18,23,24]

▸ Retaliate against employees who reject your sexual advances or who file a claim of discrimination or harassment against you or your organization.[25]

What You Can Do

At the risk of belaboring the obvious, I will say that if you reread the lists in the previous section and restate the items in their converse, you will see the essence but not the detail of what you, as a manager, *can* do. Still, I will not deal with each point separately. Instead, I'll talk about some of the less obvious situations that can create a manager's thornier problems.

Guidelines for Safe Maternity Leave Policies

The courts have ruled that Title VII, as amended in 1978, explicitly includes pregnancy-related disabilities within the scope of "sex" discrimination:

> [Women] affected by pregnancy, childbirth, or related medical conditions shall be treated the same for all employment-related purposes, including receipt of fringe benefits under fringe benefit programs, as other persons not so affected but similar in their ability or inability to work. . . ."[10]

The EEOC and the courts have said not to deny benefits or impose burdens on employees on maternity leave that you would not similarly apply to employees on disability leave for any other reason. They have also supplied some rules for guiding your organization's maternity leave practices:

1. Grant employees disabled by pregnancy-related conditions the same paid leave privileges on the same basis as other medically disabled employees, e.g., a guarantee of the same job and job status (seniority).

2. If you have a waiting period before a medically disabled employee receives paid leave, impose the same terms on pregnancy-disabled employees.
3. If you require that a medically disabled employee produce a doctor's okay before returning to work, require pregnancy-disabled employees to do so also.
4. If you allow disabled employees unpaid leave of absence when their accumulated sick leave benefits expire, allow leave privileges on the same basis to employees with pregnancy-related conditions.

In sum, the rules for medically disabled employees, including pregnant or childbearing employees, should ensure the same terms for anyone experiencing a long-term medical absence.[11] At least four states (California, Connecticut, Massachusetts, and Montana) and Puerto Rico have laws requiring *preferential* treatment for pregnancy. Other states (e.g., Hawaii, Kansas, Illinois, New Hampshire, Ohio, Minnesota, and Washington) have adopted regulations that have the effect of law. The U.S. Supreme Court, deciding a California case, said that Title VII merely establishes a floor beneath which pregnancy disability benefits may not drop, rather than a ceiling above which they may rise. Therefore, states, within certain limits, may require employers to provide preferential treatment.[10] You should check or have someone else find out what the laws in your state say.

Maternity Benefits for Spouses

An important collateral issue is the status of maternity benefits for spouses. According to the Supreme Court, you or your organization should provide equal coverage.[14]

In 1983 the Supreme Court heard a case that charged the employer with providing women employees hospitalization benefits for pregnancy-related conditions to the same extent as for other medical conditions, but not extending the same benefits to pregnant spouses of men employees. The married men employees complained that the company's insurance provided them less comprehensive protection than it provided married women employees, and the Supreme Court agreed with the men. The Court would not agree with a lower court's opinion that employees' spouses were not covered by the pregnancy amendment to Title VII; Congress, it said, did *not* expressly limit it to "women employees" or intend that the "basic purpose" of the amendment was to protect "women employees" only.[13]

If an employer provides complete health insurance coverage for the dependents of its female employees and no coverage at all for the dependents of men employees, it would clearly violate Title VII. Likewise, limits placed on pregnancy-related benefits for employees' wives penalizes married men *if* the plan offers more extensive coverage for employees' spouses for *all* other medical conditions requiring hospitalization. They would then receive a benefit package for their dependents that was less inclusive than the dependency coverage provided to married women employees.[14]

A few employers try to get around the high cost of equal benefits by offering men a "baby bonus" instead of comprehensive maternity benefits. The Seventh Circuit Court has nixed that idea.[26] The most creative idea is not necessarily the best.

Equal benefits do not stop with benefits for current employees. A conversion health insurance policy for former employees should include pregnancy coverage for former women employees or for wives of former male employees. That the insurance policy is a matter between the former employee and the insurance company is irrelevant. The employer is ultimately responsible for a discriminatory fringe benefit plan even if third parties are involved in adopting it.[27,28]

Equal Treatment for Pregnant Women

A pregnant woman is entitled to fair and equal treatment, and as I said before, in some states she is entitled to preferential treatment not only with respect to maternity benefits but other management decisions as well. For example, you could lay off a pregnant woman to answer a downsizing problem but only if you can defend that reason on the basis of "legitimate nondiscriminatory reasons." To lay off or discharge a pregnant employee because she plans to leave when she has her baby means treating this employee differently from others merely because of her pregnancy. To even consider the woman's plan to leave is a smoking gun.[15]

You do not have to *fire* a pregnant woman or one planning to bear children to get in trouble. Under Title VII, any decisions adversely affecting a woman employee that appear correlated with information about her intentions of raising a family could end in a lawsuit for constructive discharge, that is, creating conditions that appear intolerable to the employee and cause her to quit.[29]

Preventing Conflicts of Interest

You can ban spouses from reporting to the same superior in order to try to prevent a possible conflict of interest. Your organization can enforce written or unwritten antinepotism rules as long as they are facially neutral and evenhandedly applied in a nondiscriminatory way, requiring a male spouse, if for example he is the junior employee, to accept a transfer or accept discharge.[16] Not separating husbands and wives working in the same department, especially if one is senior to the other, could result in a conflict of interest, and as such antinepotism policies serve a legitimate business interest.[17]

Conflict of interest is not the only legitimate reason for antinepotism rules. A close personal relationship could produce interpersonal conflicts unrelated to business or generate unwarranted favoritism. Awkward situations can develop between any members of the same family working closely together.[30]

Antinepotism rules usually apply to married couples, but cohabitating unmarried couples may as well be married as far as some organizations care. Whether or not you can take action to separate these employees on the job, to require them to marry, or to discharge them depends on the circumstances in which you conduct your business. Let's take, for example, a situation involving a public position, such as that of a librarian who as a part of her job spends a lot of time with children. If cohabitation clearly violates community standards, the librarian's conduct can serve as a compelling business necessity for requiring the couple to separate, marry, or accept discharge.[22]

Community standards such as these can become subjective if they fail to take into account that social and personal values have changed. The changes have created new conflicts between personal privacy and organizational good that have hidden in the folds of sex discrimination. Invade a woman's private life, and you invade us all.

Separating the two provinces, personal and organizational, forms the basis of effective personnel management. Personnel policies are not themselves as important as how you implement them. If you have a human resources department, it will police your policies, especially if you call some of the questions raised here to the department's attention. Still, you can manage better if you use these tips for proactive handling of personnel matters in the following areas:

▸ *Privacy.* Recognize and respect employees' rights to their own private lives. As long as their personal life-styles do not interfere with their job performance or with the conduct of your organization's mission, you have no business interfering in their lives.

▸ *Fairness.* Policies are written to benefit the organization and to guide employees in the directions that best benefit the organization with the least amount of inconvenience to the employees, where possible. But policy effectiveness depends on how managers manage.

You may not intend to discriminate against women, but the rules regarding antinepotism, unwed parents, and alternative life-styles, for example, tend to work against women, racial minorities, and homosexuals. But, while the rules apply "in general," actual decisions apply "in particular."

▸ *Alternatives.* Thinking beyond superficial issues requires you to suspend your immediate judgment in order to consider only legitimate business necessities. Marital status is not the issue; conflict of interest or non-work-related conflicts, ability to work with and communicate with other employees or with the organization's customers are. Likewise, transferring either person, separating workstations, promotions, and so on, are possible solutions *in addition to discharging the woman.* Creative *and* lawful decision making is called for.

But can you expect equal treatment from the courts? It depends on the factors that determine the factual basis of a legitimate business reason. Appealing to "community standards" could be a subjective factor, about which I cautioned you in Chapter 4.

Rejecting Women Employees for Promotion

No law says that when men and women compete for the same job you have to promote the women over the men. The laws say only that you should prevent subjective criteria from tainting your promotion decisions. Here are some guidelines, taken from a court case,[31] that can help:

1. Do not allow a supervisor's recommendations to be the most important or only component in the selection process.
2. Produce written instructions delineating appropriate criteria to apply when making promotion decisions; apply objective measures anywhere possible.
3. Caution supervisors about using vague or undefined criteria; conduct proper training programs that include written instructions on the proper use of objective criteria.
4. Notify all employees of the selection criteria; use an open-posting system.
5. Produce safeguards to prevent discriminatory practices, e.g., a review committee that includes members of protected classes.

Acting on Complaints of Harassment

The courts and the EEOC recognize that "sexual attraction may often play a role in the day-to-day social exchange between employees" and distinguish between "invited, uninvited-but-welcome, offensive-but-tolerated, and flatly rejected" sexual advances.[32] Let's revisit the idea of "unwelcome."

Personal relationships always muddy business waters, but relationships between sexually active adults create serious issues for managers to consider. When does an innocent flirtation become sexual harassment? How serious is *one* incident? How do you determine culpability? Then, once you do, what do you do about it? Jobs, reputations, families, and lives are at stake here, and care must be taken.

Since harassment is in the eye of the beholder, mistaken intentions could result in inappropriate charges. Friendliness, thoughtless or innocent remarks, bids for attention can all be misread. To help out, the EEOC published guidelines* in early 1988 stating that "a single incident or isolated incidents of offensive sexual conduct or remarks generally do not create an abusive environment [unless] the conduct is quite severe [*Section C2*]."

The Commission quotes the U.S. Supreme Court: "[The] mere utterance of an ethnic or social [or sexual] epithet [that] engenders offensive feelings in an employee would not affect the conditions of employment to a sufficiently significant degree to violate Title VII."[33]

With regard to quid pro quo, frequently a single incident offense is sufficient for action. On the other hand, a hostile environment exists only when there is a *pattern* of unreasonable conduct.

The EEOC spells out how to judge the merits of a harassment complaint when, upon investigation, the alleged harasser denies that the advances were unwelcome.[33] How do you decide?

First, the victim, say, a woman, should have communicated her displeasure, asserting "her right to a workplace free from sexual harassment." For example: "Stop it. I don't like what you're doing"; "I have no wish to see you socially"; "Please stop making sexual remarks or jokes around me." These and similar statements clearly indicate that the behav-

---

*"EEOC Policy Guidance on Sexual Harassment," Washington, D.C.: The Bureau of National Affairs, 1988.

ior is unwelcome. Nonverbal behaviors, such as pushing away an offensive person or facial expressions of annoyance also show that the advances are unwelcome.

Still, this type of protest is *not necessary* for creating credibility. The victim may come to you without ever telling her perceived persecutor how she feels because she may fear repercussions, e.g., being fired, and not confront her harasser directly. Then, you are obligated to conduct a thorough investigation (which I describe later in this chapter).

Second, the plaintiff strengthens her case if she makes a "contemporaneous" complaint, i.e., a complaint made at the time the harassment occurs or shortly after it stops. The EEOC calls a complaint contemporaneous even if it is made *after* the victim quits her job as long as "she notified her employer of the harassment at the time of . . . departure or shortly thereafter," which often happens for the same reason the victim does not confront the harasser directly: because of fear. The employer is still obligated to investigate thoroughly, to determine whether the employee quit as a result of a constructive discharge.

Third, you need to determine if the plaintiff had ever given the alleged harasser reason to believe that sexual advances were welcome. For example, in a 1983 decision, the EEOC ruled against one of three women because she responded in kind to sexual horseplay and gave her employer reason to believe his behavior was acceptable to her.[9]

Investigating Claims of Harassment

To prevent being held liable for the acts of other people, you need to thoroughly investigate claims of harassment. The U.S. Supreme Court hedged on employer liability when it said employers are not "automatically liable" for the actions of their supervisors.[33] Each case must be taken on its own merits, but the principle of agency is consistent with the intent of Title VII and with EEOC Guidelines on Sexual Harassment (Section 1604.11c):

> An employer . . . is responsible for its acts and those of its agents and supervisory employees with respect

to sexual harassment regardless of whether the specific acts complained of were authorized or even forbidden by the employer and regardless of whether the employer knew or should have known of their occurrence.

What any co-worker, supervisor, or recognized third party does while doing business for or with the employer becomes the employer's responsibility.

Prompt Remedial Action

In some cases of relatively minor consequence, all that is needed to prevent employer liability for sexual harassment is prompt remedial action; no one expects "instantaneous redress" for all infractions.[23] The law does not require an employer to fire an employee for harassment. It requires only that the employer take prompt remedial action reasonably calculated to end the harassment.

On the other hand, if the complaining employee had been coerced, propositioned, placed in a threatening situation, or had experienced a job detriment, promising to transfer the offended party or slapping the offender's wrist may not be sufficient. A organization's remedy to a complaint should be weighted against the seriousness of the offense. A more dramatic yet *reasonable* action may be necessary after you conduct a serious investigation. The punishment should fit the crime.

Just what are reasonable standards for (1) preventing sexual harassment in the organization and (2) taking remedial action should harassment occur?

Set aside the law for a moment. A manager's response to the threat of a hostile environment in which sexual, racial, or any other form of harassment exists must be swift and effective. You want a productive, profitable work environment, one in which your most important resource, your personnel, feels safe from harm and from unreasonable interference with work performance. This is a management concern, not merely a matter of law.

A Question of Policy

You probably do not determine policy, but you can influence it. If your organization does not have a written policy prohibiting harassment, you might produce, or ask personnel to produce, a statement that includes the main points in the suggested antiharassment policy statement shown in Figure 8-1.

A Matter of Training

Policies have little value unless training informs managers about the policies and how to administer them. If your organization does not have such a training program, encourage it to implement one simultaneously with the publication of the policies.

Effective Investigation

To determine whether or not discrimination or harassment exists in your organization, first determine if any of *your* own behavior is discriminatory or unreasonable by asking the following questions:

"Do I share power with the people I work with—that is, do I treat them as equals?"

"Do I say or do things behind a protected person's back that *I* would *not* say or do if he or she were present?"

"Would I accept what I say or do if the remarks or actions were directed at *me* or at something that distinguishes me from other people?"

"Would I want what I say or do to appear in the evening newspaper or on the TV news?"

A no to any of these questions should raise a red flag for you.

Now change the pronoun *I* to *other managers* or *my co-workers* and answer the questions again. You might even ask the other managers and your co-workers to give themselves this little self-assessment.

(text continues on page 160)

Figure 8-1. Sample antiharassment policy statement.

PURPOSE

This policy ensures that all employees will enjoy a safe work environment free from unreasonable interference, intimidation, hostility, or offensive behavior on the part of managers, co-workers, or visitors. It also acknowledges that harassment, sexual or otherwise, is against the law and will not be tolerated by this organization.

POLICY

[*Organization's name*] will maintain a workplace free of harassment of any kind and from any source, either management, co-workers, or visitors, while treating all complaints fairly and evenhandedly in order to prevent frivolous or malicious accusations.

DEFINITIONS

unreasonable conduct Treating someone as if that person were inferior to you. This includes condescension (refusing to take someone seriously), verbal abuse (making negative or derogatory comments), exclusion (overlooking or denying someone access to places, people or information, especially when opportunities for advancement are involved), and tokenism or "window dressing" (including selecting one or few members of a group for very visible positions).

discrimination Employment decisions implicitly or explicitly based on factors other than job-related considerations or treating one employee differently merely on the basis of a protected characteristic, e.g., sex.

harassment Repeated, unwanted, or unwelcome verbalisms or behaviors of a sexist, racist, or ageist nature or with overtones related to a protected characteristic, e.g., sex, race, ethnicity, religion, age, disability, or military status.

hostile environment Conduct that has the purpose or effect of unreasonably interfering with a person's job performance or creates an intimidating or offensive work environment.

quid pro quo sexual harassment (1) Making submission to sexual demands an implicit or explicit term or condition of employment; (2) making decisions affecting someone's employment or compensation on the basis of whether the person submits to or rejects sexual demands.

unwelcome behavior   Conduct that the employee did not solicit or incite and that the employee regards as undesirable or offensive.

RESPONSIBILITIES

Employees

1. Be sure beyond a reasonable doubt that the conduct you find offensive is discriminatory or harassing. Find witnesses or other substantiation.
2. Let the offending person(s) know you find the conduct offensive and ask that it stop immediately.
3. If it does not stop, or if it recurs, file an official complaint with [name of appropriate channel].

Management

1. Refrain from all forms of discrimination or harassment at all times.
2. If observing discriminatory or unreasonable conduct, ask the offending person(s) to stop immediately, explaining what the conduct is and how it offends.
3. If the conduct continues or recurs, file an official complaint with [name of appropriate channel].
4. The [title of organization's officer] will handle the complaint by making a complete investigation and writing up the complaint and the results of the investigation within [number of days].
5. The investigators will make every reasonable effort to determine the facts and a resolution of the situation.

SANCTIONS

The organization has the right to apply any sanction or combination of sanctions to deal with unreasonable conduct or discrimination:

Figure 8-1. *(continued)*

1. Counseling with the offender(s)
2. Transfer
3. Probation, with a warning of suspension or discharge for continuing or recurring offenses
4. Suspension with or without pay (depending on the seriousness of the offense)
5. Discharge for cause

If you receive a complaint of harassment, take the complaint seriously and act professionally, even if the story appears sensational or titillating. The victim is entitled to a fair hearing, but so is the alleged harasser.

When evaluating a story of harassment, recognize that unreasonable behavior, especially sexual harassment, usually occurs in private and without witnesses. Sometimes what appears to be consenting sexual behavior often results from fear rather than agreement, and a complaining employee may have held back his or her complaint for fear of retaliation. You should therefore accept the victim's complaint at face value until you have completed a proper evaluation of the evidence. Take the following steps before reporting an incident as a bona fide complaint:

1. Ask the complaining party to be specific, asking for as objective an account as possible (e.g., "Please describe what happened during your last encounter with that person"), and do not put words in his or her mouth by asking laundry-list or multiple-choice questions.
2. Get all the facts needed for proceeding with an investigation, including the frequency of the harassment, the length of time it has been going on, the steps the alleged victim has taken to let the other person know that he or she is offended and wants the behavior to stop, etc.
3. Ask for witnesses' names or for corroborating evidence.
4. Do *not* ask *why* the alleged victim did or did not do something, e.g., complain earlier.

5. Find out what the alleged victim expects or what he or she wants you to do next, and do not ask leading questions, e.g., "Do you want a transfer?"
6. Ask for permission to conduct a thorough investigation, and if he or she denies permission because he or she fears reprisal, reassure him or her that no reprisals will occur for bringing the complaint or for permitting an investigation.
7. Contact the right officer in your organization to find out how to proceed and how to apply the organization's harassment policies properly.

Some dos and don'ts for talking with the alleged harasser and with witnesses (if any) are listed in Figure 8-2 (a sample policy statement appears in Figure 8-1).

Conclusion: Proactive Management

Use effective management practices to establish acceptable criteria for your actions, become aware of cultural attitudes and values that interfere with rational decision making, and avoid irrelevant or extraneous comments.

A slogan of the 1960s was, "If you're not part of the solution, you're part of the problem." Take a stand—not only against sexual harassment, which is probably the most common kind of harassment today, but also against *any* form of harassment. A manager abuses his or her resources only at the risk of losing his or her business. You cannot be an effective manager unless you consider your employees as your most valuable asset.

CASEBOOK

A few sample cases should help you reinforce what you learned in this chapter and give you the opportunity to take a closer look at your own and your organization's management practices with respect to sex discrimination and sexual harassment.

Figure 8-2. Dos and don'ts of looking into charges of harassment.

DO	DON'T
Talking With Alleged Harasser	
Talk in private and promise confidentiality.	Don't confront or be combative, especially in public.
Take the situation seriously and come directly to the point— for example: "A sexual harassment complaint has been brought against you."	Don't make light of the situation or minimize its importance or seriousness.
Maintain objectivity and be as unbiased as possible.	Don't take sides or talk about rumors as if they were facts; also, don't preach or be judgmental.
Inquire into the history and circumstances of the complaint, asking about what the person may have done, not about what he or she intended—for example: "Did you put your arms around someone this morning?"	Don't ask about intentions until you ascertain the truth of the complaint.
Keep the discussion on track.	Don't get sidetracked.
Keep each allegation separate and ask for a response to each one separately.	Don't confuse issues, but be patient if the alleged harasser is confused.
If the person admits to the charges, insist that the behavior stop, and identify the consequences or next steps should the behavior continue or reoccur.	Don't be patronizing or judgmental; deal with the facts, law, and policy only.
If the person denies the allegations, explain the steps the investigation will take to determine the truth.	Don't make accusations or threaten punishment.

Document the meeting.

Take the appropriate next steps as spelled out by policy.

Check to see if the alleged unwelcome behavior has stopped.

Don't rely on memory.

Don't let the matter die of its own accord; it won't go away.

Talking With Witnesses

Talk in private and promise confidentiality.

Take the situation seriously and come directly to the point— for example: "You were identified as a witness to an incident this morning, and I'd like us to discuss the matter."

Maintain objectivity and be as unbiased as possible.

Inquire into the history and circumstances of the complaint, asking about what the witness might have seen or heard.

Keep the discussion on track.

Don't confront or be combative, especially in public.

Don't make light of the situation or minimize its importance or seriousness.

Don't take sides or talk about rumors as if they were facts; also, don't preach or be judgmental.

Don't ask about assumptions or opinions or make judgments about the situation or the people involved.

Don't get sidetracked.

Is Maternity a Disability?

An Illinois-based communication company automatically reinstated employees returning to work from a disability leave to their former jobs. It did not offer the same assurance to women returning from maternity leave. Yes, they could be placed in comparable positions, if available, or they could be placed on extended unpaid leave.

In addition, disabled employees accrued full seniority while on leave. Women on maternity leave accrued no more than thirty days.

Company policy also allowed disabled employees to extend their leave on a day-by-day basis, but women on maternity leave were required to take a set six-month leave. However, the women could request an early return.

Seven female employees, supported by their union, filed a complaint, claiming that the company's maternity leave policies violated Title VII. The company's policies regarding seniority, reinstatement, job status, and duration of leave, together and individually, treated maternity-disabled employees differently from employees disabled for other reasons.

What are your organization's maternity policies? How do you think they would fare in court?

Disabled Is Disabled

The Northern District Court in Illinois ruled for the women on two major counts. First, the company's postleave reinstatement policy clearly violated Title VII because it treated maternity-disabled employees differently from other people returning from disability leave. Second, the court found the company's seniority policy to be in violation of Title VII because it had an adverse effect on female employees when they returned from maternity leave. However, the company's six-month leave requirement stood because a procedure existed whereby the employee on maternity leave could request an early return; it was not, therefore, gender-based discrimination.[10]

How Do You Handle Special Needs or Requests?

Donna Steinitz could not believe that she was fired as staff assistant to the company's president; they had discussed performance deficiencies in the past, but none were serious enough to warrant firing.

Particularly appalling was a belated memo written at her boss's request that included the criticism that when giving reports "her manner of presentation and attire was the 'ultrafemale' approach so that she would not get eaten up by one of the boys." The personnel director recommended that she be given "a golden handshake" to forestall claims of "sex harassment and discrimination." Poor performance documented by that memo was the reason given when Donna took the employer to court.

Donna claimed that prior to being fired she requested that her woman secretary travel with her on business trips for two reasons:

1. On two earlier business trips, the secretary had been particularly helpful as a liaison between field managers and the president's staff.
2. Her husband, Tom, did not like her to travel alone. "It is often uncomfortable traveling with male members of the staff. Put quite frankly, although it is flattering, the [inevitable] rumors are becoming quite stale. Although I once kiddingly [implied] that my love life was less than monogamous, the opposite is true as I am certain you are aware."

After waiting for an answer to her written request, she wrote another memo in which she said, "I'm particularly sensitive about traveling alone at this point in time; I'll get over it, so please be understanding and patient."

The president responded with angry, negative comments about women and advised Donna that her job was in jeopardy. A month later, she was fired. When she requested a year's severance pay, the president ordered the personnel director to prepare the belated memo described earlier.

These events, Donna charged, were the real—and discriminatory—basis on which she was fired.

How would you handle a request for a specific companion to accompany a female employee on business trips?

A Matter of Response

The federal court did *not* decide whether the plaintiff's requests were proper or necessary, or whether denying the travel requests is discriminatory, or what accommodations, if any, an employer must make for a female executive faced with actual or perceived sexual harassment or the possibility of defamatory rumors when traveling alone or with men. Instead, the court dealt with the employer's *response* to the woman's requests and ruled it to be discriminatory.

Because the plaintiff had never been threatened with termination for poor performance before (she had, in fact, received excellent evaluations, a bonus, and a promotion), the employer's reasons were pretextual. The president also ordered the personnel department to "build a file," a suspect procedure.

The employer's response was more severe than it would have been had the plaintiff been a man, the court concluded. The president's anger and inopportune remarks and the personnel director's belated memo were clear evidence of discrimination and formed the basis of the court's decision.[18]

Anger, in short, is not the appropriate response to an employee's request. Emotions and management rarely do mix. How you conduct yourself on the job can become an issue in the court.

Can You Be Sued for Giving Preferential Treatment to a Lover?

In working with women colleagues, Clay Anderson would touch them sexually. When he did that often to Ellen Davis, she told him angrily and just as often to "keep your hands off" and "would you please stop this."

Eventually Clay stopped, finding a willing sexual partner elsewhere in the group. Even though the lover's job performance was deficient in a variety of ways, she was given plum assignments. Winking women tolerating the affair were also given preferences. Ellen was fired for supposedly poor job performance.

Is promoting someone who consents over someone who refuses sexual advances a form of sexual discrimination?

Adverse Working Conditions

The decision in this 1986 case reinforces one made in 1983. In the earlier case, Title VII was applied when the plaintiff was denied opportunities granted to a co-employee who had consented to sexual advances.[6] In the present case, according preferential treatment to a female employee who submits to sexual advances and other sexual conduct violates Title VII because the manager demonstrates through his conduct that job benefits are conditioned on an employee's tolerance of sexually charged conduct or advances.[7] The law clearly prohibits such behavior.

It does not matter that a female is ultimately selected for promotion or preferential treatment. Another female employee, *perceiving* that better employment opportunities are predicated on submitting to sexual conduct, *and* that had she been a man she would not have been treated that way, is free to charge the offending supervisor with sexual discrimination. The liability is fairly clear.

Need we spell out the moral? Whether you be a male or a female manager, if you feel it necessary to approach an employee sexually, take care not to deny employees opportunities merely because they refuse to submit to your sexual advances or favor employees who do. Better still, unless you are talking about a case of "true love" (followed by marriage or alternative arrangement), avoid intimate relationships with employees, period.

Is Showing a Lack of Respect Discriminatory?

Julia Dougherty enjoyed her job as account manager for a major cosmetics company. She always received satisfactory evaluations and won an Outstanding Achievement Award. All seemed right with her world until a new regional director, a man, came on the job.

From the start, Julia and other women employees had difficulty working with him. They were not accorded the same degree of authority and responsibility permitted to men account managers. They were not given the courtesy given to the men of negotiating sales goals or being included in decision making. Although the new boss gave the men valuable feedback and coaching, he was highly critical of the women. They received no credit for their opinions, whereas the men employees' recommendations were usually accepted.

Julia's boss contacted the women account managers' clients without their knowledge, but never those of the men managers. He demanded that the women's reports be hand-delivered if they were finished too late for mail delivery. He even threatened Julia's job because of late reports but never threatened the men for the same conduct.

In court Julia called upon the other women, the men, and her boss to testify to these facts. No one contradicted her, not even the regional director.

The question is not whether the facts were true. They were. The court had to decide if that behavior was liable under Title VII.

Would you treat women employees that way?

Disparate Treatment

The regional director's behavior demonstrated his attitudes toward women employees: condescending, demeaning, unreasonable, harsh, and nonsupportive when help was needed. He treated the men employees in just the opposite way.

Employees are employees, be they men or women, and under the law they must be accorded the same professional respect and courtesy. To refuse to treat women employees the way you treat men employees amounts to unlawful discrimination. If the woman employee quits as a result of such unequal treatment, you could be liable for constructive discharge as well. So said the southern district court in Ohio in 1982.[34]

Discourtesy to women is common, as you can see from the fact that women are often fired for their appearance,[19] whereas men are usually only reprimanded. Some states (including the District of Columbia) have included protections against such conduct in their human rights legislation. Narrow-minded male attitudes often lead to severe contradictions in the workplace.

Can You Choose Your Partner on the Basis of Gender?

In 1982 Abigail Garner was turned down for a partnership in a Big Eight accounting firm. A specialist in preparing, securing, and managing government contracts for large-scale computer-based systems, she had won major contracts worth anywhere from $34 to $44 million to the firm. Still, her petition for partnership was turned down on the alleged grounds that she was overly aggressive, unduly harsh, demanding, and in general lacking in interpersonal skills needed for handling the staff. Feeling blocked, she quit, formed her own consulting firm, and filed against her former employers under Title VII.

In court, the company maintained that it had legitimate, sex-neutral business reasons for denying her the partnership. Several partners testified that she was in fact overbearing and difficult to work with. However, one partner admitted advising her to "walk more femininely, talk more femininely, dress more femininely, wear makeup, have her hair styled, and wear jewelry" to improve her chances.

Could a woman be promoted in your organization if she did not meet the criteria spelled out to Abigail Garner? How do you think the U.S. Supreme Court ruled in this case seven years later?

Men's Perceptions

The testimony last quoted sealed the woman's "mixed-motive" case: The partnership decision involved sex-based as well as sex-neutral considerations. As the trial court concluded, the firm "had filtered" her candidacy through a system documented by expert testimony in which men evaluators make decisions based on unconscious sexual stereotypes and outmoded attitudes toward women.

Title VII, Justice Brennan wrote, protects women (an employer may not "make gender an indirect stumbling block to employment opportunities"), while preserving the employer's "remaining freedom of choice." The Court had no problem finding that "an employer who objects to aggressiveness in women but whose positions require this trait places women in an intolerable and impermissible catch-22: out of a job if they behave aggressively and out of a job if they don't. Title VII lifts women out of this bind."[20, 21]

At the same time, the plurality of the Court agreed that

the firm was wrongly required to show by "clear and convincing evidence" that the woman would not have been made a partner regardless of gender. The proper standard for the employer's rebuttal is a preponderance of the evidence, rather than reliance on objective evidence that shows how the same employment result would have occurred without the discriminatory motive.

When Does Consent Violate Title VII?

Everyone, including her supervisor, Bob Kraft, called Lisa Engels the prettiest employee at National Savings and Loan. Kraft often told her that he hired her mainly for that reason.

He also often told her that unless she had sex with him, he would have her job and make employment anywhere else in town just about impossible. Frightening her with his power, he forced himself on her both during and after bank hours. He fondled her in front of others, followed her into the women's restroom where he exposed himself to her, and several times raped her at work. Overpowering and intimidating, he reduced her frequent and strenuous protests to a silent glare. Soon, he tired of her and stopped his attacks.

Fear overcoming anger, Lisa kept silent for a year. When she finally realized that she would have to submit to Kraft again if she ever wanted advancement, she filed a Title VII suit in federal court and with the EEOC against both Bob Kraft and National Savings and Loan charging sex discrimination (creating a hostile working environment) and sexual harassment. Both respondents claimed innocence.

According to Kraft, the sexual relationship was voluntary; Lisa agreed to having sex with him. Their only dispute came about when he complained about her job performance. He asked for a dismissal of the charges on the basis of mutual consent.

The management of National Savings and Loan washed their hands of the incident, pleading that they had had no knowledge of the sexual relationship and therefore were not responsible. Besides, the relationship was between two consenting adults, and they could not have reasonably known about it. They too asked for a summary dismissal.

After six years, the case worked its way up to the U.S. Supreme

Court. According to the EEOC, in its Policy Guidance on Sexual Harassment, the case posed three key questions:

1. Does unwelcome sexual behavior that creates a hostile working environment constitute employment discrimination on the basis of sex?
2. Can a Title VII violation be shown when the district court found that any sexual relationship that existed between the plaintiff and her supervisor was a "voluntary one"?
3. Is an employer strictly liable for an offensive working environment created by a supervisor's sexual advances when the employer does not know of, and could not have reasonably known of, the supervisor's conduct[?][33]

What say you? Can consent and harassment coexist? Can harassment form a basis for sex discrimination? And can you, as an employer or manager, be held liable for the actions of one of your supervisors?

Involuntary Consent

Yes. Yes. Yes. The Supreme Court upheld the plaintiff's charges on all three counts. According to Justice Rehnquist: When a supervisor sexually harasses a subordinate because of a subordinate's sex, that supervisor discriminates on the basis of sex."

Unwelcome sexual advances, requests for sexual favors, or other verbal or physical conduct of a sexual nature mark sexual harassment. The key word is *unwelcome.*

By definition, behavior harasses if it is unwelcome. It is unwelcome if the person experiencing it says it is. The person would not experience that conduct, in most cases, if he or she were of the same sex (although in 1981 and 1983, homosexual harassment came under the protection of Title VII).[4,5] Therefore, sexual harassment creates a hostile environment predicated on sex differences and is a form of sex discrimination that violates Title VII.[1]

Even if "consent" is "voluntary," the court responded to the second question, that the demands are unwelcome is sufficient to support the charge of harassment.

The fact that sex-related conduct was "voluntary," in the sense that the complainant was not forced to participate against her will, is not a defense to a sexual harassment suit brought under Title VII. . . . The correct inquiry is whether [the victim] by her conduct indicated that the alleged sexual advances were unwelcome, not whether her actual participation in sexual intercourse was voluntary.

"Consent" at gunpoint is less than "willing participation"; therefore, the complaint is enforceable under Title VII.

Is There a Title VII Violation If There Is No Job Detriment?

When Sarah Beckwith's boss in the city administration made additional job training contingent on her going to bed with him, she reached her limit of tolerance. She had been the victim of repeated sexual remarks, verbal insults, and aggressive assaults long enough. She quit and went to court, alleging that her supervisor created a hostile and offensive working environment for women, that her resignation constituted constructive discharge because her working conditions had become intolerable, and that her supervisor created a job detriment by limiting her access to training.

The employer asked for a dismissal on the grounds that Sarah voluntarily resigned without pressure from the organization. And the district court did dismiss the case, ruling that Sarah did not show that a tangible job detriment resulted from the manager's demands and therefore could not show that the man created a hostile and offensive working environment under Title VII. Additionally, constructive discharge can give rise to a Title VII claim if a hostile environment exists, but the judge agreed that Sarah resigned for reasons other than "a sexually demeaning work environment." Finally, he said that Sarah had not shown that additional training was in fact conditioned on responding to the manager's sexual demands. Sarah then appealed to the Eleventh Circuit Court.

What would happen in your shop if an employee complained that future training appeared contingent upon sleeping with the boss?

Tangible Detriment Not Always Required

The Eleventh Circuit remanded two of the three charges back to the district court for further hearings on the facts: (1) that the manager did in fact create a hostile environment and (2) that training was in fact contingent on submitting to having sex relations. The circuit court agreed that the plaintiff did not suffer constructive discharge because she did not resign under pressure from her employer.[1]

But the facts are not as important to us here as are the criteria that the court set in this case.

"Under some circumstances," the court rules, "[creating] an offensive or hostile environment due to sexual harassment can violate Title VII [even if] the complainant [does not suffer] tangible job detriment." Discriminatory working conditions can exist where a pattern of harassment subjects a person to disparate treatment regardless of whether or not the employee also proves she has lost a tangible job benefit. These are the three tests the claim must pass to qualify under Title VII:

1. That the employee is a member of a protected group
2. That the unwelcome sexual harassment based on the sex of the employee affects a "term, condition, or privilege" of employment
3. If the employer is to be held liable for the hostile environment created by a supervisor or co-worker, that the employer knew or should have known of the harassment in question but failed to take remedial action

Concerning the first point, the court would not recognize a Title VII liability if the supervisor's or co-worker's sexual behavior was offensive to men and women alike; the conduct created disparate treatment based on gender. But the court's use of the phrase *term, condition, or privilege of employment* raises an important issue.

According to the court, an employee's psychological state may be included in the above phrase if the sexual harassment is so *pervasive* that it creates an "abusive" work environment. Under these conditions, a tangible job detriment need not be shown.

This criterion underlies a later 1985 decision in which an appellate court upheld a female employee's claim that her male supervisor sexually harassed her by physically grabbing her arm and preventing her from leaving the office. The court rejected the employer's argument that although the supervisor exerted unnecessary force or violence, because there were no sexual overtones to the incident, it did not qualify under Title VII. The use of physical force toward a woman employee that would not have been applied in a similar circumstance to a man employee, if sufficiently pervasive, can form an illegal condition of employment under Title VII according to the court.[35] How you treat someone significantly different from you, e.g., a member of the opposite sex, does matter.

A pervasive atmosphere poisons a workplace, and you, as a manager, should be on guard to prevent it from creating a hostile or abusive situation. Even directing sexual advances at consenting, noncomplaining female employees or allowing fellow managers to be crude and foul-mouthed in front of female employees could jeopardize your shop.

If you ignore promotions co-managers give to subordinates who are their lovers, a female employee could sue your organization although she herself does not directly experience sexual harassment. She might have a case if she feels forced to work in an atmosphere in which such conduct is pervasive, especially if she feels harassed by having to watch willing sex partners receive preferential treatment to her detriment.[36,37] The EEOC, in its 1988 guidelines, made it clear that how you as a manager act with regard to your organization's overall situation can influence the outcome if push comes to shove.

Even cases of quid pro quo harassment, in which the Supreme Court *always* holds an employer liable, often come up for debate. For example, what if the employer does not know about the problem?

Can You Escape Liability?

Zoe Ann could not believe that on a two-day business trip with Bart Madison she had watched him drop his pants in front of other passengers while waiting to board a plane, she had been repeatedly mauled (he several times touched her hips and breasts), and she had been "playfully" choked during a business dinner. The last was too much for her, and she dashed off to the ladies' room sobbing. Consolation from her immediate supervisor was not enough.

The next day, Zoe Ann complained to the company's president, who assured her that she need only forbear for the day and a half remaining in the then-current assignment. After that, she would never have to work with Bart again. But that, too, was not enough. Zoe Ann resigned before the assignment ended and immediately sued for constructive discharge and sex discrimination.

If you received a call from an employee describing something similar to what happened to Zoe Ann, how quickly would you act? What would you do?

Prompt Remedial Action

The Fifth Circuit Court sympathized with the plaintiff: Her colleague's conduct was "public, clownish, and boorish." But, it added, the company's remedial action—the president's personal reassurance that she would not have to work with this colleague again—was sufficiently prompt to prevent liability for sexual harassment. One cannot expect "instantaneous redress."

If the plaintiff had been coerced, propositioned, placed in a threatening situation, or had experienced a job detriment, the company's action might not have been sufficient. An organization's remedy to a complaint should be weighed against the seriousness of the offense. Boorish, clownish behavior may be offensive, but not to the extent of sexual harassment as defined by law and EEOC guidelines. Therefore, the remedy was proportional to the offense.[23]

Yet a promise to change a complainant's assignment may not always be sufficient to prevent liability. A more dramatic action may be necessary, such as the one a bank management took when a man employee, while sitting in a car next to a female employee, took advantage of the opportunity to make suggestive remarks to her and to touch her suggestively. He felt encouraged when an assistant manager at the bank seemed amused and condoned the behavior. The only one not amused was the woman.

She complained to the bank management but was not satisfied with the punishment: a warning and ninety days' probation for the aggressor, and a reprimand for the assistant manager for not standing up for the female employee. So she sued, claiming that the bank's investigation and its action were superficial. She wanted to have both men fired.

The Eighth Circuit Court, applying the standard of *reasonable* action, found that the bank officials conducted a serious investigation, interviewing all three employees and two other employees who had attended the seminar and were witnesses to the misconduct. The punishment, in the court's estimate, fit the crime.[24]

Cases

1. 682 F.2d 897, 29 F.E.P. Cases (BNA) 787 (11th Cir. 1982).
2. 830 F.2d 1554, 45 F.E.P. Cases (BNA) 160 (11th Cir. 1987).
3. EEOC Decision No. 84-3, 34 F.E.P. Cases (BNA) 1887 (February 16, 1984).
4. 25 F.E.P. Cases (BNA) 5656 (N.D. Ill. 1981).
5. 36 F.E.P. Cases (BNA) 1644 (M.D. Alabama, 1983).
6. 570 F. Supp. 1197, 32 F.E.P. Cases (BNA) 1401 (D. Del. 1983).
7. 98 F.R.D. 775, 40 F.E.P. Cases (BNA) 208 (N.D. Cal. 1986).
8. Massachusetts Commission Against Discrimination (June 3, 1987).
9. EEOC Commission Decision No. 84-1.
10. 509 F. Supp. 6 (N.D. Ill. 1980).
11. 807 F.2d 1536, 42 F.E.P. Cases (BNA) 1141 (11th Cir. 1987).
12. No. 85-494 (January 13, 1987).
13. 680 F.2d 1243, 29 F.E.P. Cases (BNA) (9th Cir. 1982).
14. No. 82-411 (June 20, 1983).
15. 486 A.2d 126 (Me. 1984).
16. 601 F. Supp. 160, 37 F.E.P. Cases (BNA) 843 (W.D. Pa. 1985), *aff'd* 779 F.2d 42.
17. 462 F. Supp. 289 (S.D. W. Va.).

18. 601 F. Supp. 243, 39 F.E.P. Cases (BNA) 1398 (D. Mass. 1985).
19. 41 F.E.P. Cases (BNA) 1489 (D.C. App. 1986).
20. 825 F.2d 458, 263, 44 F.E.P. Cases (BNA) 825 (D.C. Cir. 1987).
21. No. 87-1167 (1989).
22. 436 F. Supp. 1328 (W.D. Pa. 1977), *aff'd*, 578 F.2d. 1374 (1978), *cert. denied*, 99 S. Ct. 734 (1978).
23. 828 F.2d 307, 44 F.E.P. Cases (BNA) 1604 (5th Cir. 1987).
24. 766 F.2d 424 (8th Cir. 1984).
25. No. 84-2233 GB (May 13, 1987).
26. 842 F.2d 936 (7th Cir. March 16, 1988).
27. 683 F. Supp. 1302, 46 E.P.D. (CCH) ¶37,868 (D.S.D. 1988).
28. 463 U.S. 1073 (1983).
29. No. 83-1557 (3d Cir. 1984).
30. USDC-DC, 4.23.79.
31. 758 F.2d 1462, 37 F.E.P. Cases (BNA) 1232 (11th Cir. 1985).
32. 561 F.2d 983, 999, 14 E.P.D. (CCH) ¶7755 (D.C. Cir. 1977).
33. 106 S. Ct. 2399, 40 E.P.D. (CCH) (1986).
34. 528 F. Supp. 1380, 30 F.E.P. Cases 1205 (S.D. Ohio 1982).
35. F.E.P. Cases (BNA) 364 (D.C. Cir. 1985).
36. 46 F.E.P. Cases (BNA) 1272 (D.D.C. 1988).
37. 538 F. Supp. 857, 30 F.E.P. Cases (BNA) 1212 (N.D. Ohio 1982).

Chapter 9

Mismanaging Disabled People

All EEO laws and regulations ebb and flow around (1) *definitions* and (2) *perceptions;* even the words the lawmakers use change with prevailing political tides. Whereas the Rehabilitation Act of 1973 refers to "handicapped" people, the Americans With Disabilities Act of 1990 calls handicaps *disabilities* (see Appendix for more detail of both laws).* Regardless of which word you use, what constitutes a handicap or a disability has more to do with definitions and perceptions than with medical diagnoses. Again, I define a few key terms before I look at what you cannot and can do; in the Casebook, I review a variety of unusual cases related to disability or impairment that show the complexities of equal opportunity issues.

The 1990 legislation, which goes into effect July 24, 1992, does not alter the definitions spelled out in the Rehabilitation Act of 1973 and that form the basis for the court decisions described in this chapter.

Definitions of Key Terms

physical impairment [Any] physiological disorder or condition, cosmetic disfigurement, or anatomical loss affecting one or more

---

*See also Julie Rovner, "Provisions: Americans With Disabilities Act of 1990," *Congressional Quarterly* (Washington, D.C.: July 28, 1990), pp. 2437–2444.

. . . body systems: neurological; musculoskeletal; special sense organs; respiratory, including speech organs; cardiovascular; reproductive; digestive; genitourinary; hemic and lymphatic; skin; and endocrine.[1]

impaired or handicapped person Any person who (1) has a physical or mental impairment [that] substantially limits one or more of such person's major life activities, (2) has a record of such an impairment, or (3) is regarded as having such an impairment.[1]

major life activities Functions such as caring for oneself, performing manual tasks, walking, seeing, hearing, speaking, breathing, learning, and working.[1]

reasonable accommodation Making an effort to manage a disabled employee's work or workplace to meet his or her special needs or to protect him or her and other employees.[2]

Not only are those definitions very comprehensive, they are quite specific; one section also identifies the importance of perception: "(iii) is regarded as having such an impairment." If you *think* someone is handicapped, you could, in fact, create the conditions whereby he or she can charge you with discrimination.

Take AIDS, for example. If you erroneously think that someone suffering from AIDS can spread the disease through casual contact on the job and, on that basis alone, treat that employee differently from the way you do others, you have admitted that the employee is impaired or handicapped.[3,4-7] You thereby make yourself vulnerable to a legal challenge.

It is largely your responsibility as an employer to identify what constitutes a disability, and an erroneous perception has the same impact (if not more so) as a correct one. You should know just what is covered by the broad legal definitions, which is not as simple as it may seem.

Epilepsy, even if controlled by medication, has been called a disability.[8] High blood pressure (hypertension) limits a person's major life activities, too, and is therefore called a disability by the courts.[9] A cancer-induced mastectomy? Yes, according to a federal court in Missouri.[10] Obesity? In some courts, yes,[11] in other courts, no.[12] Alcoholism or other substance addictions? In some courts, yes,[13-17] in other courts, no.[18] You probably should seek legal advice before making personnel decisions that could possibly adversely affect a handicapped person's job opportunities or conditions of employment.

What You Cannot Do

What are your boundaries when you manage handicapped people?

You cannot fail or refuse to hire any person because he or she is handicapped as long as she or he is capable of successfully and safely performing the duties of the job. When you do manage someone who is disabled, you cannot:

1. Discriminate against him or her with respect to compensation, terms, conditions, or privileges of employment.
2. Limit, segregate, or classify employees in any way that would deprive or tend to deprive a person of employment opportunities or have an adverse effect on the person's status as an employee.
3. Fail to provide training to a person because he or she is disabled.
4. Discharge any person because he or she is disabled.
5. Retaliate against any employees or applicants for employment because they made a charge, testified, assisted, or participated in any manner protected by the Rehabilitation Act of 1973.

What You Can Do

You, too, have rights. You can deny a disabled or impaired person a job if the disability or impairment would interfere with the person's ability to successfully perform the duties of the job or would pose a direct threat to property or to the safety of other people. You cannot fire a person merely on the basis of a disability, but you can fire or otherwise discipline someone for good cause, or if the disability creates a burden on your ability to conduct business or to guarantee the employee's safety or the safety of other people.

Three general guidelines can help you manage disabled people, including those suffering from alcohol or drug addiction:

1. *Be flexible.* You cannot be rigid in your approaches to employees suffering from any kind of disease, be it AIDS or alcoholism or diabetes. You need to develop new ways of perceiving a person's abilities or capabilities and new ways of thinking about disease.

2. *Be patient and forbearing.* Satisfying a "reasonable accommodation" standard requires patience and forbearance as well as compassion, especially if the person's ability to perform job functions satisfactorily has not been impaired. If performance begins to slip, it is your responsibility to find out why and to do what you can to help before summarily dismissing the offending employee.

Here is the point. Even if the steps you take do not work, you have to take them before you can decide to not hire or to fire an otherwise qualified but disabled person. That this "reasonableness" rule applies to meeting religious or military obligations as well as physical or mental needs makes this point most important.

3. *Be observant.* Failing to recognize the cause of a performance or behavior problem will not exempt you from liability should you take an adverse action against a disabled or impaired person. Erratic performance should be a red flag for a manager to investigate the cause or causes of the slippage; and should an impairment be responsible, the employer should offer the person an opportunity to receive treatment.[17]

To execute these guidelines, here are some steps you can take:

1. Make reasonable allowances for absences.
2. Reorganize the person's work assignments.

182   *Safe Management Practices*

3. Reassign him or her to a different job or workplace if safety is a concern.
4. Encourage medical or psychiatric treatment.

Because alcoholics and drug addicts often go through a period of psychological denial of their problems and frequently become belligerent and rebellious when confronted directly, the steps for dealing with addictions differ in one respect: Instead of confrontation, it is best, regardless of the type or severity of the disability, to observe performance relative to objective standards. When an employee's work suffers in comparison to those standards, deal with *that fact* and do not accuse him or her of anything. Your responsibility extends only to uncovering and dealing with a performance problem. If performance does not improve or if the employee cannot perform an available alternative function in your business, then you have a basis for firing him or her. If you accuse someone of drinking or using drugs, you run the risk of being sued for defamation.

Drinking alcohol is not illegal, and only some drug usage is. Alcohol or drug use becomes your affair only if drinking alcohol or using drugs during work hours violates company policy. If you catch an employee in the act, you have a basis for challenging alcohol or drug use. Without calling the person an alcoholic or addict, refer a problem employee to two forms of counseling: performance counseling first and, if he or she admits to drinking or drug use, substance abuse counseling second.

If counseling does not bring about a desired change, offer a leave without pay, if paid leave is not available or is exhausted. As long as a disability is correctable and the person is likely to respond to treatment, as is an alcoholic, leave is reasonable if reassigning the employee to a less difficult or demanding position is not possible.

Let the employee receive disability benefits, especially if the impairment results from a work-related injury. If performance, attendance, or behavior problems stem from a health-related condition, require a medical or psychiatric evaluation. If you have to consider firing an employee, offer him or her a "last chance" or "firm choice" option between rehabilitation or discipline (including dismissal).*

I am not suggesting that managing a disabled employee is no different than managing nondisabled employees or that it is always easy. But a wise Native American proverb gives good counsel: "Before you judge any other man, walk in his moccasins along a pebbly shore."

CASEBOOK

Making safe decisions about managing people is never simple. Making safe decisions about managing disabled or impaired people is exacerbated by the fact that so much vagueness and so many ambiguities clutter up the situations in which you make your decisions. Test yourself with the cases that follow.

Is a Beard a Handicap?

Few employers today insist that men be clean-shaven, that they not wear beards, but a fire department in Michigan did. When a black fire fighter refused to shave off his beard, the department discharged him. The fired employee then went to court charging discrimination on the basis of a handicap.

He explained to the court that he wore the beard only because he suffered from *pseudofolliculitis barbae,* an illness that affects mostly black men. Cuts from shaving the bumps raised by ingrown hair stubble infect and produce permanent scarring. Normal medical treatment involves cultivating a beard. The court had to decide whether this condition falls under the heading of "handicap" within the meaning of the Michigan Handicappers' Civil Rights Act.

Does your organization have an appearance code? Which rules could possibly be covered by EEO laws or guidelines?

---

*For a thorough description of some steps an organization can take to help its addicted employees, see *HR Magazine on Human Resource Management* (April 1990), pp. 46–49, 50–54, 55–58, 61–62.

Definition

The Michigan Court of Appeals settled the issue by noting that *pseudofolliculitis barbae* occurs genetically and that no cure exists other than allowing a beard to grow. Therefore, the fire fighter's beard fits within the meaning of "handicap" as defined by state law. Firing or otherwise disciplining him for noncompliance with a grooming code requiring men to be clean-shaven could be a form of discrimination. The court then remanded the case back to the lower court to decide if the man's handicap would prevent him from reasonably performing his job duties (where the trail ends).[19]

What Constitutes a Physical Impairment?

Lisa Adams's bouts with tuberculosis kept her from her duties at the elementary school where she taught. Her doctors thought they had cured it, but after she suffered three relapses the school board moved to dismiss her, not only cutting off her income but her medical insurance as well.

When her attorney brought suit under the Rehabilitation Act of 1973, the school board argued that the Act did not cover persons with contagious diseases. The board saw its action as a necessary precaution against communicating the disease to other people.

How would your management handle Lisa's claims?

Limited Major Life Activities

The Eleventh Circuit Court ruled that the Act, not the intent, violated the law. The Rehabilitation Act covers the plaintiff and anyone suffering from "a physical or mental impairment that substantially limits major life activities." The disease in this case significantly impairs respiratory functions as well as other major body systems, and even the employer acknowledged that the teacher had a record of the impairment as defined in the law and regarded her as having an impairment. By definition and by perception, the subject suffers a protected disability.[20]

Some states, including Kentucky and Georgia, have statutes specifically excluding persons with contagious diseases. So the school board appealed to the supreme court, arguing that (1) contagious diseases are not covered and (2) even if they were, under the circumstances the plaintiff was not qualified to teach school.

The Supreme Court upheld the Eleventh Circuit's interpretation of the definition of "impaired person," but remanded the case back to trial court to determine whether the plaintiff was qualified to teach. The first issue is a matter of legal interpretation, the second is a matter of fact.[1] The first decision concerns us because this is the ruling that provided us with several definitions at the beginning of the chapter, which serve as the cornerstone for all cases of this type. A 7–2 majority agreed that Section 504 of the Rehabilitation Act covers employees afflicted with a contagious disease.

The question of contagion also forms a major part of this decision. The school board, supported by the Justice Department, rested part of its case on the fear that this teacher could contaminate other people. This fear, they argued, provides legitimate justification for dismissing her.

The court answered that the argument begged the question; we cannot meaningfully separate the contagious effects of a disease from the disease's physical effects on the patient. The plaintiff's contagiousness and her physical disability resulted from the same underlying cause: turberculosis. Employers cannot, the court emphasized, use the distinction between the effects of a disease on others and the effects of a disease on the person to justify discriminatory treatment. A person with a contagious disease is covered.

The question of whether or not contagion limits the person's qualifications for performing his or her job is a matter of fact, which the lower court had not settled. Hence, the case was remanded back to that court to determine (where, again, the trail ends).

The question you must answer if you are confronted by this sort of situation is: Does a person qualified for a job lose his or her rights if that person poses a significant risk of communicating an infectious disease to others in the workplace, if reasonable accommodation will not reduce or eliminate the risk?

For example, in our case, if the teacher's TB had been active and contagious, the school board would not have had to return her to a classroom with children. If the disease had not been active and contagious, the board would have been obligated to return her.

Now, if she could not return to classroom teaching, the court might ask if there were any other position for which she was qualified that she could fill without endangering anyone else. The courts can answer such questions only case by case.

As more employers are confronted with an increasing number of AIDS patients, the decision I just discussed becomes extremely important. Some states—for example, California, Massachusetts, Oregon, and Texas—with court support, have written legislation protecting AIDS-infected employees. How about the state where you work? And what has your organization done to accommodate the possibility of having an AIDS-infected employee?

How Important Are Your Perceptions?

After becoming ill, Dennis Kroyan sought medical attention that produced a large number of absences. In spite of a doctor's note explaining that Kroyan was under his care (which satisfied company demands), Dennis's supervisor, Ira Shankman, insisted on knowing the reasons for the medical appointments.

"I'd rather not say," Dennis replied. "It's very personal."

Ira pressed him anyway. "C'mon, Dennis. I'm your friend, not just your supervisor. You can trust me to keep a secret."

"Okay," the employee reluctantly conceded. "I think I've got AIDS and something the doctor called ARC."

Shocked and concerned about the spread of AIDS in the company, Ira went straight to his supervisors, who would have been kinder had they fired Dennis. Instead, they made his condition known to his co-workers.

Not long afterwards, Dennis received life-threatening phone calls from other employees. Frightened by the calls, he did not return to work and entered the hospital, where tests confirmed the diagnoses. Distressed by the way they had treated him, Dennis took his employers to court for discrimination on the basis of disability. "My supervisors disclosed private information about my health in violation of Massachusetts General Laws, C. 151 B Section 4(16). If I suffered from any other disease, no one would have said anything to anyone."

"We had a legitimate business interest in getting and publishing the information from Kroyan," the company countered. "We must consider the other employees when a contagious disease is present. In that situation, we had to balance the individual's right to privacy against the population's right to know, and the right to know won."

How do you feel about this matter? If one of your employees were to contract AIDS, how would you or your company react?

Facts vs. Perception

If you sided with the company, you made the same mistake it did. The Superior Court of Massachusetts concluded that, under Massachusetts law, AIDS is a qualifying disability. In drawing its conclusion, the court cited the statute and a publication of the Massachusetts Commission Against Discrimination, "AIDS Policy." The law says that an employer may not discriminate against any person because of his or her disability where the person "[is] capable of performing the essential functions of the position involved with reasonable accommodation." Only if "the employer can demonstrate that the accommodation . . . would impose an undue hardship to the employer's business" would the employer be exempted from the law or the commission's policy on AIDS (which says that AIDS victims are entitled to protection under this law).[3] Other decisions also have provided AIDS victims with equal protection.[4–7]

This case establishes that an AIDS victim may qualify for remedies because his or her manager *erroneously perceived* that the victim is contagious to co-workers. Under both Massachusetts law and the Rehab Act, if an employee is not likely to spread AIDS, which medical evidence shows cannot be spread by casual contact, then the erroneous perception indicates that the employer regards the employee as impaired or disabled. Discriminating against that person—in the present case, divulging privileged information—violates the law to the same extent that discrimination on the basis of a *correct* perception violates it.

The privacy issue in this case was measured against the standard set by the Massachusetts Supreme Judicial Court in 1984[6] that requires the employer to show that a legitimate business interest is served by prying into or disclosing privileged medical information. That interest is a matter of fact, rather than a matter of law, that the company in this case could not substantiate. The company discriminated against the disabled employee and invaded his privacy as well, all on the basis of an erroneous perception that through casual contact an AIDS victim endangers the general population.

When an employer adversely affects a disabled person's job opportunities merely on the basis of a disability, he or she risks litigation. Before making a decision that affects or limits a disabled person's right to opportunity, you should become more aware of the disability itself and of local and federal laws or regulations governing accommodating disabled people. You would ensure compliance *and* reap the rewards of tapping a person's potential.

What Constitutes Reasonable Efforts to Accommodate?

When the managers of Williamson's Wood Works realized that Bob Pantella suffered from a serious illness that brought on physically uncontrollable seizures, they became quite alarmed. They encouraged him to seek medical help, and when he did he found out that he suffered from diabetes mellitus and a hyperactive thyroid. Several seizures later, management transferred him into a less dangerous work environment in which he would not have to operate a forklift, but where he could still contribute and keep his job. After four more seizures that came without warning, the company let him go.

In court Pantella charged that, under Oregon's laws, the company discriminated against him on the basis of "a physical or mental impairment [that] with reasonable accommodation by the employer, does not preclude the performance of the work involved." He also claimed his condition was controllable and under control.

The company's attorney countered with an enumeration of the steps his client took. One, they maintained a position for the man over nine months during which time he suffered four uncontrollable seizures. Two, they transferred him to a safer environment from a part of the warehouse where he worked close to potentially dangerous machines and posed a considerable safety hazard to himself and others. Three, they eliminated the need for him to operate a forklift, the operation of which posed a safety hazard to both the employee and others had he continued to drive one. The managers, in short, had shown their willingness to accommodate Pantella's disability, but his condition was uncontrollable and they had to let him go.

Do you think the employee had a case? How far would your company have gone to accommodate someone in this situation?

Unsuccessful but Sufficient

Score one for the managers. According to the district court in Oregon, the employer had made several efforts to accommodate the employee, including transferring him and reassigning his work in order to protect him and other employees. Although unsuccessful, the efforts sufficed to satisfy Oregon's reasonable accommodation standard.[2]

No general rules define *accommodation*. However, an employer is *not* required to exhaust *all* possible avenues to ensure meeting an employee's special needs. In the sample case, demanding that the managers move hazardous equipment or redesign the warehouse's physical layout to satisfy the employee's safety needs would have caused an unnecessary and undue burden for the employer. The court agreed that the managers took reasonable steps to accommodate the employee, and that is all that matters.

Do You Have to Accommodate Alcoholics and Drug Addicts?

The company's finance and insurance manager, Doug Frala, called in sick and remained absent for several days. The doctor's diagnosis was hepatitis complicated by drug withdrawal symptoms. He prescribed a month at a residential drug treatment facility where Doug could receive treatment for both problems. However, when Doug asked the company's president for a one-month leave of absence, he was fired. "We can't afford to be without you for that long, Doug. It'll be better if we just replace you now," his employer explained.

Would your company have let Doug go? Why or why not?

When in Ohio

Ohio statutes define "handicap" in broad terms:

> A medically diagnosable, abnormal condition [that] is expected to continue for a considerable length of time, whether correctable or uncorrectable by a good medical practice, which can reasonably be expected to limit the person's functional ability . . . so that he cannot perform his everyday routine living and working without significantly increased hardship and vulnerability to what are considered the everyday obstacles and hazards encountered by the non-handicapped.

Medical testimony in this case supported the plaintiff's contention that addictions, including alcoholism, create a debilitating chemical imbalance that is an abnormal physical condition. It can limit the addict's individual functional ability, including physical endurance, mental capacity, and judgment. Treatment can produce remission, but the effects of a drug may remain for a significant period of time. Alcoholism is therefore covered in Ohio law.[13]

Nevertheless, Ohio law also permits the employer to discharge the employee if he or she cannot perform his or her duties and responsibilities or some other duties necessary for the conduct of the employer's business (reasonable accommodation). The court in this case ruled that the plaintiff had been a good employee, and, had he not admitted to his alcohol addiction and requested the leave of absence, he probably would not have been fired. The company had granted lengthy leaves of absence to other employees, one with phlebitis and another who had suffered a heart attack. The only distinguishing condition here was the nature of the plaintiff's disability. Therefore, the company was guilty of discrimination under Ohio law.

The company would have been guilty under Iowa law, too.[14] And the federal courts have said that unless an employer gives an alcoholic employee a "firm choice" between rehabilitation and serious disciplinary action, it has not made reasonable accommodation.[15] In a 1984 case, the Supreme Court held that the employer's efforts before discharging an employee suffering from alcoholism were taken "with compassion and tolerance, and more patience than many employers would have shown," but the efforts fell short of the statutory mandate for accommodating disabled employees for three reasons:

1. The employer failed to give the employee a "firm choice" either to get appropriate therapy or face suspension or other disciplinary action; the employer vacillated for several months while the employee's attendance deteriorated further.
2. The employer failed to evaluate all available evidence to determine whether the employee's alcoholism was responsible for his unacceptable performance, relying instead on a physician's report that attributed the employee's absences to job stress while ignoring a psychiatrist's report laying the blame on drinking.
3. The employer failed to evaluate whether an alternative arrangement, such as leave without pay, would create an undue hardship on it.[16]

The laws in some states do not recognize alcoholism and drug abuse as disabilities and do not go along with federal guidelines with respect to reasonable accommodation. Cases that come before courts in these states are usually decided in the employer's favor.[17] Still, you should look into the specific laws in your own state before sighing with relief.

Cases

1. 475 U.S. 1118, 43 F.E.P. Cases (BNA) 81 (1987).
2. 618 F. Supp. 41, 36 F.E.P Cases (BNA) 1849 (D. Or. 1985).
3. No. 80,332 (Mass. Super. Ct. Aug. 15, 1986).
4. No. 14,940/85 (N.Y. Sup. Ct., Queens County, Feb. 11, 1986), 10 Mental and Physical Disability Law Rptr. 133–135 (1986).
5. 54 U.S.L.W. 2330 (December 11, 1985).
6. 392 Mass. 5098 (1984).
7. No. F.E.P. 83–84 (February 5, 1987).
8. No. 86-1571 (9th Cir. April 22, 1987).
9. No. C250,870 (Cal. Sup. Ct. October 28, 1982).
10. 46 F.E.P. Cases (BNA) 971 (W.D. Mo. 1988).
11. No. 179 (N.Y. Ct. App. May 7, 1985).
12. 415 N.W.2d 793 (N.D. 1987).
13. 250 Ohio St. 3d 279 (1986).
14. 366 N.W.2d 522 (Iowa Sup. Ct. 1985).
15. 598 F. Supp. 126, 36 F.E.P. Cases (BNA) 425 (D.D.C. 1984).
16. No. 83-3160 (D.D.C. January 14, 1985).
17. U.S.D.C. Miami, Fl. March 1, 1988.
18. 676 P.2d 602 (Alaska 1984).
19. 33 F.E.P. Cases (BNA) 650 (Mich. Ct. App. 1982).
20. 772 F.2d 759, 39 F.E.P. Cases (BNA) 9 (11th Cir. 1985).

Chapter 10

Employee Action Rights and Labor Laws

So yours is a nonunion shop. No contract obligations. No shop stewards. No grievance committee. What does the National Labor Relations Act (NLRA) have to do with you? Labor laws do not affect you, right? Well, until you read what these laws say you cannot and can do even in a nonunion shop, you should not be too sure of that.

What the Laws Say

The four federal laws that affect most labor-management relations are: (1) the National Labor Relations Act, (2) the Labor Management Relations Act, (3) the Fair Labor Standards Act, and (4) the Labor-Management Reporting and Disclosure Act. Each of these laws protects nonunion employees on the job and extends employees' rights to organize on their own behalf, including the right to form unions. They therefore affect management practices with regard to pay (e.g., minimum wage and overtime), concerted action, disciplinary procedures, and discharge policies.

1. *National Labor Relations Act of 1935 (NLRA).* This law protects employees' rights to take concerted action, that is, work together, to alter work conditions by:

- Using any bulletin boards that publish general community information
- Holding meetings during work hours, with no loss of pay or threat of retaliation, to discuss safety or other working conditions

It allows *all* workers to engage in other concerted activities for the purpose of collective bargaining through their own representatives—including forming, joining, or assisting labor organizations—or other mutual aid or protection. (At the same time, it prevents nonunion employees from being forced or coerced into joining a labor organization or engaging in collective bargaining except where membership in a labor organization is a condition of employment and is created by contract.) And, companies cannot have the right to interfere with any employee attempting to organize the employees for the purpose of collective action, or to discriminate or take steps to discipline, discharge, or retaliate against him or her for doing it.

2. *Labor Management Relations Act of 1947 (LMRA).* The Taft-Hartley Act, as this Act is also called, amends the NLRA and provides additional support for mediation in labor disputes that affect interstate commerce, equalizes legal responsibilities of labor organizations and employers, gives the President emergency powers, and allows for other actions designed to protect the nation's general welfare.

3. *Fair Labor Standards Act of 1938 (FLSA).* Also known as the Wage-Hour Act, this law establishes fair labor standards in employments in and affecting interstate commerce, and for other purposes. It protects all workers, including children and women by establishing minimum hourly wages and distinguishing between nonexempt employees (those to whom you must pay overtime for hours in excess of forty hours a week) and exempt (those to whom you do not have to pay overtime).

4. *Labor-Management Reporting and Disclosure Act of 1959 (LMRDA).* This law, subtitled the Labor Reform Act, forms an umbrella that covers nonsupervisory nonunion as well as unionized employees by preventing labor organizations, em-

ployers, or their officers and representatives, including labor relations consultants, from distorting and defeating the policies of the LMRA.

What You Cannot Do

Each of the four labor laws limits managers in its own specific way.

The National Labor Relations Act

This Act created the National Labor Relations Board (NLRB) and also defines "unfair labor practices by employers."

It says that you, as a manager, cannot interfere with, restrain, or coerce employees exercising their rights. You cannot dominate or interfere with the formation or administration of a labor organization or contribute financial or other aid to it; however, you are required to allow employees to meet with you during working hours without a loss of time or pay to discuss issues of collective interest. Along those lines, you cannot refuse to bargain collectively with the employees' representative, either. (However, see below under "What You Can Do" with regard to rejecting proposals.)

You cannot discriminate in hiring or tenure on the basis of union or nonunion membership. You cannot use the term or conditions of employment to encourage or discourage membership in a labor organization, except where an agreement exists that requires membership. And you cannot fire or otherwise discriminate against an employee for filing charges or giving testimony under this Act.

Labor Management Relations Act, 1947

Under this amendment to the NLRA, you cannot conduct unwarranted or sudden lockouts. You cannot pay, loan, or deliver money or other assets to a union, union official, union welfare fund, or employee involved in a labor dispute, and, in your role as a manager of your organization, you cannot make direct contributions to political candidates.

Fair Labor Standards Act

You probably know that under this Act you cannot employ children under age 16 ("oppressive labor") and certain categories of children ages 16–18. You may also know that this is the legislation that created the minimum hourly rate, which tends to fluctuate from time to time and which is sometimes superseded by minimum wage standards mandated by state laws. And this law says you cannot work "nonexempt" employees for more than forty hours a week unless you pay them at least time and a half their "regular rate of pay" for the overtime.

Less well known is that the Act also specifies that you cannot use gender as a basis for discriminating in wages, except where wages are based on a seniority system, a merit system, a piecework or commission or bonus system, or on a factor other than sex. The law also specifies that you cannot simply lower the wage rate of any employee just to end wage disparities.

Finally, in agreement with the NLRA, you cannot discharge or otherwise discriminate against any employee for taking part in a collective action of mutual benefit with respect to wages or other working conditions. Likewise, you cannot discharge or otherwise discriminate against any employee for filing, instituting, or causing to be instituted a complaint relating to the Act, or for testifying or being about to testify in an action protected by the Act.

Labor-Management Reporting and Disclosure Act, 1959

In language similar to that used in the NLRA, this law says you cannot interfere with employees' rights to work, to organize, to choose representatives, bargain collectively, or engage in concerted action for their mutual aid or protection.

What You Can Do

Yes, managers do have rights under these acts. Again, taking them in the order presented above, let's take a look at what you can do and in some cases must do.

National Labor Relations Act

As long as you do not interfere with your employees' right to take collective action or form a union, you can freely express your own viewpoints, arguments, or opinions in writing, print, graphics, or visuals about unions or collective bargaining. While ensuring that what you say does not threaten reprisal or force for forming or joining a collective bargaining unit or promise benefits for not forming or joining one, you can express your opinion and reject proposals or requests for concessions.

Where a union exists, you can hear employee grievances and adjust them without union representation as long as the adjustment is consistent with the terms of a contract or agreement in effect, and as long as the bargaining representative has been given an opportunity to be present.

Decisions on grievances taken to the NLRB are not final; the law says you can appeal any such ruling in any appropriate U.S. circuit court of appeals.

Labor Management Relations Act, 1947

This law prohibits wildcat strikes as well as unwarranted lockouts. The law gives you the right to make every reasonable effort to reach an agreement with your employees on rates of pay, hours, and working conditions, including notice of changes, and to arrange promptly to hold a conference to settle any differences between you. If a conference is not successful, the law requires that you both participate fully in meetings called by the Federal Mediation Service.

The Federal Mediation Service was created to try to avoid industrial controversy by offering services either on its own initiative or by request from you or your employees. The service's main goal is to try to reach an agreement through conciliation within a reasonable time. If the service's director cannot produce an agreement, he or she will try to get you and your employees to find other means of settling the dispute without resorting to a strike, a lockout, or other coercion (e.g., submitting the employer's last offer to a secret ballot of the employees).

Now you do not have to agree with the mediator's solutions, because failure to agree is not a violation of any duty or obligation imposed by the law. On the other hand, if the mediator sees the situation as posing a serious threat to the general welfare of the nation, the service will advise the President of that perceived threat. The President, in turn, is empowered to direct the attorney general to petition any appropriate district court to stop a threatened strike or lockout or to end one or the other in progress. If the court agrees that a strike or a lockout will adversely affect an entire industry or substantial part of it or would threaten the national health, safety, or security, it can stop the strike or lockout or take other appropriate measures.

Fair Labor Standards Act

Many employers see this law as unfriendly toward them. However, it does allow you some freedom to decide on what you can do with regard to specific forms of compensation or benefits not covered by the law:

1. Gifts, special bonuses, rewards for service
2. Payments made for occasional periods in which no work is performed, for travel expenses, or other reimbursable expenses
3. Recognition for service awards
4. Contributions irrevocably made to a trustee or third party in a retirement, pension, or insurance plan
5. Extra compensation paid on a premium rate for:
   a. Overtime after a regular eight-hour day
   b. Overtime on a nonwork day
   c. Work outside normal hours as agreed on through collective bargaining
6. Compensation through a guaranteed wage plan based on a bona fide individual contract or collective bargaining agreement

By creating a class of employees called "exempt employees," the law allows you to *not* have to pay overtime to some people if they work beyond forty hours a week. You are a member of this class, because it covers executives, managers, and first-line supervisors, as well as employees whose jobs require making decisions and using personal judgment, creativity, or innovativeness but who are not classified as managers. Teachers and educational administrators, salespeople, and other people working on commission or for tips for service, employees of service organizations in which more than 50 percent of the organization's gross income derives from *intra*state as opposed to *inter*state commerce—these are all people to whom overtime need not be paid.

Labor-Management Reporting and Disclosure Act, 1959

This law does not prescribe employers' rights so much as it describes what you must do to comply with them. It identifies a number of reports you must file with the secretary of labor, including the several reports relevant to safe management that I have listed in the legislation summaries in the Appendix.

Conclusion

Some managers see these laws, e.g., the minimum wage law, as heavy burdens. Other managers recognize that this legislation has been, in part, responsible for the strength of the U.S. economy and for the standard of living we all enjoy. In some respects, they guarantee that employers and employees alike work to meet each other's needs, while they protect the welfare of both individuals and the nation.

CASEBOOK

Only about 20 percent of U.S. workers belong to unions. Still, the force and power of unions have been felt in all industries and in society as a whole. And, yes, these labor laws I have been discussing have given those unions greater voice in the economy than their numbers would suggest they should have. Just how important these laws are to society is well illustrated in the following cases.

When Does Innocence Cross Over Into Unlawful Interference?

Both Phyllis and Fred, low-level supervisors, had a personal interest in what was happening when a union began its organizing campaign at their food processing plant. "How are things?" Phyllis asked one of her line employees, referring to the union campaign.

"Okay," was the noncommittal reply.

"Think the union will come in?"

"Guess so," the employee responded. "Talk around here is that it will."

"I don't know," Phyllis replied. "What I've heard seems to indicate it could go either way."

Fred stopped another employee and raised the same issue. "Think the union will come in?" When the employee did not respond, Fred added, "I'm just curious. You know, person to person."

"I guess so," the woman answered.

"Why? Do you think you've gotten a bad shake from the company?"

"I really don't want to talk about it."

"Don't mean any harm," Fred reassured the woman. "We've known each other a long time, and I'd like to know, personally."

"Well, I think it'll make it on the first ballot."

Two innocent conversations, independent of each other and each a matter of curiosity, or so it seemed to the supervisors.

Not from the union's perspective. After the union lost the election, it alleged that those two conversations constituted unfair labor practices that violated the NLRA.

How about it? Does chitchat such as that constitute unlawful interrogation that has the effect of restraining or coercing employees engaged in concerted organization activities?

A Time and Place for Everything

If you answered yes to that question, you agreed with the NLRB when it said that even if the conversations had been just "small talk," the law still prohibits any such discussion during an organizing campaign. The conversations were unlawful because they served "no legitimate purpose" and could have had a chilling effect on the exercise of the employees' union activities. Even an innocent and friendly conversation can be called "interrogation," the technical term denoting "illegal questioning of employees about their union membership, activities, and desires."[1]

When Does the Information You Disseminate Cross the Line?

The law allows managers to explain their positions about a particular union and offer their personal opinions, urging employees not to sign up. They can also explain that the organization need not agree to anything promised to employees by a union unless the union is certified and a contract is signed. So what is the big deal about innocent conversations?

How about these preelection statements? First, a question and answer fact sheet an employer sent to all employees with the intent to delineate the employees' legal rights under the Act claimed:

Question: Can I lose my job if the union calls me out on strike?

Answer: If the union calls you out on strike to try to force [the organization] to agree to union promises, [the organization] is free to replace economic strikers. This means that when the strike is over, you may no longer have a job, and the law does not force [the employer] to rehire you.

In a letter to the employees, the same employer stated:

Most important of all, you could lose the right to speak and think for yourself. If a union is certified, you will have to deal through union representatives and may not be permitted to go directly to [the employer] about particular problems you may have.

The union lost and went straight to the NLRB, charging that the employer violated the NLRA by issuing a technically inaccurate

statement and a second that was "implicitly threatening" to employees. The NLRB agreed.

Can you spot the two offensive statements? What disqualifies
them?

Error and Overstatement

Reread these two sentences.

> This means that when the strike is over, you may no
> longer have a job, and the law does not force [the
> employer] to rehire you.
>
> *and*
>
> Most important of all, you could lose the right to
> speak and think for yourself.

The first statement seems correct but is a technical mis-
statement. An employer may lawfully, permanently replace
economic strikers, but while the word *rehire* implies a total
severance of employment, the law gives an economic striker
the right to reinstatement as long as his or her position is still
available.

The Board also found the second statement objectionable
because, although the statement seems to be accurate, it is not
technically correct and thereby forms a "retaliatory threat."
The statement, the Board said, suggests that if employees form
a union the employer would sever their right to deal directly
with management. That is a threat, not a piece of information.

The terms of a collective bargaining agreement could, and
often do, prevent employees from taking a grievance directly
to management, but in the Board's opinion this statement
implies that management itself will deny employees their right
to direct access if the union wins. So, although the employer
won the battle at the ballot box, it lost the war in front of the
NLRB.[2]

Most people do not realize that even a single, offhand
comment can result in the NLRB's overturning the results of
an election, if in its opinion that comment might have tainted
the results because it appeared to be coercive. Because it is the

Board's objective to ensure that a union election be conducted in an "atmosphere" free of coercion, the Board cautions supervisors to become aware of the T.I.P.S. formula: do not *T*hreaten, *I*nterrogate, *P*romise benefit, or engage in *S*urveillance.

Cases

1. 265 N.L.R.B. No. 182 (1982).
2. 265 N.L.R.B. No. 135 (1982).

Section III

Safe Firing Practices

Once upon a time, you could fire anyone you wanted, anytime you wanted, for virtually any reason or for no reason at all. U.S. employers took their freedom to discharge employees (the doctrine of employment/termination at will) as a matter of law rather than as what it is: a labor-management philosophy that most courts recognized as an implied contract favoring the rights of employers.

The Freedom to Discharge Employees

Employment at will presumes that employers hire and fire people for and at their own convenience. The theory allows employers, in the absence of a written agreement, to hire someone for an unspecified period of time and fire him or her with or without cause, with or without notice—in short, to employ and terminate at will. Of course, the philosophy assumes the employee has the equal right of quitting at any time, with or without cause, with or without notice.

However, times are changing. Society, through contract law and public policy, constrains managers in many new ways. Organizations themselves, by publishing employee handbooks, constrain them in still other ways. Employees constrain managers by becoming more aware of their own rights and by attacking the at-will notion of employment in many courts that are friendly to the plaintiff.

To reduce the risk of legal challenges to your personnel decisions, you need to have a clear sense of what employment (or termination) at will means and how the doctrine is being attacked. In this introductory chapter, I will look at the definitions of key terms that underlie many of the issues related to disciplining and firing employees. In the chapters that follow, I will spell out what you cannot and can do with regard to safely disciplining or terminating employees, including issues related to public policy and age discrimination.

Definitions of Key Terms

contract An agreement in which one party promises to do something or provide something for another, in return for consideration—something of value, which may or may not be tangible (e.g., money). In an employment contract, the promise to pay someone for his or her labor is consideration.

explicit contract A written or oral agreement that offers consideration and spells out the terms and conditions of employment. An employment agreement is a bilateral contract.

bilateral contract An agreement in which *both* parties knowingly offer to participate in some endeavor and to provide something of value in return for something of value—e.g., to give money in return for services.

unilateral contract An agreement in which only *one* party offers something of value. The other party may *not know* the contract exists or that an offer has been made. For example, if you make a specific promise (even orally)—an offer—when someone accepts a position, that offer can, in some states, bind you. Promising *not* to fire someone "unless [he or she] screws up badly" could come back to haunt you in court.[1]

implicit (implied) contract Any statements you make, oral or written, that an ordinary, reasonable person can interpret to set specific terms and conditions of employment; could possibly be construed as an implied, binding, usually unilateral contract.

Various state courts often differ as to the nature of an implied contract or how binding one is. The Pennsylvania Supreme Court, in 1974, ruled that the absence of an explicit contract does *not* mean that an employee handbook or a personnel guide creates an implied contract.[2] Employment is at will.

Some courts agree with Pennsylvania's, but, in 1980, when an employee challenged his firing by saying the company promised not to discharge anyone without just cause, the Michigan courts called the promise a contract. The company, the courts said, had to, but did not, show cause when it fired him. In so saying, the Michigan courts recognized the existence of implied contracts in employee manuals. They also held that, in the absence of explicit contracts or specific disclaimers, circumstances can dictate that an implied contract *supersedes* written policies.[3,4] Now, some courts agree with Michigan's. Where do your state's courts stand? It's hard to tell without a scorecard.*

good faith, fair dealing A special case of implied contract. The covenant of good faith and fair dealing, although poorly defined, has been adopted by several states, notably Alaska, California, Connecticut, Massachusetts, and Montana. This doctrine imposes contractual constraints on promises made in employment relations by recognizing the importance of trust in negotiated agreements. For example, discharging a salesperson to avoid paying a large commission is a bad-faith action that violates the covenant because the salesperson trusts you to make good on your promise to pay what you agreed to pay.[5] Some courts have extended the covenant to include the failure to follow internal grievance procedures, to employ reasonable appraisal procedures, or to keep explicit promises prior to terminating someone.[6,7,8,9]

outrageous conduct Conduct any reasonable person would consider exceeds the limits of socially acceptable employer practices. Has been added by some states to the standards for breach of contract. The complaint of severe mental and emotional harm often accompanies this charge and, in some cases, actually defines the outrageous conduct. This, among other claims, was the situation in Oregon when a company security officer denied an employee suspected of violating company rules her right to remain silent and threatened her with arrest.[10]

disclaimer An explicit statement declaring employment at will as

---

*See Thomas J. Condon, Esq., *Fire Me and I'll Sue, a Manager's Survival Guide to Employee Rights* (New York: Alexander Hamilton Institute, 1988), for a state-by-state list of current positions taken by the courts and legislatures.

company policy; this statement usually safeguards the employer's position. A well-written disclaimer, which I will provide later, can prevent an employee handbook from creating an implicit contract.

constructive discharge A type of wrongful discharge exemplified when an employer intentionally or unintentionally creates or allows conditions to exist that lead an employee to believe he or she has only two options: (1) to accept a personally adverse situation or (2) to resign.

Our review of essentials of wrongful discharge should help you grasp many of the things you can and cannot do with respect to disciplining and firing employees. It should also help you examine your own organization's stance via-á-vis employment-at-will issues and help you understand how employment at will is being attacked.

Cases

1. 779 F.2d 101, 121, L.R.R.M. (BNA) 2169 (2d Cir. 1985).
2. 456 Pa. 171, 319 A.2d 174 (1974).
3. 408 Mich. 579, 292 N.W.2d 880 (1980).
4. 495 F. Supp. 344, 117 L.R.R.M. (BNA) 2702 (Mich. 1980).
5. 373 Mass. 96, 364 N.E.2d 1251, 115 L.R.R.M. (BNA) 4658 (1977).
6. 181 Cal. App. 3d 813, 226 Cal. Rptr. 570 (Cal. Ct. App. 4th Dist. 1986).
7. 226 Mont. 69, 733 P.2d 1292 (1987).
8. 666 P.2d 1000, 115 L.R.R.M. (BNA) 4254 (1983).
9. See also 393 Mass. 231, 471 N.E.2d 47, 118 L.R.R.M. (BNA) 2406 (Mass. Sup. Ct. 1984).
10. 63 Or. App. 1423, 664, P.2d 1119, 118 L.R.R.M. (BNA) 3019 (Or. App. 1983).

Chapter 11

Safe Discipline and Firing Practices

Economic and political winds create new or different judicial tides that ebb and flow over time and with the economy and state of the nation. During periods of high unemployment, for example, people are reluctant to quit in a fit of pique and go to court. Likewise, newly elected judges or new federal court appointments take the tides on still another turn; what direction they will take is often anyone's guess. All I can say is that the eddies in these legal tides have weakened the foundations of the employment-at-will doctrine.

Until fairly recently, the creed of employment at will seemed impregnable, a ready-made defense against employee retaliation for unfair or outrageous treatment. But the growth in human rights, especially since the turn of the century, has generated a new legal climate in the United States that not only produced the civil rights laws of 1964 but has also produced frequent judicial reviews of the at-will defense, especially where legal rights are involved. Inspired by the human rights movement, employees now look to their own interests under the common laws of contract.

Workers defend themselves in court against breach of contract or wrongful discharge more frequently than before, and the courts have sided with employees in almost any kind of personnel decision a manager might possibly make. No longer merely bitter and resentful, resigned to their fate when they feel improperly treated in compensation or promotion or when fired, employees don't just get angry, they get even.

The days when employers could treat employees however they wished have become a relic of history. Pressures created by the labor movement have stayed the employer's free hand. Managers today must pause before punishing or discharging an employee, whether or not they believe they have just cause. Both common law and statute law, including the various EEO laws I have already discussed, have balanced the employer-employee relationship; *how* one goes about disciplining or discharging an employee, the subjects of this chapter, can become a court matter.

Does your organization reserve the right to fire someone with or without cause, with or without notice? Has it published an employee handbook that spells out terms or conditions of employment that could lead to lawsuits? Has it trained you and other managers how to administer its policies and how to avoid making loose promises or implied threats? You should be prepared to deal with the changes time has wrought.

What You Cannot Do

Managers' hands have been stayed in two broad areas: discipline and policy administration.

Discriminatory Discipline

You cannot administer disciplinary policies and procedures that could in themselves have "a meaningful adverse effect on an employee's working conditions."[1] Reprimands, especially if filed in a personnel jacket, may affect an employee's future promotion opportunities and have a permanent impact on his or her ongoing work life. This in turn could affect the employee's daily life and psychological well-being. When a disciplinary action affects the person's terms or conditions of employment, it could have a discriminatory effect if the person's status places him or her in a protected group.

Let's take wage garnishment, which minority employees

(given their social conditions) experience more frequently than do others, as an example. A policy that would discipline an employee for numerous garnishments could have a disparate impact on minorities, and that policy, even if it results in just a reprimand, may constitute an unlawful employment practice because of the disparate impact.[2-5] Personnel policies and decisions should have a clearly defined business basis and should not have an adverse impact on people whose social status makes them especially vulnerable.

Provisions of the Employee Handbook

You cannot ignore the provisions of an employee handbook *if* the employee can show that:

1. The employee handbook has become a part of an employment contract
2. The job security provisions in an employee handbook are enforceable
3. A summary dismissal is a breach of an employment contract[6]

Personnel handbook provisions can form a *unilateral contract* and therefore become enforceable as an employment contract if they are distributed to the general population of employees, of if they are used for any purpose other than as a guide for supervisors, or if they are not delimited by a disclaimer that can prevent a printed policy manual from suggesting promises you do not intend to keep. Policy statements should then be used only as a general guide for *managing supervisory behavior.*

You cannot promise job security. Phrases such as "career situation" or "job security" might not form the basis of a contract, but specific job security provisions in an employee handbook, disseminated to all the employees, can be so construed. Those provisions could then override a terminable-at-will construction of an employment contract. Check your manual to see if a job security provision could affect your ability to fire someone, and if so, call the situation to your personnel officer's attention.

Replacing or amending the old manual presents you with
another situation. A second employee handbook or an amendment does not necessarily usurp the earlier one. In a 1987 case,
a federal court ruled that a company's at-will revisions of its
original employee manual did not *automatically* supersede the
termination-for-cause contractual relationship embodied in
the handbook's earlier version.[7]

For the court to accept the revisions, you must show that
an employee contesting an at-will discharge had accepted the
new handbook as his or her amended contract. If, at the time
you issue the second handbook, you require employees to sign
an acknowledgment that they have read it, that they understand the terms that affect the conditions of employment, and
that they are willing to work according to those terms, you are
on safer ground.

If your employee handbook promises that certain procedures will be followed before an employee is discharged, then
your disciplinary policy contains sufficiently *definite language*
to form an offer of a *unilateral contract.* Under those circumstances, according to some courts, a summary dismissal can
constitute a breach of contract. Check out the key words in one
specific policy statement that lost in court:[6] "If an employee
has violated a company policy, the following procedure *will
apply* [*italics added*]."

That this policy with those words was distributed to all
employees nailed down the contract. In this case, the court
held that the employer's argument that employees are at will
was without merit because the termination procedures were
contractually binding.

Read your policy manual carefully. Ask your personnel
officer to check the state's legal precedents in cases such as
these. A goodly number of states agree with these
decisions.[8-16]

How you administer policies is as important as the policies
themselves. If you have a personnel policy that creates enforceable contract rights, it is essential to follow it to the letter;
failure to do so can be seen by the courts as a breach of
contract.[17]

Let's say your organization's employee handbook prescribes a five-step progressive disciplinary procedure. The first two steps call for counseling, the third for a written reprimand, the fourth for a three-day suspension, and the fifth for discharge if another incident occurs. The handbook also includes statements that promise fair and objective consideration for employees with job-related problems, and that you, the employer, will adhere to a policy of progressive discipline tempered by the seriousness of the offense. Let's also say that your organization has published these statements but has not trained your managers in the proper application of the rules or monitored your *management performance.*

All those policy statements could form the basis of a contract that supersedes employment at will, or so the Wyoming Supreme Court concluded. If under the circumstances I outlined you follow all the steps but discharge the employee even though he or she did not commit another offense warranting discipline, which violates the rule of the fifth step ("if another incident occurs"), you probably will be sued and lose.

Substantial compliance with the discipline procedure is an insufficient defense. In the court's opinion *strict* compliance can be the only standard by which the procedures can be judged. You cannot follow most, but not all, of the steps. You must follow *all* of them. The failure to do so is a breach of contract for which the wrongfully discharged employee could possibly receive damages.

The little things are important as well, especially if an employment contract has been reduced to writing. The following language can cause you much trouble if you fail to adhere to it closely:

> Unless you or the company give written notice of termination, this agreement will be automatically extended on December 31 of each year.

If the contract calls for *written* notice, the courts have said, oral notice is not enough.[18] If you have any doubts as to how your personnel policies commit you and the other managers, ask your personnel officer to get a professional opinion from an attorney who specializes in employee relations in your state (opinions will differ from state to state). You might also ask that the attorney conduct a seminar for you and your fellow managers. In the meantime, there are things you can do personally to improve your safety.

What You Can Do

That the courts have come to recognize employee contract rights as well as civil rights is not an occasion for management handwringing. The courts also recognize employer rights as long as policy books are properly written and policies properly administered. In what follows, I try to show you some ways in which you can protect yourself with well-written disclaimers and policy statements that have withstood many court challenges.[19–42]

Protect Your Right to Fire

If your organization has published an employee handbook, check to see if it contains language that specifically reserves to you your right to employ at will or to modify the organization's employment rules. If the handbook says there is no employment contract, then you cannot breach any contract.[43]

Even though courts in different states, at different times, disagree with the Pennsylvania Supreme Court, that court's basic outline of what constitutes the at-will doctrine provides a clear statement of what to consider when looking at your own organization's published rules under which employees can be discharged:

1. If the employer publishes a handbook, the at-will policy is preserved if the book includes specific language that assumes the employer's unilateral right to modify its policies. That reservation of rights precludes the possibility of creating a just-cause contract.

2. The at-will policy is further protected if the employer states that published reasons for discharge are merely illustrations, not exclusive causes. That claim then gives the employer

the right to decide on a case-by-case basis what constitutes just cause or to ignore just cause altogether.

3. If, when they receive the handbook, employees are required to sign an acknowledgment that they received it, they give up their right to being discharged for only just cause.

Publish Disclaimers

Well-written disclaimers and policy statements offer some protection against lawsuits. Check out your organization's job application or handbook to make sure the disclaimers do the following:

1. Uphold the idea of employment at will.
2. Explain that employment is for no specific duration.
3. Explain that either party can end the relationship at any time, with or without cause, with or without notice.
4. Explain that no one but the highest management authority in the group can alter the terms described in the organization's documents.

Check any written policy manuals that have been distributed to any of the nonmanagement employees for language that does the following:

1. Clearly spells out the limitations on employment.
2. Explains to both managers and employees that the personnel policies in the manual act as guidelines for conduct, not as a contract.

Finally, make sure that if your organization has published disclaimers and policies, the employees have also acknowledged by their signatures that they have read and understood them. If your managers rewrite anything that could materially change the conditions or terms of employment, ask that they have the employees sign a written acknowledgment of having read and understood the revisions as well, and ascertain that they are willing to work under the new terms and conditions.

The recommended disclaimer and acknowledgment shown

in Figures 11-1 and 11-2 have been modeled after several that have passed court tests, and should in most cases hold up if ever challenged. Even if you use them verbatim, have a labor attorney check the statement for consistency with what has been upheld in your state. Local precedent is the only valid test, although favorable precedents are not guarantees that you will win in court.

Because organizational needs vary widely from group to group, each organization has to write its own personnel policies and procedures accordingly.

Effectively Written Policies and Procedures

If your organization has or develops a personnel manual, your personnel officer should distribute it to each manager in your organization and ask for a signed acknowledgment that the manager has received and read it. A seminar on how to read, interpret, and use the manual would be a very good idea.

Figure 11-1. Recommended disclaimer for employee handbook.

ABOUT THIS HANDBOOK

This handbook spells out the goals, standards, values, attitudes, beliefs, and benefits that [company name] believes are important and that management encourages. The standards of conduct govern all employees, including management personnel, and are intended to help us all get along in a friendly and productive atmosphere. [company name]'s policies are also designed to promote your personal productivity and career advancement.

At the same time, this handbook serves only as a general guide to what we can reasonably expect from each other in the conduct of our business. Therefore, neither this handbook nor any of its provisions constitute an employment agreement or contract of any kind or a guarantee to continued employment. Because circumstances and situations change, we will have to change or amend these guidelines from time to time. We will notify you in writing when we do.

Figure 11-2. Recommended acknowledgment by employee.

Acknowledgment

I have read the *Office Employment Handbook* and understand and agree that it is only a general guide that does not constitute an employment contract or guarantee of continued employment. I also understand and agree that my employment is for no definite period; that my employment and compensation can be terminated with or without cause, with or without notice, at any time, at the option of either [*company name*] or myself; that no representative of the organization other than [*name of person heading organization*] has any authority to enter into any agreement for employment for any specified period of time or make any agreement contrary to the foregoing.

This manual should identify a set of guidelines with regard to goals and objectives (policies) and procedures or rules. It should explain the values the organization holds and what work-related values and conduct it expects of employees. It also should detail for managers what they are supposed to do in the event an employee does not follow the rules. If your organization does not distribute such a manual, you should discuss the matter with your personnel officer; there may be a good reason for not doing so. Then, again, there may not be.

The sample antiharassment policy statement that appears in Chapter 8 on sex discrimination (Figure 8-1) illustrates what a well-written and complete policy and procedures statement should look like. If your organization publishes policies and procedures, you can use the guidance that follows to measure just how well written and complete they are (or aren't).

At the same time, each new employee should receive a copy of an employee handbook that distills information from the personnel manual. This abridged version of the personnel manual should consist primarily of policy statements (the goals and objectives) hedged in disclaimers, some procedures, and the organization's values, expectations, and basic rules of conduct.

Policy Statements

A policy by itself is a guideline for thinking or for making decisions, and not necessarily a guide to specific actions, and it should not make any promise that can be construed as establishing a contractual obligation. Check your organization's policy statements to see if they meet the criteria described below.

A complete policy should follow a format that includes separate sections for each part of the policy:

Policy:	The policy statement itself
Procedures:	Steps used to apply or implement the policy
Management responsibilities:	What managers are expected to do, methods for monitoring or controlling how the policy statement is implemented
Consequences:	Statements concerning what will happen in the event the policy is not enforced, as well as statements concerning consequences if policies are not followed; positive statements related to the value of following the policy would be helpful (e.g., "To ensure the cooperation of all employees, this policy. . . .")
References:	Quotes or summaries of specific legal documents if legislation or common law is involved

A policy should be:

‣ *Broad,* in the manner of a goal statement, and leave room for discretion and interpretation, making application flexible but under the direction of the policy. It could start with "It is our [organization's name] intent to. . . ."

▸ *Comprehensive*, covering every aspect of the relevant personnel activities. Words such as "all cases of this kind," "in no circumstance can anyone authorize a contract other than. . . ." should be prominent.

▸ *Livable*, fitting the realities of both the organization and the world around it. For example, a policy statement can begin with "Given the ratio of minority employees to majority employees in [organization's name]. . . ."

▸ *Inviolate*, allowing no exceptions unless the policy itself fails to apply in special circumstances. In some cases, the policy might read, "This policy does not apply to employees on an unpaid leave of absence."

▸ *Authoritative* (though not authoritarian), identifying responsibilities, accountabilities, and both positive and negative consequences of decisions made within the context of the policy. For example:

> If you are a first-line supervisor, you will be held responsible for the daily attendance of the employees reporting directly to you. Failure to take timely corrective action for unexcused absences could result in disciplinary action for you as well as for the employee. If you report 100 percent attendance for the quarter, you will receive one day's time off in the quarter immediately following the quarter in which the 100 percent attendance occurred.

▸ *Applicable*, used frequently by managers to ensure that their decisions are fair, consistent, and in line with executive management's thinking and wishes. A policy might deny a supervisor the right to offer full-time permanent employment to an applicant without the agreement of human resources: "To prevent the appearance of contractually obligating the organization to any one applicant, you must discuss all decisions to hire with the vice-president of human resources, and an agreement to extend an offer to that person must be reached."

Even if the policy statements are broad and comprehensive, they could still fail to communicate their intent to everyone because they either do not say what they mean or they are expressed badly. Figure 11-3 lists the right way and the wrong way to write policy statements. In which column would you say your organization's policy statements fall?

Procedures

A procedure is a sequence of steps to be performed and, in this context, usually describes how to implement a policy. Policies usually evolve slowly but procedures are subject to frequent, sometimes sweeping, changes or amendments. Whereas a policy statement is a broad statement of intent (a goal), procedures are specific and action-oriented. They explain how a rule of conduct (which is a requirement for action or inaction) is enforced and how managers are supposed to use their authority or exercise their control. For example, a procedure related to hiring policies might say, "If an applicant does not fill out all relevant blanks in the application for employment (e.g., a

Figure 11-3. Rights and wrongs of policy statements.

Right Way	Wrong Way
Short sentences that use an economy of language	Technical jargon or other language that might not be readily understood by everyone
A friendly, responsive tone	
Personal pronouns (e.g., *you*) rather than impersonal words (e.g., *managers*) to allow readers to see how the policy applies to them	Legalistic language, even talking about the law
	A choppy or abrupt style
Clear, ordinary language that says what the organization really means	Ambiguity or fuzziness that allows managers to make inappropriate or improper decisions by implication
Action-oriented language expressed by active verbs	Overuse of lists or outlines

gap appears between employments), you should ask the person what happened during those years between employments."

Miscellaneous Items

Other materials can be added to a personnel manual to help managers understand what they cannot or can do. For example, the manual should include a section in the back that contains summaries of relevant pieces of legislation or common law concepts (such as those in this book). That and other devices can help an organization protect itself, its managers, and its line employees from wrongful discharge suits.

Conclusion

Employees have found their voice through the courts and other government agencies, a voice long reserved for employers. On the bright side, the new balance struck by the courts between employee and employer rights, if maintained, will help you develop effective management standards and practices that will benefit all concerned. You and your organization can help yourselves if you follow these suggestions.

Use and follow progressive disciplinary procedures whenever possible. When you do have to fire someone, make sure you have backup documentation that you have shared with higher management before making your final decision. In short, do not get caught "building a file," which can lead to an assessment of damages.

Check your policy manual to see if it lists clearly stated offenses for which immediate discharge is possible. Make sure the list is accompanied by a disclaimer saying that the list only illustrates the types of offenses that could result in immediate discharge, that it is not exclusive of other possibilities. The list coupled with a well-written disclaimer makes employment at will an organizational policy; discharge for cause is not necessary and is not restricted to rules of conduct spelled out in a policy manual.

Decide whether you have been given appropriate guidelines about what to say to other people once you have discharged an employee. If you fire someone for cause—e.g., theft, destruction of property—you need merely mention the incident in brief, neutral, matter-of-fact terms to those employees who have a need to know (e.g., immediate co-workers). Firing someone for poor performance can be acknowledged merely by saying that the organization and the employee agreed to disagree and separate. Both ways of explaining things should help you avoid charges of defamation.

But written policies are not enough. Your organization should train you and your co-managers in how to enforce company codes of conduct and how to follow the guidelines for avoiding litigation when hiring, appraising, promoting, or firing employees. If the organization does not offer the training, ask for it.

You can discipline or fire an employee. No one says you cannot. But, if you do, you have to ensure that in the process you have not breached a contract, explicit or implicit, or violated public policy (which I will discuss in the next chapter).

At issue is the balance between employer and employee rights, rights governed by laws of contract as well as civil rights laws. As employer, you have the right to dismiss any employee you want, for whatever reason you want, and with whatever notice you want to give as long as you do not have a definite employment contract limiting your actions.

On the other hand, where no definite employment contract exists, you should be prepared to defend yourself against any charges an employee you dismiss brings against you or your organization. Although no law requires your organization to publish specific personnel policies, they are still good protections against lawsuits. However, they can also be the source of lawsuits, if those policies, as you have read, produce disparate treatment or adverse impact—or, more likely, if they are not carefully implemented.

CASEBOOK

Although I could produce many volumes with breach of contract cases, I will include only a few illustrative samples through which you can test your own awareness and against which you can test your organization's disciplining and firing policies.

How Can You Preserve Your Right to Fire?

When Barbara Price ran her "for sale" ad in the newspaper published by her employer's competitor, she had no idea she would lose her job over it. In court, she claimed that the language of the employee handbook created a contract that limited employee discharge to "just cause," i.e., actions that violate very specific rules or expectations: "The following actions violate the standards of conduct of the *Tribune* and therefore represent cause for disciplinary action." The handbook then listed eleven separate actions common to most handbooks: dishonesty, possession of intoxicants or illegal substances, unexcused absences, and so on.

The publication's attorney argued that the employer had the right to terminate anyone at any time, with or without cause, or to determine what other than the eleven items listed could be called "just cause." To bolster the employer's case, the defendant read into the record two other excerpts from the handbook:

[The eleven separate actions] enumerat[ed] here [are] by way of illustration and shall not be deemed to exclude any other just causes.
It must be remembered that as circumstances change, rules often must change. Therefore, the *Tribune* may from time to time amend some rules to meet changing needs.

Does your organization list reasons for discharge? How does the employee manual protect your freedom to discharge someone?

At-Will Supported

The Pennsylvania courts provide the basic outline of what constitutes the at-will doctrine. The Pennsylvania Superior Court decided for the defendant, refusing to undermine the at-will employment doctrine prevalent in that state. According to the court, without a clear statement of the *employer's* intent to agree to any other arrangement, at will must prevail.

In this case, because the handbook's language specifically reserved the right to modify the employment *rules* (not at-will employment), the employer's right to discharge at will held.[43] Discharging the employee was not in breach of contract because *no such contract existed*, either implicitly or explicitly. Additionally, because the employee signed an acknowledgment, the employer had protected itself completely.

To sum up, the substance of the employment-at-will doctrine consists of the employers' right to hire and fire people for and at their own convenience. In the absence of a written agreement, an employer may hire someone for an unspecified period of time and fire him or her with or without reason (cause), with or without notice. But, don't forget, the employee has the equal right of quitting at any time, with or without cause, with or without notice.

How Can Your Procedure Manual Interfere With Your Decision to Lay Off a Worker?

The managers of a major airline carrier thought they had produced a good procedure for their reduction in force, one that provided guidelines and instructions to all managers for carrying out their responsibilities. However, one employee in Colorado, finding himself on the street, cried foul. "The procedure manual's a binding contract that spells out the steps management has to take before firing someone. They were not followed in my case," he told the court.

"No," the airline argued. "The manual explains management guidelines and does not have the intent or the force of a contract."

With which argument do you think the federal court agreed? Have you checked your own manual lately?

A Manual as a Contract

Often the individual's rights win against employer rights, as in this case where the court ruled on behalf of the plaintiff and against the traditional doctrine of termination at will because without *written agreements* to say differently, this employee manual had given rise to *implied* contract rights that govern laying off people. The company more than failed to follow its own rules. It ignored them and thereby violated the contract established in its own manual.[44]

As in many recent cases, this court reinforces the employees' awareness that common laws of contract protect them from what they see as arbitrary management decisions harmful to themselves, that those laws protect them from wrongful discharge. Many courts, as in this case, have adopted the philosophy of entitlement in the workplace as well as in social and political arenas. Employees as well as employers are entitled to equal protection under the law.

Can Your Disciplinary Procedures Form a Contract?

Peter Strauss had worked as a loan officer for State Bank for a year and half when a routine audit uncovered a number of technical exceptions in its loan portfolio. Without a hearing, he was fired.

In turn, he took the bank to court, claiming that it breached his employment contract by dismissing him without cause and in violation of the bank's prescribed disciplinary procedures. To bolster his case, he cited three provisions of the employee handbook that the bank had adopted and distributed to the employees while Strauss was employed but that it did not follow when it discharged him: performance review, job security, and a four-stage disciplinary action procedure. The first provision said:

> All employees want to know "where they stand." Our performance evaluation program is designed to help you to determine where you are, where you are going, and how to get there. Factual and objective appraisals of you and your work performance should serve as aids to your future advancement.

The second citation, "Job Security," extolled the stability of employment in the banking industry.

Employment in the banking industry is very stable. It does not fluctuate up and down sharply in good times and bad. . . . We have no seasonal layoffs and we never hire a lot of people when business is booming only to release them when things are not as active.

The job security offered by [*State*] Bank is one reason why so many of our employees have five or more years of service. In return for this, management expects job security from you, that is, the security that you will perform the duties of your position with diligence, cooperation, dependability, and a sense of responsibility.

The third provision described a four-stage "disciplinary policy."

In the interest of fairness to all employees, the company establishes reasonable standards of conduct for all employees to follow. . . . [They] are not intended to place unreasonable restrictions on you but are considered necessary for us to conduct our business in an orderly and efficient manner. If an employee has violated a company policy, the following procedure will apply:

1. An oral reprimand by the immediate supervisor for the first offense, with a written notice sent to the executive vice-president
2. A written reprimand for the second offense
3. A written reprimand and a meeting with the executive vice-president and possible suspension from work without pay for five days
4. Discharge from employment for an employee whose conduct does not improve as a result of the previous action taken

State Bank's attorney argued that all three provisions were irrelevant inasmuch as Strauss was employed at will.

A jury awarded Strauss $27,675 in damages for being terminated in breach of contract and without good cause. The bank took its case to the state supreme court.

What has your organization published with respect to performance appraisal, job security, and disciplinary procedures? If it lost a case before a jury, how could your state supreme court possibly rule?

Got 'Em, Follow 'Em.

The Minnesota Supreme Court ruled in favor of the plaintiff on all three counts and provided me with the answers to the three broad questions I discussed in the text: (1) Can an employee handbook become a part of an employment contract? (2) Can job security provisions in an employee handbook be enforced? (3) Can a summary dismissal, as in this case, breach an employment contract? The court answered yes to all three.[16]

First, personnel handbook provisions can form a *unilateral contract* and may therefore become enforceable as an employment contract if they are distributed to the general population of employees, or if they are used for any purpose other than as a guide for supervisors, or if they are not delimited in some manner (e.g., with a disclaimer).

Second, phrases such as "career situation" and "job security" might not form the basis of a contract, but job security provisions in an employee handbook, disseminated to all the employees, can be so construed. The job security provisions in the employment contract would then override a terminable-at-will construction of the contract.

Third, a disciplinary policy is binding when it contains sufficiently *definite language* to form an offer of a *unilateral contract* promising that certain procedures will be followed before an employee is discharged. The phrase "If an employee has violated a company policy, the following procedure will apply" is definite language in this case.

Cases

1. 707 F.2d 1274, 32 F.E.P. Cases (BNA) 142 (11th Cir. 1983).
2. 99 Lab. Cas. (CCH) Section 10,639 (N.W. Ohio 1983).
3. 99 Lab. Cas. (CCH) ¶10,640 (D. Mass. 1983).
4. 122 L.R.R.M. 2344 (E.D. Miss. 1986).
5. Reported in *Resource*, The Journal of the American Society for Personnel Administration, 8:1 (January 1989).

6. (Minn. Sup. Ct. April 29, 1983).
7. 753 F. Supp. 871 (E.D. Va. 1987).

Examples of Employee Manuals as the Basis of Enforceable Contracts

8. No. 84-2554 (1st Dist. Ill. September 15, 1985).
9. 708 P.2d 110 (Ariz. Ct. App. 1985); see also 141 Ariz. 544, 688 P.2d 170 (1984).
10. No. 49592-1 (Wash. Sup. Ct. July 5, 1984).
11. 215 Neb. 677, 340 N.W.2d 388 (Neb. 1983).
12. 672 P.2d 629 (Nev. 1983).
13. No. 84-CA-1508-MR (Ky. Ct. App. April 12, 1985).
14. 486 A.2d 798 (Md. Ct. App. 1985).
15. No. WD 36426 (Mo. Ct. App. April 9, 1985).
16. No. A-98-82 (May 9, 1985).
17. 704 P.2d 702 (Wyo. 1985).
18. 609 F. Supp. 627 (N.D. Ill. 1985).

Cases Upholding a Disclaimer or Other Employee Manual Procedures

19. 100 Lab. Cas. ¶10,793 (Ala. Sup. Ct. 1983).
20. 474 So. 2d 1069 (Ala. 1985).
21. 495 So. 2d 1381 (Ala. 1986).
22. 199 Cal. Rptr. 613 (Cal. App. 2d Dist. 1984).
23. 113 Idaho 581, 746 P.2d 1040 (Idaho App. 1987).
24. 2 I.E.R. Cases 1568 (Ill. App. Ct. 1987).
25. No. 87-1622 (Ill. App. Ct. June 24, 1988).
26. 738 S.W.2d 824 (Ky. Ct. App. 1987).
27. No. 84-824 (La. Ct. App. Dec. 12, 1985).
28. 495 F. Supp. 344 (E.D. Mich. 1980).
29. C.A. No. 81-73233 (E.D. Mich. October 18, 1982).
30. N.W.2d 529 (Mich. App. 1984).
31. No. 71,773 (Mich. Ct. App. Nov. 4, 1985).
32. No. 76,014 (Mich. Ct. App. 1985).
33. 122 L.R.R.M. 2153 (6th Cir. 1986).
34. 417 N.W.2d 496 (Mich. Ct. App. 1987).
35. 413 N.W.2d 146 (Minn. App. 1987).
36. 2 I.E.R. Cases 1799 (Mo. 1988).

37. 220 N.J. Super. Ct. 135, 531 A.2d 757 (N.J. Super. Ct. 1987).
38. 356 S.E.2d 357, 2 I.E.R. Cases 269 (1987).
39. No. 49,770 (Ohio Ct. App. December 5, 1985).
40. 1 I.E.R. 476 (Pa. 1986).
41. 715 S.W.2d 60 (Tex. Ct. App. 1986).
42. 116 L.R.R.M. (BNA) 3092 (Wis. Ct. App. 1984).
43. 354 Pa. Super. 199, 511 A.2d 830, 1 I.E.R. 476 (Pa. 1986).
44. 574 F. Supp. 805 (D. Colo. 1983).

Chapter 12
Public Policy

In Chapter 11 I made a reference to "public policy" without defining or explaining the concept. The reason should now be obvious: Any discussion of firing someone in violation of public policy requires its own chapter.

Giving employees time off for voting or for serving on a jury is the best-known public policy issue, but it represents only the surface of a constantly expanding body of issues. The concept covers every aspect of a citizen's social and political rights and obligations; firing someone in violation of public policy, if the charge is substantiated, is always an exception to termination at will.

It pays, therefore, to define this key term before grappling with the questions regarding what you cannot and can do that the concept raises. You need to see if your organization's policies and practices could, in some way, jeopardize you or the organization itself.

public policy   Laws and resolutions of the state, common law, the state's constitution, judicial decisions, and public morals form public policy and create rights and obligations. Society believes it cannot function effectively without essential social standards, such as honesty in business dealings. To satisfy this social demand, the courts have established the concept of public policy. The matter of violations of public policy ranges far and wide because most states, including those that accept employment-at-will as their theory of management, e.g., Pennsylvania and Illinois, have specific laws protecting a person's rights and always *except* actual violations of public policy.

What You Cannot Do

Sexual-specific violations of public policy deserve special consideration. Managers commit the following "sins" too frequently:

1. *The obvious.* You cannot refuse to give someone time off for voting if the polls are not open during the person's non-working hours. You cannot refuse to give a person time off to answer the call for jury duty. You cannot fire someone for meeting his or her civic obligations. Employers abridge or interfere with voting rights, jury duty, courtroom testimony, and so on, at their own risk, and very few employers today abridge these rights; but, from our definition it is clear that matters of public policy do not stop here. Most cases where someone feels abused for exercising rights preserved or mandated by law relate to more subtle issues: the right to answer a subpoena, the right to file a workers comp claim, the right to refuse to violate a standard of conduct, and so forth.

2. *Fire someone for refusing to violate public morals.* You cannot fire someone who refused to do anything he or she believes is contrary to *public* morals (as distinguished from *personal* morals, which by themselves do not define or form a source of public policy). Values created by social and legal processes determine public morals and can be used to call you to court if you discharge someone who feels wrongfully discharged in violation of public policy.[1]

3. *Fire someone for refusing to violate a law.* You cannot ask someone to violate or conspire to violate a local, state, or federal statute and fire him or her for refusing to do so. It does not matter if the law was actually violated or if the employee can prove conclusively that a law was broken. The employee does not even have to take the complaint to the authorities, which action is also protected under law. The employee need

only show in court that he or she was fired for discussing with management his or her reasonable belief that certain actions are illegal. The firing itself is an instance of wrongful discharge in violation of public policy.[2]

4. *Fire someone for refusing to commit perjury.* You cannot ask someone to lie in court or in a sworn document, or to lie in the normal course of doing business, and fire him or her for refusing to do so.[3] This rule also covers instances in which a statement could possibly be false.[4] A person has a social obligation to refrain from making statements the truth of which is unclear or questionable,[5] and firing him or her for not making them would be retaliatory.

5. *Fire probationary employees if they are fulfilling a legal obligation.* Let's say you have an employee, a woman employee, you have placed on probation for excessive absences and tardiness. You have given her written warning that she will be fired if she misses work during the probationary period. Let's also suppose she receives a subpoena to make deposition in a lawsuit in which she is the defendant. Feeling caught between the proverbial rock and hard place, she answers the subpoena. Can you fire her for being absent during her probationary period?

No, say the courts. You cannot. An employer must give a person time off to make deposition or answer a subpoena regardless of the circumstances.[6] It makes no difference if the request to attend a deposition hearing is oral, delivered by counsel, or under subpoena. The employee's attendance record notwithstanding, the *threat* of the loss of a job because he or she fulfills her legal obligation interferes with the judicial process and injures the public.

6. *Prevent an employee from exercising legal rights.* Asking an employee to sign a waiver of rights, for example, to sign away his or her right to file a workers compensation claim, could be seen as an attempt to deny that employee his or her legal rights. Firing the person after he or she signs the waiver can be seen as an exception to termination at will in violation of public policy.[7]

Managers should be on guard anytime an employee is

entitled to exercise legally protected rights. If a waiver of rights is used, especially if the person cannot read English, advising the employee of the agreement's contents and having him or her acknowledge the explanation could help protect the release's proper wording. Even so, it might not stand up in court. The wisest course of action in a situation such as this is for you or your organization to adhere to the spirit and letter of the law.

This is particularly important in the case of workers compensation because the purpose of such statutes is to provide medical cost protection in the event an employee is injured during the conduct of the employer's business. To infringe on the remedial spirit of the law not only jeopardizes your employees, it also injures your ability to hire and retain employees.

7. *Violate an employee's First Amendment rights.* You cannot fire someone for "whistleblowing," i.e., complaining to authorities about illegal, immoral, or dangerous-to-the-public business practices.[8] Connecticut, for example, has two laws that apply.

The first, the Free Speech Act, enjoins employers from retaliating against someone exercising his or her First Amendment rights:

> [Any] employer . . . who subjects any employee to discipline or discharge on account of the [employee exercising his or her] rights guaranteed in the first amendment of the United States Constitution or section 3, 4, or 14 of article [1] of the [state's] constitution, provided [that] activity does not substantially or materially interfere with the employee's bona fide job performance or the working relationship between the employee and the employer, shall be liable to [the] employee for damages caused by [the] discipline or discharge.

The second law, the Connecticut Whistleblowing Statute, extends the first law to cover whistleblowing:

No employer shall discharge, discipline or otherwise penalize any employee because the employee . . . reports . . . a violation or suspected violation of any state or federal law or regulation or any municipal ordinance or regulation to a public body, or because an employee is requested by a public body to participate in an investigation, hearing, or inquiry held by that public body, or a court action.

The Connecticut District Court gave teeth to these statutes when, in an important case in 1986, it ruled that rather than conflict with each other, one law complements the other.[8] This way, a court could award the plaintiff two different sets of remedies. Under the Whistleblower Statute, relief is limited to reinstatement, back pay, and benefits. The Free Speech Act entitles the aggrieved to collect damages, including punitive damages. Interfering with an employee's guaranteed rights anywhere, not just in Connecticut, could get expensive.

You cannot require someone to lobby on your organization's behalf, and fire him or her for refusing. Because public policy compels employers to recognize society's interest in an employee's freedom of political expression, such action could be seen as interfering with an employee's freedom from discharge because of his or her political beliefs. A person can be a loyal employee even if he or she does not hold the same political opinions as his or her employer does.

In a landmark case,[9] the Third Circuit Court in Pennsylvania weighed an employee's right to political freedom against the employer's right to effectively conduct business by asking these four questions:

a. Did the employee's behavior prevent the employer from fulfilling its responsibilities?
b. Did the employee's behavior prevent him from carrying out his responsibilities?
c. Did the employee's behavior interfere with necessary, close working relationships?
d. Did the employee's behavior occur at a time, in a

manner, and in a place to interfere with the employer's business operations?

If the court had answered any one of those questions in the affirmative, the employee would have lost his case. Because none of them were applicable to his behavior, he won. Before you let anyone go in a situation such as this, make sure you base your decision on rational rather than emotional grounds.

8. *Deny someone due process.* You can fire someone you merely suspect of wrongdoing, but you should not deny him or her due process when you do it. You should give him or her the opportunity to show that he or she did not commit the wrongful act.

Appearances can sometimes deceive. It is dangerous to assume you are in the right when you think someone did harm or injury to your organization. While in many courts around the country employers have won the right to discharge employees suspected of wrongdoing, even though the case against the employee was not proved, in many other courts the failure to extend *due process privileges* to the accused has cost employers the right to terminate for cause.

What You Can Do

When it comes to public policy, your best bet is to understand your limits under local, state, and federal law. What you cannot do translates into what you can do to manage safely within the constraints of public policy.

At the same time, you can protect yourself if you think an employee's actions or failure to act interferes with your business operations. The decision to which I referred earlier (by the Third Circuit Court in Pennsylvania) highlights several important tests of self-defense.[9]

Before even thinking of taking action against someone who has engaged in some arguably protected activity, especially a political activity, consider whether or not *you* have the *protections* you need. Consider:

1. The nature and motive(s) of the employee's conduct
2. The sorts of interests both you and the employee are trying to advance
3. Your countervailing interests against those of the employee
4. How near or close the employee's conduct is to the time and act of interference you allege
5. What in the nature of the particular relationship between you and the employee might lead you to expect the employee to comply with your organization's agendas
6. Society's interest in protecting freedom of belief and action against any contract interests that may exist between you and the employee

Your defense would have to show that the employee intentionally and maliciously acted in a manner to harm your ability to conduct business: that your business interests have greater social and economic value than the employee's personal interests do, that the employee acted adversely on or about the time of the harm, that the employment contract created an expectation of loyalty (including political loyalty), and that society's interests are better met by the organization's agenda than by the employee's. That defense is as tough to create as the sentence describing it is long.

Again, it is in your own interest to pay attention to what the law protects before firing someone for anything other than poor performance or gross misconduct.

Conclusion

The recognition of contract rights comes at the same time employees have learned that they cannot be denied the right to vote, to serve on a jury, apply for workers compensation or unemployment insurance, or attend to other legal matters. They also know they have the right to protest or refuse if they have been asked to violate a law or a standard of social conduct. All such strictures violate the rights granted by the dictates of public policy. But what constitutes public policy?

No matter how morally outraged an employee may be by what the employer requires or does, undesirable personal morals *alone* cannot define or become the source of *public* policy. Rather, public policy is based on common law, the state and federal constitutions, state and federal statutes, judicial decisions, and public morals. Only by looking at values created by those processes can public policy be determined.

Inasmuch as public policy issues vary from state to state and jurisdiction to jurisdiction, no blanket prescriptions can be written for keeping your decisions out of court. There are no guarantees.

Rather, in matters where running up against public policy is possible, give yourself a chance to reflect on your decision before acting on it; perhaps call an attorney before doing something about a decision that seems jeopardized by the judicial tide of the time or place.

CASEBOOK

Most personnel officers can talk knowledgeably about public policy, but few managers can. Their ignorance of the law often puts them at risk and jeopardizes their organizations; and that is why you should read each case carefully and grapple with the question that begins each one.

Compare your decisions with the courts' in the cases. Could you or your organization be jeopardized in some way similar to the one described in the cases? How can you use the court's ruling in a given case to help you or your organization protect or defend yourselves?

Can You Fire Someone for Refusing to Go Along With a Prank?

A camping trip in the Arizona desert with your supervisor and co-workers should be a lot of fun. At least that is what paramedic coordinator Ellen Braun thought until the party began. To her embarrassment everyone was expected to defecate and urinate in public. She was also expected to take part in a skit, a parody of the song "Moon River," that would end with all the performers pulling down their pants and "mooning" the audience, exposing their bare back-sides to the spectators. Braun would not go along with any of that.

Before the camping trip, so the plaintiff claimed, she had received consistently favorable performance appraisals. Afterward, her supervisor regularly criticized her performance and attitude. The relationship between the paramedic coordinator and the supervisor deteriorated, culminating in Braun's discharge.

The aggrieved claimed retaliatory discharge. The hospital countered with charges of a lack of cooperation and poor performance.

Assuming that such a skit is acceptable, how would you react if an employee refused to go along with it? With whom do you think the court sided?

No Laughing Matter

This case seems trivial and extreme, but because it carried all the way to the Arizona Supreme Court it helps clarify the meaning of the public policy exception to termination at will that I described in the beginning of this chapter. Its importance, therefore, cannot be emphasized enough.

The court ruled that the employee should not have been fired; the supervisor's actions *were* punitive and retaliatory. Firing someone who refuses to engage in a prank he or she thinks is contrary to *public morals,* as well as contrary to his or her own, may violate public policy and form the predicate for a wrongful discharge lawsuit.[1]

While individual cases or violations of public policy may differ, the general rules for application created by the Arizona Supreme Court seem essentially the same for all courts in all states. The court agreed that in one sense the incident was trivial (people at play), but in a larger sense, it was quite serious. As Braun claimed, the act of "mooning" itself could be considered a violation of the criminal code: Exposing one's anus or genitals is contrary to public standards of morality. Firing the plaintiff for refusing to "moon" the audience therefore violates public policy.

So people at play turned into a major court case. One person's fun can turn out to be another's discomfort and the source of everyone's great misery. Managers have to take care that pranks do not get out of hand, and if they do, take care of how people who do not want to join in on the "fun" are handled.

That does not mean that every disagreement leads to a violation of public policy. Another case underscores the importance of *public* perceptions of right and wrong.

In this instance, the court found that an employee, fired for complaining about his employer's mismanagement, had the right to disagree with management's decisions, but management also had the equal right to fire him. Even if the employee was right to be offended by poor management, the court said, the employer violated no matter of public policy; *the conflict was over personal values*, not over public morals, conscience, or policies.[10]

Can You Fire Someone for Refusing to Violate a Law

"The plan may not be legal," Eric Freedman complained to his CEO. "The methods are definitely not generally accepted accounting procedures, and they may violate federal securities law."

The company's stony-faced president mulled over the problem before answering his chief financial officer. "Just restate some accounts. Discount the purchase of production equipment as income and restate the African safari accounts to bring things back into line."

"I'm sorry, Gene. That won't work. It overstates income and inflates asset valuation, which, in my opinion, violates federal law."

"We need team players here, Eric. You should know that."

Freedman steadfastly refused to accept the accounting procedures the company finally used. In response to his complaints to management, he was fired.

In court, when Freedman sued Worldwide Publishing for wrongful discharge in violation of public policy, the company's attorney argued that *state* law does not mandate a set of accounting procedures; therefore, public policy is not at issue here. Additionally, no one ever proved that their procedures violated any laws. In accordance with the company's termination-at-will policies, they fired Freedman for not complying with the company's wishes.

What do you think? Do you think the company has a case? Do you think your organization would fire a senior vice-president for complaining internally about accounting procedures?

No Gaps in GAAP

Your company might not have fired Freedman, but the one for whom the plaintiff worked did, and the Illinois Court of Appeals, Fifth District, took it to task.[2] Basing its judgment partially on an earlier Illinois decision,[11] the court ruled that not just state statutes apply to the principle of public policy. Federal laws duly enacted in Congress, national in scope, mandate public policy in all the states.

Federal law mandates the use of GAAP (generally accepted accounting principles). Therefore, asking the finance officer to accept deviations from GAAP amounted to asking him *to conspire to violate a federal law as well as accepted social standards.* Firing him for protesting unaccepted standards violated public policy with regard to reporting practices: full disclosure, truthfulness, and accuracy in the financial reports made to governments. In making this decision, the Illinois court applied federal law to issues of public policy in the states.

This decision is one of several that demonstrate that taking refuge behind the doctrine of employment at will does not always work. Both the violation of public policy and the promise not to discharge an employee without cause constitute exceptions to the doctrine.

The moral of this story might be, if you are going to violate the law yourself, do not try to drag anyone along with you or fire him or her for not cooperating. You will be hit twice, once for breaking the law in the first place and second for firing someone for not helping you do it.

How about your organization? What safeguards prevent a manager from ever asking someone to commit a possible felony?

Can You Fire Someone for Refusing to Possibly Defame Someone Else?

Frank Sullivan was fired. When he applied for unemployment insurance, Ed Polanski, a supervisor, refused to sign upper management's statement describing the reasons for dismissal. He claimed the report was untrue, falsely accusing Sullivan of poor work habits and immoral behavior. Without Polanski's signature, management could not file its counterclaim; they fired the supervisor as well.

But Polanski went to court, arguing that his discharge was retaliatory and is the same as cases in which an employee is fired for refusing to commit perjury or for refusing to alter OSHA or EPA (Environmental Protection Agency) reports. His attorney also used the argument that accepted standards of social conduct and public policy require honesty in business relationships and the employer fired the supervisor for his honesty.

The company defended itself by claiming that the truth or falsity of the statement was a factual question that management resolved internally. It was Polanski's opinion against theirs. They had good cause to fire him: insubordination.

How would your organization handle this type of situation? Who do you think won after a long, difficult fight?

Honesty the Best Policy

Here's the question: Is refusing to make a *possibly* false statement protected by public policy?

A jury said it is and awarded the plaintiff damages. But the appeals court reversed, ruling that even though public policy favors honesty in business, refusing to sign the report on the basis of one's personal opinion of what constitutes honesty or dishonesty is not protected. The report's honesty is a factual matter that was settled. An exception would undermine the doctrine of termination at will.

Furthermore, the opinion said, this case does not resemble wrongful discharge claims in which someone is to asked to commit purgery. *Statutes* protect such instances, but no statute protects honesty per se. Damages need not be paid.[4]

Not so, answered the Oregon Supreme Court in a decision one year later. Pay the plaintiff damages. Oregon *case law* protects him from being discharged because he refused to sign a report that is *arguably defamatory*. Given the nature of the allegations against his colleague's work habits and moral conduct, the plaintiff had a social obligation not to defame him.

Public policy *is* violated by discharging someone on that ground.[5]

The debate between the courts in this case shows how significant the issue is and how dependent upon definitions court rulings can be. The Oregon Supreme Court's decision further extends the meaning of public policy by calling upon social obligations instead of laws against purgery. The decision seems to say, "Honesty in business is merely good business, for both employers and society. Why compound dishonesty in doing business with wrongfully discharging someone for refusing to be dishonest?"

Does a Signed Waiver of Workers Comp Rights Protect You If You Fire the Person?

Jack Berkowitz, an Eastern European immigrant, hurt himself on the job badly enough to require hospitalization and time off. Not even the doctors were sure he would be able to return to the job he had. After his employer, Handicraft Industries, had him sign a severance agreement in which he waived all his rights, including the right to file a workers comp claim, he was fired.

A year later Berkowitz filed the workers comp claim. When the company fought back, he went to court stating that his firing was retaliatory in violation of public policy, designed to prevent him from filing his claim.

In response, the company waved the signed severance waiver and asked for a summary dismissal of the case.

Berkowitz's attorney responded that since the immigrant could not read or write English, some manager or another was obligated to read and explain the document to him, which no one had done.

What do you think? Should this case go to trial? Would your organization do something to prevent an employee from filing a bona fide workers comp claim? Under what conditions?

Make It Clear

A waiver of rights, such as the one contained in the severance agreement, may not head off a retaliatory discharge lawsuit (especially if the employee does not understand the terms of the agreement).

The Illinois Appellate Court in this 1985 case said, "Go to trial." The allegations were sufficient to create factual questions about the employer's intent. The court pointed out that the employee need not show that he, in fact, had filed a claim. He need merely show that he was fired to *prevent* him from exercising his legally guaranteed rights. If the employee did not understand he was signing a waiver that jeopardized his rights, and the employer knew the man could not read or write, the waiver could appear to have been an intentional ploy to have the man relinquish his right.[7]

When it comes to an employee's legal rights, beware any attempt to interfere. If you are not sure of where you stand, check it out with an attorney. The time and expense of safe management shrinks in the face of a possible lawsuit.

Can You Fire Someone for Refusing to Reimburse Your Organization for a Work-Related Loss?

When an allegedly stolen payroll check showed up in the Community Credit Union's statements, it bore an apparently forged endorsement. Diana Bonds, a teller, cashed the check, and for that, without having an opportunity to explain how she came to do it, she was told to reimburse the credit union for the loss. When she refused to do so, management discharged her.

Her attorney complained in court that the discharge violated Section 103.455 of the Wisconsin statutes, which prescribes procedures for imposing the burden of paying for a work-related loss on an employee accused of causing the loss. Under this law, the accused must be given the opportunity to show that the loss was not his or her fault. Community Credit Union failed to follow those statutorily prescribed procedures, the suit alleged.

The employer retorted that the cashing of a fraudulently endorsed payroll check falls outside the purview of the law cited. The possible felony justifies immediate dismissal.

What do you think? Was immediate dismissal justified? Is that how your organization would handle this sort of situation?

Due Process

The Wisconsin Supreme Court did not think that immediate dismissal was justified. It agreed that the statute did not expressly prohibit firing someone in this sort of situation, but that was beside the point. Rather, firing the employee contravened the public policy embodied in the legislation.

According to the court, the law's main purpose is to avoid coercing an employee to carry the full burden of a work-related loss without due process, which includes the opportunity to show that he or she did not cause the loss either through carelessness, negligence, or willful misconduct.[12]

What Can You Do If Someone Tells the Painful Truth?

Kristine Shultz responded to a subpoena in a co-worker's insurance claim against Health Care Associates, their employer, and told the truth. Her testimony helped the co-worker win the case.

Her employer, seeing her testimony as an act of disloyalty, went as far as saying, "Maybe you should seek other employment because you testified against us." That's what Kristine alleged in court after quitting.

To Kristine's attorney's charge that his client was forced out, the employer answered that she quit voluntarily.

How would you react to Kristine's testimony. Would you have fired her? Whose side do you think the court took?

To Tell the Truth

You can find yourself in the same deep trouble that the employer brought on itself if you fire someone in violation of some aspect of public policy. The court ruled that the employer forced the plaintiff to quit by telling her to find employment elsewhere because she fulfilled her obligation to testify honestly when subpoenaed to do so. Continued employment there would only have led to intolerable conditions for her. For the court, this was a case of both *constructive discharge* and a violation of *public policy*.[13]

Cases

1. No. 17646-PR (Ariz. Sup. Ct. 1985) (en banc).
2. 101 Ill. Dec. 251, 498 N.E.2d 575 (Ill. App. Ct. 5th Dist. 1986).
3. 328 S.E.2d 818 (N.C. Ct. App. 1985).
4. 670 P.2d (Or. Ct. App. 1983).
5. 681 P.2d 114 (Or. Sup. Ct. 1984).
6. 2 I.E.R. Cases 589 (Mo. Ct. App. 1987).
7. 478 N.E.2d 1039 (Ill. App. Ct. 1985).
8. 105 Lab. Cas. ¶55.608 (D. Conn. 1986).
9. No. 83-5101 (3d Cir. October 26, 1983).
10. 489 A.2d 828 (Pa. Super. Ct. 1985).
11. 108 Ill. 2d 502, 92 Ill. Dec. 561, 485 N.E.2d 372 (1985), *cert. denied*, 106 S. Ct. 1641 (1986).
12. 104 Lab. Cas. ¶55,555 (Wis. 1986).
13. 620 F. Supp. 1268, 120 L.R.R.M. (BNA) 3233 (D. Kan. 1985).

Chapter 13

Safe Management of Older Employees

Americans used to look up to and, in some cases, revere the elderly. Ironically, today, when longevity has become more the rule than the exception, young people often think of the older generation as economic obstacles. Resentment then expresses itself in forms of prejudice usually associated with racism: discrimination in hiring, promotion, firing. Older employees are harassed, belittled, mistreated in the workplace rather than sought out for their experience, skills, and wisdom. "Move over, old person. Make way for younger blood."[1]

So we need special interest laws such as the Age Discrimination in Employment Act (ADEA) to protect our aging but still productive workers. That is also why you need to consider how to prevent *ageism* when you make personnel decisions, especially when laying off employees during a reorganization or downsizing effort. First, let's see what the law says it protects before I look at what you cannot and can do.

What the Law Says

If you wish to read a summary of the law's provisions, turn to the Appendix. I can sum up the statute as it pertains to this chapter by saying that since the law intends to promote the employment of older persons, to prohibit age discrimination in employment, and to help employers and workers find ways of meeting problems arising from the impact of age on employment, it protects all persons aged 40 years or older. As do other EEO laws, this one requires you to make employment opportunities available to its protected group, and it prevents you from otherwise discriminating against any person over 40 with respect to compensation, terms, conditions, or privileges of employment merely because of age. The terms "otherwise discriminate" means that you cannot use age as a basic consideration for discharging someone or forcing someone to retire.

If you do fire, lay off, or otherwise discriminate against employees aged 40 or over, tuck this fact into the back of your mind: They have the incentive to fight back. ADEA provides it by awarding significant damages if the aggrieved can prove age discrimination: *double* the amount of pay *and benefits* an employee *would have* earned between the time he or she was turned out and the time the court decides in his or her favor. ADEA also permits jury trials, and juries tend to allow the older person's age to work to his or her advantage. The very reason you might let him or her go becomes the motive for ruling against you.

What You Cannot Do

You cannot fire or lay off older employees as freely as you might wish. The law makes that abundantly clear. And ways around it can be easily blocked, mainly because length of service, higher salaries, and age usually go hand in hand. If high salaries, seniority, or tenure enter into your employment decisions (e.g., demotions or layoffs), you run the risk of discriminating against employees on the basis of age; any additional reasons you invoke can be judged to be "pretextual," especially if the employees involved have had long records of unimpeachable service.[2,3]

As in other forms of discrimination, beware retaliatory motives. Harassment, building a case against an employee, or otherwise making his or her working conditions intolerable after he or she threatens to or has brought action against you for age discrimination can provide your employee with a "smoking gun."[4] What you say or do to an older employee can, and probably will, be used against you in a court of law or before the EEOC.[5]

The EEOC often considers seemingly innocuous statements as evidence of age harassment: "more accident prone than younger employees," "unable to learn new tasks because he or she is too old," "less efficient than younger employees." Making older employees the butt of jokes or barbs because of their age, poor health, or other medical problems, while younger employees' illnesses are overlooked, are more shots from the gun. Other forms of evidence include:

- Identifying performance problems only after an employee reaches a certain age, e.g., 65
- Suggesting that an employee sign up for Social Security or take early retirement
- Expressing concerns about the cost of health benefits of older employees
- Taking action against older employees with supposedly poor performance records (e.g., demoting or discharging them), but not taking similar action against younger employees with as bad or worse records
- Basing personnel decisions on "employee potential," i.e., that the older employees do not have the career or income-generating possibilities that younger employees do
- Placing unreasonable standards on older employees that make it difficult or impossible to meet the demands placed on them[6-10]

Safe management demands that managers handle work-related matters or act on the basis of legitimate business interests in a timely and reasonable manner. Arbitrarily replacing a member of a protected group, in this case an older employee, by a member of a nonprotected group, a younger employee, can open up an organization to a lawsuit. ("Arbitrary replacement" means the lack of a sound business reason for taking the action.) Offhand remarks about older employees and "new blood" policies can be used as evidence of discrimination. The facts underlying an action determine the value of that action.[11]

The courts want facts and documentation. For example, ADEA provides employers with an exemption for bona fide employee benefit plans in which the employer is not required to provide identical benefits to all employees regardless of age. The law requires only that the employer *spend* equally on all employees, but the exemption is limited to achieving *equivalency* in the cost of providing benefits to younger and older workers alike. To take advantage of the exemption, an employer must demonstrate that the nature and extent of the cost savings realized by specific reductions in its benefit plan merely *balanced costs*.[12]

The ability to balance the needs of the organization against the needs of its employees provides one mark of effective management. Particularly, the way in which management handles layoffs, an ever-present fact of contemporary economic life, to prevent an adverse impact on a protected group (especially on people over the age of 40) separates effective managers from those who are likely to wind up in court.

Demoting Older Employees to Save Money

You cannot reduce your costs at the expense of older employees' salaries. Older employees usually enjoy the seniority and higher compensation scales that tempt managers to manipulate those earnings in order to cut corners. However, do not count on the demoted employees or the courts agreeing with you.[13,14]

Using a Reorganization as an Excuse

You cannot vindicate laying off older employees on the basis of a need to reorganize, as long as they are the only target of the reorganization. Additionally, if your organization must downsize or shift people around, take care that neither you nor your fellow managers shoot yourselves in the foot by discussing the "reorg" in discriminatory terms, e.g., "can't adapt to change" or "need a few good, young people."[15]

What You Can Do

Once more it seems your hands are tied. But that is not true. You can demote or fire employees if they merit it, regardless of their age, but you must guarantee that your actions are bona fide and legitimate by keeping records of poor performance, written warnings, and so on.[16]

Implementing Reductions in Force

You can downsize if financial difficulties require it. However, be sure that the decision makers have as much distance as possible and are insulated from the people about whom they are making the layoff decisions. Lower-level managers can recommend people to lay off, but they must base their recommendations on business-related factors only.[17,18]

Making Legitimate Business Decisions

Follow these six commonsense rules to guide what you can do when managing older employees, especially if you have to make tough demotion or firing decisions:

1. *When managing anyone, keep detailed records of all disciplinary actions.* In the event that an older employee feels mistreated because of age, your documentation of a history of performance problems is your best defense.[19] "Building a file" is clearly a case of too little too late.[20]

And keep your records until the statute of limitations runs out (or longer): two to three years from a firm date of termination. Failure to identify a firm date or to maintain production or other records could work against you and your organization.[21,22]

2. *Offer older workers the same counseling or training opportunities you offer younger employees.* You sure can teach older people new tricks. Most of them have the education, training, or experience necessary for transferring old skills to new jobs, and they should be allowed the opportunity to try. Especially

if you are faced with a reduction in force (RIF) or job discontinuance, consider other alternatives for your employees with the greatest amount of seniority before letting them go. A layoff based on seniority is not solid grounds if the older employees are capable of performing other jobs or learning how to do them.[23]

At the same time, you are not *obligated* to retrain or relocate an employee whose job is eliminated due to a RIF if to do so would create an unacceptable burden for you, the employer. If retraining or relocation would cost more than your organization can reasonably afford or if no other positions exist and would have to be created, you can justify your decision. Again, the issue becomes a matter of "legitimate business reason."[24-26]

3. *Prevent harassment on the basis of age.* If you are in a policy-making position and your organization does not have an antiharassment policy, create one. Use the guidelines in Chapters 2 and 8. And train your managers to prevent harassment on the basis of age, just as you would train them to prevent harassment on the basis of sex, race, disability, or veteran's status. Calling people "old and overpaid" is not only unfair and cruel, it can also be used as evidence against you if an older employee quits and sues for constructive discharge or if you fire him or her for some other reason. Your comments *condition* the discharge.[27]

4. *Help protect older employees during a RIF or other cost-cutting actions.* Even if you do not make the layoff decisions, give careful consideration to whom you recommend for demoting or cutting and how you execute the decisions. Listing employees' ages and years of service could be used as direct evidence of age discrimination.[28] Using a proportionate classification system in which you lay off and also retain a proportionate representation of women, minorities, and employees over age 40 could be seen as a pretextual scheme rather than an affirmative action plan.[29] Such a plan could also pose a problem in states, e.g., New York, that prohibit discrimination against young workers. However, you can use other methods for making your layoff decisions that could hold up in court. Check with your attorney.

Offering early retirement, based on an existing pension plan, to people who want to take advantage of it is acceptable as long as the following are true:

- No other avenues for cost saving are available.
- Employees are not pressured or coerced into accepting it or being fired.
- The employees are given sufficient time to study and accept or reject the offer.
- The employees are given sufficient and proper counseling as to the terms of the offer.
- Exceptions are based on bona fide business reasons, e.g., essential employees or employees covered by a collective bargaining agreement that you cannot unilaterally alter.
- Criteria for eligibility are clearly spelled out and do not discriminate against the older retirees in favor of the younger ones.[30-33]

I cannot overemphasize the need for rational, legitimate business reasons for taking cost-cutting actions that adversely affect older employees. Time and again the courts have ruled that if an employer eliminates an employee's job for legitimate business reasons, it is not obligated to create or locate another job for the employee. ADEA does not demand that heavy obligation, even if the organization has an informal policy that offers that assistance.[34] Should the appearance of discrimination lead you into court, the documentation of nondiscriminatory reasons can lead you safely out of court as well.[35]

5. *Ask employees taking early retirement to sign a release in which they acknowledge having read and understood the terms of the agreement, having received sufficient time and counseling for making a reasoned decision, and having voluntarily accepted or rejected the offer of early retirement.*[36] A release is *useful* in the event you are challenged in court, but it is not a surefire defense. Your release should clarify all the terms of the plan, explain realistically the consequences of signing the release, leave open the opportunity to negotiate the terms and conditions of the plan, and make it clear that coercion was not used

(that acceptance was voluntary). Compare the two *actual* release statements shown in Figures 12-1 and 12-2 and decide which one survived the court challenge.

Legal language or not, Release 1 cannot bind the terms of the retirement package the company offered its employees. Vague and ambiguous, the document falls far short of binding language. Release 2 holds its own not because it is more complicated but rather because it is more thorough.

The first paragraph in Release 2 dates the document, clarifies its purpose, and signals that its signing is voluntary: "The Employer and Employee mutually desire to enter into this Agreement whereby the Employee voluntarily elects. . . ." It indicates that a bona fide and established pension plan exists: "early retirement under the Employer's retirement plan." This paragraph also refers to a valuable consideration, an essential ingredient for binding any contract, when it says "in consideration of an additional sum of money, specified in paragraph 2, below."

The release specifies an effective date from which tolling begins (two to three years). It also names the plan to which the first paragraph refers, Pension Program for Nonunion Employees, and binds the retirement allowance to the terms of the program. It specifies the consideration given in return for signing the release before asking the signer to release and discharge the company et al. from any and all claims arising under the laws pertinent to such causes: Title VII of the Civil Rights Act of 1964 and the Age Discrimination in Employment Act. The last paragraph then affirms that the "Employee has read this Agreement, understands its terms and the release in

Figure 12-1. Release statement 1.

In consideration of the foregoing, you, [*employee name*], hereby release [*company name*] and all of its subsidiaries, divisions, and related corporations from any and all actions, causes of action, claims, and demands, whatsoever, which you, your heirs, executors, or administrators ever had, now have, or may have against such entities by reason of any matter, course, or thing whatsoever.[37]

Figure 12-2.   Release statement 2.

SPECIAL EARLY RETIREMENT INCENTIVE PROGRAM AGREEMENT

This Agreement is entered into this ____day of _____,
19____ between [*company name*] ("the Employer") and [*employee name*] ("the Employee"). The Employer and the Employee mutually desire to enter into this Agreement whereby the Employee voluntarily elects early retirement under the Employer's retirement plan in consideration of an additional sum of money, specified in paragraph 2, below.

1. The Employee's retirement will become effective on _____,
    19__. The Employee will thereafter receive his or her monthly retirement allowance as provided in the Pension Program for Nonunion Employees.
2. In addition to the monthly retirement allowance described in paragraph 1, above, the Employee will receive $_____ in one lump-sum payment.
3. The Employee releases and discharges [*company name*], its officers, agents, and successors, from any and all claims arising under Title VII of the Civil Rights Act of 1964, as amended, 42 U.S.C. 2000e *et seq.*, The Age Discrimination in Employment Act, 29 U.S.C. §621 *et seq.* [*and any relevant state law*].
4. The Employee has read this Agreement, understands its terms and the release in it, and voluntarily accepts its provisions.[36]

---

it, . . ." and it reaffirms that the employee "voluntarily accepts its provisions."

Measure any similar document your organization has used or is considering using against the standards set by the successful Release 2. If it lacks any of the terms we identified, it too will fail in court.

Should an employee threaten to sue no matter what efforts were made to help or protect him or her, an early settlement out of court may be a more humane as well as less expensive tactic. Do not forget that the employee, not you, has the incentive to fight. However, if you or your organization believe that you are in the right, take whatever action you deem appropriate. Do not forget our constant warning: Before doing anything, consult an attorney.

6. *Communicate clearly but cautiously with all your organization's constituencies.* Everyone with a need to know, that is, everyone who will be affected by cost cutting, reorganization, or downsizing (officers, board members, employees), should know what is happening. Communications should include the organization's economic condition and the steps being taken to improve it or to do away with the organization or some part thereof. However, be careful that when you produce communiqués, you do not trigger another smoking gun by using discriminatory language or by penetrating the insulation that protects the top management decision makers (which I will talk about in the Casebook).

Conclusion

It is not only in society's best interest to hire, train, and promote all possible workers regardless of sex, race, national origin, creed, or *age*. It is also in your best interest as a manager.

Isaac Newton, when writing about his discovery of the universal laws of gravity, refused to take credit for his own genius. Instead, he gave credit to those geniuses who came before him. "I stood," he said, "on the shoulders of giants." Your older employees, because of their years of training and experience, are the giants on whose shoulders you stand.

CASEBOOK

Employees are getting older. That is not just a mindless truism about the average age of employees. It is, rather, a warning.

By the end of the century, all the "baby boomers" will have crossed 40, most of them well into their fifties, and most of them will be "plateaued" (i.e., will have reached the highest level in the organization they can). At the same time, they will be healthy, energetic, and productive. You may be one of them. How will your managers and your organization treat you?

Study these cases and see how prepared your organization is for safely managing a graying work force. Consider the issues that surface from the point of view of what you yourself are doing and what will happen in the future with respect to how older employees are treated.

Can You Save Money by Demoting Employees?

Milt Jonah lost his supervisory position and was demoted to lead worker just after his fifty-third birthday. He was still smarting from the news when he found out he was being replaced by someone 40 years old. "They demoted me just to save money," he told the court. "They're going to close the plant in a few years, and they'd have to pay me more separation pay than they will my younger replacement. Our seniority plan requires it. To prove it, I found out that when they made the decision to demote me, they called in a benefits expert who reviewed who would get what when the closing came."

The company responded that money saving was an issue, but still, because Jonah was the least experienced supervisor in the group and had poor performance evaluations, they had a reasonable and legitimate business reason for demoting him.

If faced with a closing, how would your organization go about reducing costs? What are some of the issues it would consider?

Pretext

If the plaintiff had received such poor reviews in the past, why did the organization take until now to do something about it? That's the question asked by the courts. The evidence linked the demotion to save money to age discrimination, because the saving of money purportedly stemmed directly from the supervisor's greater seniority.[13]

An employee is not required to take a demotion to satisfy

a company cost-saving plan. If an employee quits under those circumstances, he or she could also charge constructive discharge, that is, making or allowing the employee's work conditions to become so intolerable that he or she has no choice but to quit.[14]

Yet your hands are not entirely tied if you can demonstrate that the demoted or fired employee merited that treatment, e.g., through poor productivity records, written warnings, and so on.[16] Just be sure that any personnel decision you make, especially if you plan to demote an older employee, can be backed by valid business reasons.

Does Your Need to Reorganize Vindicate You?

In 1971 a major consumer goods company found its 50 percent decline in sales sufficient reason to cut costs by making a substantial structural reorganization and firing a large number of executive employees within a relatively short time span: more than 100 employees between 1971 and 1973. It just so happened that most of the laid-off employees were older than 40.

The company argued that nondiscriminatory business reasons justified its actions: Key accounts had not been called upon, some managers had not worked with their salespeople for several years, no new methods had been adopted for ten years or more, and the managers did not even know their business had been falling off. Age had nothing to do with the decisions.

What criteria would your organization use for identifying people for discharge?

Loose Lips and Pink Slips

Without a doubt, the company had pressing needs for a "drastic reorganization" and had indeed considered factors other than age in making its firing decisions. However, age was one determining factor in choosing which particular employees to discharge. How did the court come to this conclusion *ten years later?*

Company pay recommendations and discharge reports

made too many offhand comments and age-related statements. Some had less than obvious relationships to age, but implied them nevertheless: "unable to conform to the new [company] philosophy," "inability to adapt to change. . . . [or] to the new configuration." Others made blatant references to age: "really good young man," "outstanding young buyer." If you couple those statements with the fact that a vast majority of sales reps hired during the reorganization were in their twenties while the majority discharged were older people, you do not need the wisdom of a judge to draw the conclusion that the company intended to discriminate on the basis of age.[15]

If you are in charge and your motives are pure, under some circumstances someone else's loose lips could sink your ship.

Who Should Make the Decisions?

When ten older employees of Sangrita, Inc., found themselves suddenly in the streets and replaced by younger employees, they wasted no time in taking their former employer to court. Because they had all received performance ratings of satisfactory or better throughout their tenure with Sangrita, the only reason they could find for their dismissal was age.

No, the company retorted. It was just a matter of money. The reduction in force was necessitated by financial difficulty. Upper management, where the final cutback decisions were made, had never made discriminatory remarks, even though the supervisors, who had submitted the names, had.

The plaintiffs alleged that the people who headed up the division in which the plaintiffs worked—the plant's general manager, Steve Rowan, and his direct report, Dan Horton (the director of the data system division)—influenced the company to terminate older employees by repeatedly making age-related references, e.g., "older employees," "older farts," and "old bastards." At one meeting, Rowan commented on his surprise that so many of the "old guard" and "old faces" were still around and that he would "like to see new blood or new ideas." At yet another meeting, Rowan allegedly told an employee, "Bob, you've been with the company a long time. You're too old to go any further. It's my policy that I'm going to make room for younger men."

The employees used that evidence to argue that, in spite of the fact that neither Rowan nor Horton was directly involved in the decisions concerning whom to lay off, the name-calling and other remarks created a bias against older employees.

How do you feel about older employees? If you think you would like to replace them, could your feelings be held against you and your organization's decision makers? If you are the decision maker, could your direct reports get you in trouble with your older employees?

Insulating the Decision Maker

Best leave layoff decisions to people far removed from the employees directly affected. That is how Sangrita, Inc., defeated the claims against it.

According to the courts in the case, the comments made by Rowan and Horton could not be considered direct or substantial evidence, not even circumstantial evidence, of discrimination on the basis of age. Their positions of authority notwithstanding, they did not have the complete authority to lay off employees in the reduction in force without approval from top management. The list they submitted was sent to the headquarters office, in a different location, and reviewed by upper management, which then made the final decisions. The court could find no connection between the biased remarks and the layoff decisions.[17, 18]

In its opinion, the court emphasized that to show age discrimination a plaintiff must draw a connection between what was said and an adverse action taken against him or her. To make that showing, the age-related comments or statements have to come from someone *directly responsible for the dismissal decision.* That another person in the chain of command makes biased remarks or statements is not sufficient evidence to conclude that the decision was the result of that person's bias.

In this case, the decision makers were insulated from the charge of age bias. But do not think that you can always hide behind that kind of insulation.

In the previous case, it seemed that distance made the managers safe, that defense may not always work.

Can Your Decisions Hide Behind Other Managers' Biases?

When Max Bowman, age 61, was laid off from the TV station where he worked, he charged management with age discrimination, even though he could not attribute age-biased remarks to anyone making the decisions. Instead, he could claim only that one of his own managers, the one who signed his "pink slip," had made the biased statements.

The trial court dismissed the case, emphasizing that it does not matter who implements the firing decision; what is important is who makes the decision. In this case, even though higher management consulted with the biased manager, the higher-level managers made the final decision on strictly business-related grounds.

Bowman appealed to the Seventh Circuit Court, where he showed that younger employees were transferred to other positions while he was let go even though he volunteered to work in another capacity. In response to his request for a transfer, his exit interviewer told him that the news bureau had grown too complex for him to handle another job and that a hiring freeze precluded using him in some other capacity. Younger employees were more favorably treated than he was; therefore, age was a determining factor in the decision that affected him adversely.

The company disagreed. The station's ratings were third among the major network stations in the community. Each department was reviewed (1) to improve the ratings and (2) to eliminate overstaffing. Fifteen vacant positions were eliminated, and a few months later the entire news bureau was closed, leaving Bowman without a job. The discharge decision, the company concluded, arose from its efforts to achieve a leaner, more efficient company.

Why would you or your organization lay off any specific employee? Have you considered the implications of such reasons?

The Value of Silence

That the TV station's upper management did not make biased remarks made no difference. The Seventh Circuit Court ruled that the triable issues concerned whether the plaintiff's age was a factor in the decision to lay off that specific employee rather than consider him for other available positions for which he was qualified.[38]

The station may have had economic reasons for its decision, but at the time management discharged the plaintiff two vacancies in the newsroom existed for which he was qualified. They were later filled by younger people. Additionally, management's hiring freeze was subject to considerable, rather than absolute, discretion. Although over fifteen jobs were eliminated after they became vacant, fifteen people between the ages of 34 and 44 were hired within a year to fill yet other vacancies. The court agreed with Bowman; the TV station's cost-cutting actions were selective and had more of an adverse impact on him than on younger employees.

Consider two points: The TV station had legitimate business reasons for a cutback, yet the court ruled against it. Why? Because management could not answer the question "Why wasn't the older employee retained in an alternative position, as were some of the younger employees?" The managers should have considered other available positions into which they could have transferred the protected employee.

Especially if you allow younger (nonprotected) employees to transfer or offer them the opportunity to transfer to or assume another available position, you must consider the older (protected) employee as well. *Offering* the older employee the opportunity, even if it happens to be lower-paying (in some cases), will prevent the assumption that he or she does not want to accept it. In this case, it was age protection, but the same applies to issues such as race, sex, disability, or veteran's status.

If the employee turns down the offer, then you should document the fact that you offered a choice but the employee rejected it. If you do not do this, the employee can come back and claim that he or she would have taken the alternative if it had been offered.

The second point underscores the issue raised at the start of this discussion: What you say can strip away the decision maker's insulation. Regardless of who makes discriminatory remarks or comments and who makes the layoff decision, if the remarks or comments *follow* the discharge decision, it can be presumed that whoever makes the remarks or comments *has been authorized* to make them. This court decision means that if your CEO makes the discharge decision and you execute it, if you make a discriminatory remark, e.g., "You probably could not learn the new technology," during the exit interview, your CEO could be held liable for age discrimination. This is only one chip in the armor of insulation; others are likely to follow.

Insulation works two ways: Federal laws also insulate most older employees, and most states have statutes as well. The Vermont Supreme Court, before the state had a law prohibiting discrimination on the basis of age, invoked public policy in a wrongful discharge suit when an efficiency consultant recommended that a company change its "retirement home image" by hiring "young go-getters." On the basis of that advice, the company fired several older employees and defended itself on the grounds that the state lacked a legal barrier to the decision.

The Vermont Supreme Court answered that the absence of statutes against discrimination does not imply the license to discriminate. Instead, there exists a clear and compelling public policy against age discrimination. An employee can sue for wrongful discharge in violation of public policy.[39] This decision therefore suggests that antidiscrimination statutes codify and acknowledge what is best for society.

Cases

1. 772 F.2d 799, 39 F.E.P. Cases (BNA) 14 (11th Cir. 1985).
2. 702 F.2d 686, 31 F.E.P. Cases (BNA) 376 (8th Cir. 1983).
3. 46 F.E.P. Cases (BNA) 519 (S.D.N.Y. 1987).
4. 822 F.2d 1249, 44 F.E.P. Cases (BNA) 268 (2d Cir. 1987).
5. 710 F.2d 76, 33 F.E.P. Cases (BNA) 977 (2d Cir. 1983).
6. 643 F. Supp. 779, 42 F.E.P. Cases (BNA) 1144 (E.D. Pa. 1986).
7. 821 F.2d 489 (8th Cir. June 17, 1987).
8. 803 F.2d 202, 42 F.E.P. Cases 185 (5th Cir. 1986).

9. 822 F.2d 52 (3d Cir. June 19, 1987).
10. 785 F.2d 458, 41 F.E.P. Cases (BNA) 714 (7th Cir. 1986).
11. 785 F.2d 584, 40 F.E.P. Cases (BNA) 508 (7th Cir. 1986).
12. 842 F.2d 1480, 46 F.E.P. Cases (BNA) 857 (3d Cir. 1988).
13. 772 F.2d 374 (8th Cir. 1983).
14. 781 F.2d 173, 39 F.E.P. Cases (BNA) 1201 (10th Cir. 1986).
15. 690 F.2d 1072 (E.D.N.C. 1982).
16. 688 F.2d 547, 29 F.E.P. Cases (BNA) 1491 (7th Cir. 1982).
17. 744 F.2d 1464, 41 F.E.P. Cases 562 (M.D. Fla. 1986).
18. See also 750 F.2d 1405, 36 F.E.P. Cases 913 (7th Cir. 1984).
19. 609 F. Supp. 1003, 38 F.E.P. Cases (BNA) 79 (N.D. Ill. 1985).
20. 768 F.2d 402, 247, 38 F.E.P. Cases (BNA) 773 (D.C. Cir. 1985).
21. 603 F. Supp. 1035, 37 F.E.P. Cases (BNA) 193 (D. Conn. 1985).
22. 833 F.2d 1406, 45 F.E.P. Cases 608 (10th Cir. 1987).
23. 832 F.2d 258 (E.D.Pa) 45 F.E.P. Cases (BNA) 212 (3d Cir. 1987), *cert. denied,* 109 S. Ct. 782 (1989).
24. 40 F.E.P. Cases (BNA) 1227 (W.D. Ky. 1986).
25. 643 F.2d 914, 25 F.E.P. Cases (BNA) 355 (2d Cir. 1981).
26. 673 F.2d 34, 29 F.E.P. Cases (BNA) 937 (2d Cir. 1982).
27. 708 F.2d 233, 31 F.E.P. Cases (BNA) 1532 (6th Cir. 1983).
28. 679 F. Supp. 751, 46 F.E.P. Cases (BNA) 1050 (N.D. Ill. 1988).
29. 424 Mich. 675 (1986).
30. No. 82-1697 (6th Cir. May 16, 1984).
31. No. 82-C-7277 (N.D. Ill. January 7, 1987).
32. 843 F.2d 190, 46 F.E.P. Cases (BNA) 1086 (5th Cir. 1988).
33. 782 F.2d 1421, 40 F.E.P. Cases (BNA) 201 (7th Cir. 1986).
34. C.A. No. 82-C-1576 (June 14, 1984).
35. 714 F.2d 556, 32 F.E.P. Cases (BNA) 1451 (5th Cir. 1983).
36. 633 F. Supp. 13, 46 F.E.P. Cases (BNA) 174 (E.D. Tex. 1988).
37. 647 F. Supp. 22, 45 F.E.P. Cases (BNA) 1054 (3d Cir. 1987).
38. No. 87-2065 (7th Cir. May 9, 1988).
39. 1 I.E.R. Cases 800 (Vt. 1986).

Epilogue

Personnel Decisions: Where Are We Now?

"A pain in the neck," one personnel manager I know calls some employees, former employees, and the laws I have discussed in this book. Armed with those laws, some employees bring trivial, sometimes frivolous, complaints into the courtroom, and they often ask for damages far out of proportion to the damage done.[1] But, then again, far too many managers, as the cases in this book have demonstrated, say or do the dumb things that make them vulnerable to attacks from employees or former employees.

I should not have to remind managers that laws of contract protect both parties to a contract, that employees have rights guaranteed by law, that equal opportunity is more than a patriotic slogan, and that society places a higher value on public good and safety than on personal (or corporate) profits. I should *not* have to remind them, but I do.

Both management and employees tend to operate off of yesterday's assumptions—class, struggle, racial and sex biases, religious prejudice—that no longer meet anyone's needs or objectives and that often lead to preventable courtroom battles. Sound management policies should try to prevent lawsuits for breach of contract or discrimination not because it is the legal thing to do or the morally right thing to do but rather because it is in everyone's, especially in the organization's, best interest.

I mentioned earlier that in this last decade of the century women will constitute the largest segment of new workers entering the work force. Minorities and immigrants fill a distant second role. The supply of able-bodied, "qualified" white males is drying up to perhaps 15 percent of the new workers entering the labor force. The work force, by its very composition, is forcing equal opportunity hiring onto the business community. Companies that do not practice fair hiring and employment methods will lose their competitive advantage.[2]

When, in Section III, I described the legal climate in the country today, I said that any employee feeling aggrieved, not just members of "protected groups," is likely to pursue legal action. As a result, the business community could suffer the consequences of long, expensive years in litigation that often end in high-priced damage awards unless it takes heed of the changes in society. Try to fit $69,575,367[3] for wrongful discharge and breach of contract into your organization's budget and see how it feels.

The 1989 U.S. Supreme Court decisions dealing with affirmative action took some pressure off employers, but the Court has done nothing to change the responsibilities inherent in daily management practices. If you do not want the *government* to guarantee equal opportunity for all employees, you need to assume responsibility for it or risk fighting more and tougher battles in the future. Although those 1989 Court decisions could aid and abet managers from other countries whose hiring and promotion practices are discriminatory when applied in the United States, even those managers are learning that U.S. employees take EEO very seriously.[4] The High Court has not seen an end to EEO suits, either. EEO legislation has made good sense and has had the influence it was designed to have. A study of how EEO/AA (affirmative action) laws have affected major personnel policies shows that most of them arose largely if not entirely from or in response to one piece of legislation or another.[5] What a terrible waste if we allow the Court decisions to weaken the social value of that legislation. At this writing, the administration under George Bush seems to understand the implications of undermining EEO/AA law; according to *Business Week*, Labor Secretary Elizabeth H. Dole has hinted that the administration may work with the Congress to overturn some of the U.S. Supreme Court's rulings.[6]

Regardless of what the courts and the government do, you first-line, middle, and senior managers play a different role than do human resources managers when it comes to affirmative action. You hire and manage the labor force. Fair, equitable hiring and management practices, hiring qualified or trainable people and treating them with dignity regardless of special characteristics, are what affirmative action is all about. The real positive changes in the work world (which in turn will create positive changes in the rest of our social fabric) must come at your level. Equal opportunity and fair treatment amount to little more than managing in good faith and fair dealing, articles on which all business contracts are established. It therefore makes sense to fully understand the key issues involved in hiring, managing, and firing people.

Key Issues: Contracts and Good Faith

Just how important are honesty and fair dealings in business? The case that follows, in which the former employee and the former employer disagree as to why the employee was fired, may answer that question.

Bert Walker says he was fired because he would have missed work to pull his jury duty. The employer says Walker was fired because he was only a temporary employee in the first place. According to Walker, his immediate supervisor told him that the company had no reason to fire him; that it had good reason to like his work. It just had to let him go.

Walker claims he was never told he was a temporary employee. He left another job, he says, on the promise of permanent employment, without which he would never have made the move. That he was fired the Friday before he was supposed to report for jury duty was "too coincidental" for him.[7]

Nearly two years later, the case is still working its way through the courts. There is no telling how long it will take to resolve the case or how much it will cost. How can you prevent this type of disagreement from damaging your organization?

This dispute speaks to something more important than to an isolated employment contract. It addresses a fundamental tenet of contracts in general: the importance of keeping your word, playing by honest rules, and honoring contractual commitments.

When we agree to work together, we make an agreement and expect each party to the agreement to deal fairly with the other. The agreement may not be an explicit or implicit employment contract, but it is a contract nonetheless, a *psychological* contract.

Honesty and candor toward your employees with respect to organizational policies and rules; with regard to employee performance, advancement, and compensation; and with regard to the future of the organization are essential ingredients of the psychological contract betweeen you and the workers. Their rights are not the only issue here. Rather, their productivity and profitability depend upon their satisfaction with the way in which you honor your contracts. Effective managers do not suffer from expensive high turnover or litigation.

When we publish written employment contracts, we merely formally and legally acknowledge what we agreed to do informally. Now, for how long do you expect to do business in a community if you do not take your contracts with your employees as seriously as you take your contracts with your suppliers or customers?

Key Issues: Public Policy and Civil Rights

Let's assume that the plaintiff's perceptions of the situation are accurate: (1) He was not told he was a temporary employee only, and (2) he was fired because he was going to miss work for jury duty. If the plaintiff is right, the employer is guilty of violating the public trust on *two* counts.

Society depends upon managers' honesty in the conduct of their business. It relies upon management's recognition of everyone's right and obligations under the law. Without honesty and social responsibility, the fabric of society would unravel.

Such issues as these give impetus to the widening discussions of ethics in business in both graduate school classrooms and corporate boardrooms.[8] What do we gain by creating a global economy if managers do not share in responsibility for improving the quality of work life and in the quality of life in the world community as well?

And of what value are unrecognized or disregarded laws designed to protect the public good or general welfare of the nation? In the Appendix, I summarize equal opportunity and fair labor laws, but no summary of laws deals with the social, intellectual, and emotional issues that produce or are affected by the laws. When the Supreme Court allowed white firefighters in Alabama to challenge their city's agreed-upon affirmative action plan, it created debates that could set back many of our nation's social gains to a pre-1964 low rather than a forum for productive accommodation.

The level to which the debate is sinking can be summed up in these statements from a 1989 newspaper article attributed to firefighters in a midwestern city.*

Black fire-fighter 1:	The court has made it more difficult for blacks to use the courts to get jobs and advancement.
White fire-fighter 1:	It pleases me that the whole United States is coming to believe that people must show merit to advance. We do not want to put people on our job that are not qualified.
Black fire-fighter 2:	[Since white officials at the department prefer to hire relatives,] the odds would have been high that I would not have been hired.
White fire-fighter 2:	Blacks are going to wake up one of these days and realize that they're going to have to hustle for these things.

Values and perceptions affect all our social dealings, not just our legal relationships. Unless laws can be used to protect

*"Black, White Firefighters Differ on Court Ruling," *St. Louis Post-Dispatch* (June 13, 1989), p. 1B.

us from our prejudices and our ignorance, we have little hope of rectifying the grievances of the past. The potential for creating new grievances in the future has now been increased.

Civil rights laws are usually reactive, responsive to the social and political issues that have gotten lost in the smoke of debate over the implications of the law.

▸ Protecting jobs for people over the age of 40 is a matter of law; understanding that the distinctions between "young," "middle age," and "old" have blurred significantly is a matter of social awareness.
▸ Protecting job opportunities for women, minorities, and disabled people is a matter of law; understanding the quality of work life that affects women, minorities, and disabled people is a matter of sensitivity to people's feelings.
▸ Protecting religious freedom is a matter of law; understanding the needs of religious minorities is a matter of becoming conscious of what other people value.

Key Issues: Age, Sex Discrimination, and Special Accommodation for Disabled People

The following sections discuss the key issues of the future. Let's consider each of them one at a time.

Age. Americans are aging. "Hire young" policies in the 1970s made room for the largest baby boom in U.S. history. Now the people who hired them are aging and the 76 million baby boomers they hired are graying. But so what?

Age does not mean what it used to. By the year 2040, only fifty years from now, the baby boomers will have reached ages 76 to 94. More than 21 percent of the population will be over 65 years of age, as compared to 12 percent today. In 1986 the average life expectancy was seventy-two years for white men, seventy-nine for white women, sixty-six for black men, and seventy-four for black women. Add at least seven years to the men's ages and twelve and a half years to women's by 2040. This will be a healthier, abler older work force than we have seen, even by today's standards, and remember that most of those new workers will be women and minorities.⁹

We need to question, as many people do, whether our definitions of old age are not obsolete. Some gerontologists divide today's age groups into four quarters instead of three: (1) *childhood and adolesence* between birth and 21, (2) *youth* between 21 and 49, (3) *middle age* between 50 and 75, and (4) *old age* from 75 on. They say that age group 2 (youth) has shrivelled, while age group 3 (middle age) is delaying marriage and child rearing. At the same time, they also say that for most people, the third quarter of life should be as productive as the second.¹¹ And why should it not be?

Medical science and physical fitness as a result of exercise and diet have expanded life expectancy and changed the quality of older workers' lives. Hard, physical labor killed our forebears before age 50. Now the Bureau of Labor Statistics defines the *older worker* as "someone 55 or older." And just as the work force will increasingly become composed of more women, it will also get increasingly older as the baby boomers continue to turn gray.¹⁰

So, the question becomes, Why not hire older workers? Why lay off or retire your older employees? They have the training, the skills, and the experience to do work for you, and they have the strength and the wisdom to do it better. They are learning new ways of doing new work as well. They are not "old dogs" afraid to or incapable of learning new tricks.

Besides, who can replace them? The time may come when it is more cost-effective to downsize by laying off two younger people than by retiring one older person, even though the older person makes a higher salary. Managers will have to unlearn negative stereotypes about older people and replace those prejudices with the recognition that older people can learn new skills, that they can transfer their old skills to new tasks, and that they can provide leadership to younger, less experienced employees.

That age is a key issue for today's managers gets support from a strange but believable source. Ann Landers reports that when she belittled a fifty-year-old woman's complaints about age discrimination, she received *20,000* letters telling her she "was off [her] rocker." Not just women wrote in. Many men did as well.[11] Still, most women suffer a double jeopardy when they reach age 40.

Sex Discrimination. Easing employees' entry into nontraditional, higher-paying roles should be the goal of the business community—not only for women, but for all previously disenfranchised workers—if for no other reason than because of the statistics cited earlier in the chapter. The size of the untapped female and minority labor pool signals the size of the untapped labor talents just waiting to get the call. The poor productivity of U.S. business and industry could very well partly be the result of not satisfying their own self-interest by hiring people qualified or trainable to do the work regardless of areas such as sex, age, or race.

The U.S. Supreme Court decisions in 1989 referred to earlier in this chapter could easily victimize women even more than blacks and minorities. The statistical ratios between women in the available labor pool and those in professional or highly paid executive positions will no longer count for much in a court of law. Getting into those positions has been difficult enough, but now proving that male managers do not hire women as readily as they hire other men will have to be considered on a case-by-case basis.

But once on the job, then what? Business as usual? Sarah Hardesty and Nehama Jacobs called the barrier keeping women out of high-level positions a "glass ceiling" through which women can see what is possible but probably unattainable.[12] And, then came "the Mommy Track" debate.

In an article in *Harvard Business Review*, Felice Schwartz, founder of Catalyst (a career development group for women), argues that employers should institute two different or separate career paths for women: a "career-primary" path for women who wish to devote their lives to their work, and a "career-and-family" path for women who are willing to forgo advancement for the sake of bearing and raising children.[13] Although mostly hostile, the response[14] to Schwartz's ideas should at least awaken managers to the need to reconsider how they treat women in the work force. There are no homogeneous stereotypes there, either.

Career women are not devoid of family feelings. Many want families and careers, but some are not willing to sacrifice one for the other. That, according to John Wilcox, contributing editor for *Training and Development Journal*, is not uncommon among career men, either.

Citing the Bureau of National Affairs report, *The 1990s Father: Balancing Work and Family Concerns*, Wilcox says corporate policy has been making room for the family-oriented male for many generations. Mid-level, slow-track positions exist everywhere to allow men to find job security, a reasonable income, and time for their families. Now that only 3.7 percent of the modern family fits the traditional family model, why should a "Mommy track" be different from a "Daddy track"?[15]

Why? Because change is hard to accept and even harder to incorporate into our world. So laws have to be written and amended, rewritten and debated in courts. Nowhere is that clearer than in racial discrimination.

Racial Discrimination. Laws prohibiting discrimination on the basis of race have been on the books since before 1866, but we still see the attitudes of slavery at work everywhere in the society. Take this case, for example:

When a major southern univesity hired its first black head basketball coach, it was quickly embarrassed by the announcement that the new coach would not get free membership in the local country club as his white predecessors did because the club would not admit blacks.

These "social" clubs are important adjuncts for doing business (just as businesses are adjuncts of society). That coach, for example, had used a club membership provided for him by his previous employer for hosting professional meetings and for coaxing sizable donations from prominent businesspeople.[16] The line between private and public is becoming thinner by the year, and managers must only push gently now to penetrate all the barriers to racial minorities (and women) before the federal government steps in again, as it is doing with the new Americans With Disabilities Act.

Disabled People. By extending the coverage of the Rehabilitation Act of 1973 from the public to the private sector,
Congress is now doing with this Act what the courts have been
doing for many years. The Americans With Disabilities Act
will require businesses employing fifteen or more people to
obey the same constraints the earlier law imposes on federal
agencies and businesses or institutions contracting with or
receiving funds from the federal government. It will also require service industry businesses, such as restaurants and
office buildings, to make accommodations for disabled people:
ramps for wheelchairs, braille signs, and so on. Why not?

Most disabled people are entitled to the same service
anyone else can get, and they can be as productive as we people
who do not suffer from disabilities. People in wheelchairs play
basketball, so why can they not operate a computer? Blind
people sing in choirs, so why can they not talk on the telephone? Some deaf people can now talk on a telephone and
hear what the other party is saying, and what they cannot hear
they can read on specially designed printer phones. Why not
hire disabled people or treat them with the dignity to which
they are entitled? In the following two cases, we see the ugly
heads of prejudice and ignorance again.

A woman writes to a newspaper column, "I'm 34, have
epilepsy, and don't work. I've tried, but as soon as they hear I
have epilepsy, there's no job."[17]

An emotionally disturbed Vietnam veteran takes his co-
workers and employer to court for harassment, charging they
terrorized him by imitating exploding bombs ("dropping ta-
bles and heavy equipment, breaking bottles, popping empty
milk cartons and paper cups, and setting off fireworks"). The
judges declared that "the human insensitivity often witnessed
in the children's schoolyard has reappeared in the adult workplace," where the co-workers engaged in and the employer
acquiesced to a "campaign of terror . . . apparently entirely for
amusement or perhaps outright cruelty."[18]

While few people quarrel with the *intent* of the Americans
With Disabilities Act, the business community quarrels over
its perception of the law's cost. For some small businesses,
accommodating disabled people could be prohibitive and work

an undue hardship on the employer.[19] That is precisely why the law specifically cites undue hardship as a legitimate business reason for not hiring disabled people.

The variety of situations this book covers should make clear that I cannot offer you a generalized set of steps for keeping all your employee decisions out of court. I can, however, suggest Ten Golden Rules of Safe Management that you can paste on your office wall.

Ten Golden Rules of Safe Management

1. Treat all applicants and employees, regardless of sex, race, color, national origin, creed, religion, disability, or veteran's status, with the same respect that you wish for yourself; permit everyone access to equal opportunities for employment and to a safe, productive working environment.
2. Treat any employee as a valuable resource who if abused or overworked will fail you when you need him or her the most; only if the organization's objectives and the employees' personal goals meet at various points can you avoid conflict.
3. Respect your employees' right to exercise their legal rights and fulfill their legal obligations, even if, as in a workers comp claim, the organization could be hurt.
4. Respect your employees' and former employees' right to privacy and dignity, protecting them from defamation, exposure to ridicule, or loss of future economic opportunities.
5. Protect yourself or your employer from lawsuits resulting from management decisions that put applicants at a disadvantage on the job or relative to other employees.
6. Protect yourself or your employer by not doing or saying anything that would suggest an implied or nonexistent contract or promise you do not have the authority to make.
7. Protect yourself, your employer, and the public by

screening all applicants thoroughly before hiring them, including evaluating gaps in employment histories, checking references, and checking with authorities for criminal convictions if the applicant's history warrants an investigation.

8. If your organization has a code of conduct, live by it yourself; model the behavior you expect from others.
9. If your organization has published rules and procedures for taking corrective action or firing employees, follow the rules and procedures to the letter.
10. Think before you speak, write a memo, make an entry into a file, or take action against an employee; seek professional or legal counsel if you need to.

Notes

1. Marshall Sella, "More Big Bucks in Jury Verdicts: Additions to the 1988 List," *ABA Journal* (July 1989), p. 69; Stephanie B. Goldberg, "Punitives in Peril," *ABA Journal* (October 1989), p. 46.
2. Paula Dwyer, "The Blow to Affirmative Action May Not Hurt That Much," *Business Week* (July 3, 1989), p. 61; Bill Cantor, "Minority Hiring Shows Problems in Corporate America," *IABC Communication World* (July/August 1989), pp. 22–25.
3. Sella, "More Big Bucks in Jury Verdicts."
4. Michele Galen and Leah J. Nathans, " 'White People, Black People' Not Wanted Here?" *Business Week* (July 10, 1989), p. 31; Stephen Labaton, "Business and the Law: Bias Rulings Aid Japan's U.S. Units," *The New York Times* (June 19, 1989), p. D2.
5. Horace E. Johns and H. Ronald Moser, "Where Has EEO Taken Personnel Policies?" *Personnel* (September 1989), pp. 63–66.
6. Dwyer, "The Blow to Affirmative Action."
7. Joan Bray, "Worker Attributes Firing to Jury Duty," *St. Louis Post-Dispatch* (May 25, 1988), p. 5A.

8. See "Business Ethics: A 50 Page FW Special Report," *Financial World* (June 27, 1989), pp. 19ff.

9. Ellen Creager, "Our Definition of Old Age: Is It Obsolete?" *St. Louis Post-Dispatch* (July 3, 1989), p. 1D.

10. "Ridding Managers of Age Discrimination Attitudes and Practices," *Management Development Report of ASTD* (Fall 1988), p. 6.

11. Ann Landers, "Age Discrimination Reports From All Over," *St. Louis Post-Dispatch* (June 5, 1989), p. 2D.

12. See Sarah Hardesty and Nehama Jacobs, *Success and Betrayal* (Touchstone/Simon & Schuster), 1987.

13. Felice N. Schwartz, "Management Women and the New Facts of Life," *Harvard Business Review* (January/February 1989).

14. Elizabeth Ehrlich, "Is the Mommy Track a Blessing—or a Betrayal?" *Business Week* (May 15, 1989), pp. 98–99.

15. John Wilcox, "Mommy Track, Daddy Track," *Training and Development Journal* (September 1989), pp. 12–14.

16. "Not Yet Clubbable," *The Economist* (May 6, 1989), p. 27.

17. Reader's letter in Diane Piastro, "Living With a Disability: Epileptic Fights Discrimination," *St. Louis Post-Dispatch* (July 8, 1989), p. 3D.

18. Norma R. Fritz, "In Focus: The High Cost of Cruelty," *Personnel* (September 1989), p. 4.

19. "New Rights for America's Disabled: Generosity is particularly easy when you choose not to foot the bill," *The Economist* (September 23, 1989), p. 19.

Appendix

What Civil Rights and Other Personal Protection Laws Say

Despite the U.S. Supreme Court decisions of 1989, equal opportunity battles will continue. What *protected groups* cannot claim, *protected individuals*—minorities of many races and ethnic groups, women, older people, disabled people—still can.

It seems that the rate of new job creation and the growth of the work force are slowing, that 90 percent of the new jobs created will be in service sectors, and that between now and the end of the century the gender distribution of the work force will evolve to fully 50 percent women. Approximately 85 percent of the new entrants into the labor pool in the year 2000 will be women and minority workers. Employers will have to offer equal opportunities by default.* With attention to cultural and social diversity and to a wide variety of needs and sensitivities fast becoming a management necessity, hiring women, minorities, disabled people, and older people will be the easy part; managing them will be the hard part.

I will not add to the many thousands of pages already written about the laws governing equal opportunity. Instead, I will summa-

*See Bill Cantor, "Minority Hiring Shows Problems in Corporate America, *IABC Communication World* (July/August 1989), pp. 22–23; Paula Dewey, "The Blow to Affirmative Action May Not Hurt That Much," *Business Week* (July 3, 1989), pp. 61–62.

rize the most important of them to provide a context to which you can relate the cases and the answers I cite about separate management issues—hiring, management practices, discharging, and so on.
Generally, each summary is divided into six parts:

1. Purpose
2. Whom/What the Act Protects
3. What Managers Can't Do
4. What Managers Can Do
5. Penalties for Intentional Violation
6. Enforcement

These summaries supply only a thumbnail sketch of what has been ruled impermissible and what has been ruled acceptable, at least up to this point in time (mid-1990). If you have any doubt about any specific situation, a call to your organization's personnel department or attorney is in order.

If a complaint is lodged against you personally, you would be well advised to say nothing to your employees; discuss the matter only with your personnel officer and your attorney.

Title VII, Civil Rights Act of 1964

(as amended)

Purpose

To protect constitutional rights, to extend the Commission on Civil Rights, to establish a Commission on Equal Employment Opportunity (EEOC), and for other purposes

Whom/What the Act Protects

Protected groups covers:

1. People of race or color other than white (now defined by the Supreme Court in terms of the Civil Rights Act of 1866: all ethnic minorities)
2. People of any bona fide religious persuasion
3. Members of either sex
4. People whose national origin is other than the United States

What Managers Can't Do

1. Fail or refuse to hire any person or to otherwise discriminate against any person with respect to compensation, terms, conditions, or privileges of employment because he or she is a member of a protected group.

2. Discharge any person because he or she is a member of a protected group.
3. Limit, segregate, or classify employees or applicants for employment in any way that would deprive or tend to deprive a person of employment opportunities or have an adverse effect on the person's status as an employee.
4. Fail to provide training to a person because he or she is a member of a protected group.
5. Retaliate against any employees or applicants for employment because they made a charge, testified, assisted, or participated in any manner in an action protected by this law.
6. Print or publish (or have someone else print or publish) any notice or advertisement relating to employment that may adversely affect members of a protected group.
7. Fail to post and keep posted in an obvious place a notice concerning the contents of this law.

What Managers Can Do

1. Hire or employ people on the basis of a bona fide occupational qualification (BFOQ), that is, a qualification demanded by the conditions of the position, e.g., an unusual or special skill, or being male in order to play a male role.
2. Apply different standards of compensation or different terms, conditions, or privileges of employment as part of a legally acceptable seniority or merit system, or a system that pays for piecework or on commission or in different locations, as long as the distinctions are not the result of deliberate discrimination.
3. Set up different compensation packages if the differences are authorized by the provisions of Section 6(d) of the Fair Labor Standards Act of 1938, as amended, if they are based on factors other than sex, e.g., a seniority or merit system or piecework or quality bonuses.
4. Hire without regard to quotas or preferential treatment.
5. Fire or otherwise discipline someone for good cause.

Penalties for Intentional Violation

1. A court order stopping the company from conducting unlawful employment practices and ordering affirmative action, which may include but not be limited to reinstating or hiring employees with or without back pay, or any other fair relief the court rules is appropriate
2. Court action to force an organization to comply (if necessary)
3. Reasonable attorney fees and other costs

Enforcement

1. Equal Employment Opportunity Commission (EEOC)
2. Attorney General of the United States (AG)

A person may file charges within 180 days after the alleged unlawful practice took place, and notice of the charge will be served within 10 days afterward. If the person filing the claim has filed charges with a state or local agency, then he or she has 300 days in which to file, or may file within 30 days after the state or local agency finishes its action, whichever is earlier.

If, within 30 days, the EEOC is not able to arrange an agreement it finds acceptable, it may bring civil action through the AG. Employee/applicant may file suit within 90 days after the right to sue notice has been issued.

[*Note:* The terms and conditions of the Civil Rights Act of 1964 have been extended to cover harassment in the workplace on the basis of race, color, religion, sex, and national origin. Not only may the individual defendant be held liable, but the organization can be held liable also if it has not taken reasonable steps to prevent harassment. The organization is particularly liable if it can be shown that organization policies or indifferences have created a "hostile environment."]

Executive Order No. 11,246

Covering Government Contractors and Subcontractors
(as amended by Executive Orders 11,375 and 12,086)

Purpose

To extend the equal opportunity provisions of Title VII of the
Civil Rights Act of 1964 by specifically prohibiting job discrimination based on race, color, religion, sex, national origin,
handicap, or veteran's status by:

1. Contractors and subcontractors operating under federal service, supply, and construction contracts
2. Contractors and subcontractors who perform under
   federally aided construction contracts and who have
   contracts in excess of $10,000 with the federal govern-
   ment
3. Nonconstruction contractors and subcontractors with
   fifty or more employees who have prime contracts or
   subcontracts with the federal government in excess of
   $50,000; such employers must develop and maintain
   written affirmative action programs

Whom/What the E.O. Protects

Protected groups covers:

1. People of race or color other than white (now defined by the U.S. Supreme Court in terms of the Civil Rights Act of 1866: all ethnic minorities)
2. People of any bona fide religious persuasion
3. Members of either sex
4. People whose national origin is other than the United States
5. Handicapped persons as defined by the Rehabilitation Act
6. Veterans as defined by the Veterans Readjustment Act

What Managers Can't Do

1. Fail or refuse to hire any person or to otherwise discriminate against any person with respect to compensation, terms, conditions, or privileges of employment because he or she is a member of a protected group.
2. Discharge any person because he or she is a member of a protected group.
3. Limit, segregate, or classify employees or applicants for employment in any way that would either deprive or tend to deprive a person of employment opportunities or have an adverse effect on the person's status as an employee.
4. Fail to provide training to a person because he or she is a member of a protected group.
5. Retaliate against any employees or applicants for employment because they made a charge, testified, assisted, or participated in any manner in an action protected by this law.
6. Print or publish (or have someone else print or publish) any notice or advertisement relating to employment that may adversely affect members of a protected group.
7. Fail to post and keep posted in an obvious place a notice concerning the contents of this law or to notify

any labor union or representative of employees with which it has a collective bargaining agreement or other contract or agreement of its commitment under E.O. 11,246.

8. Fail to include the following information in a written bid:

   a. Whether the organization has an affirmative action program and supporting documentation on file, unless exempted by E.O. 11,246 or by an administrative exemption;

   b. Whether it has participated in any previous government contract or substract subject to E.O. 11,246 and its equal opportunity clause;

   c. Whether it has filed all reports due under the applicable filing requirements.

9. Fail to require prospective prime contractors and subcontractors to submit a written certification that the contractor does not and will not maintain segregated facilities.

10. Fail to complete accurate annual reports of compliance.

11. Deny the administering agency and the secretary of labor access to its books, records, and accounts to investigate or determine compliance.

What Managers Can Do

1. Apply for an exemption if the exemption is in the national interest, e.g., security clearance requirements.

2. Hire or employ people on the basis of a bona fide occupational qualification (BFOQ).

3. Apply different standards of compensation, or different terms, conditions, or privileges of employment, as part of a legally acceptable seniority or merit system or a system that pays for piecework or on commission or in different locations as long as the distinctions are not the result of deliberate discrimination.

4. Hire without regard to quotas or preferential treatment.
5. Fire or otherwise discipline someone for good cause.

Penalties for Violations

1. Sanctions imposed by the Office of Federal Contract Compliance Programs (OFCCP), which could include loss of any part or the whole of a federal contract, debarment from further contracts, publication of violators' names, recommendations to the Justice Department for action under E.O. 11,246 and to the Equal Employment Opportunity Commission or the Justice Department for action under the Civil Rights Act of 1964, Title VII.
2. Criminal action for furnishing false information in connection with the procurement of a federal contract.
3. Injunctions stopping the company from conducting unlawful employment practices ordering affirmative action, which may include but not be limited to reinstating or hiring employees with or without back pay or any other fair relief the court rules is appropriate.
4. Court action to force an organization to comply (if necessary).
5. Reasonable attorney fees and other costs.

Enforcement

1. OFCCP, Department of Labor
2. Attorney General of the United States (AG)
3. Federal district court

A person may file charges within 180 days after the alleged unlawful practice took place, unless the time limitation is extended by the OFCCP upon a showing of good cause and notice of the charge will be served within 10 days.

Sex Discrimination Guidelines Under E.O. 11,246 (41 C.F.R., Pt. 60-20)

Purpose

To interpret legislation banning preference, limitation, or discrimination based on sex

Whom the Guidelines Protect

Anyone, regardless of gender, unless gender is a bona fide occupational qualification (BFOQ)

What Managers Can't Do

1. Specify sex in recruiting, job posting, or advertising to hire, unless sex is a BFOQ.
2. Distinguish in any manner on the basis of sex in personnel policies.
3. In any way prohibit, limit, or discriminate on the basis of sex when filling available positions, unless sex is a BFOQ.
4. Make distinctions based on sex in employment opportunities, wages, hours, or other conditions of employment.
5. Favor married over unmarried people, people with no

children over people with young children, or people of one sex over people of another sex.

6. Use limitations of physical facilities to accommodate people of both sexes as a reason for discrimination.
7. Rely on state labor laws that protect women in order to deny them employment for which they are qualified.
8. Penalize women because of their need for time away from work for childbearing.
9. Use mandatory or optional retirement age to discriminate on the basis of sex.
10. Use seniority lines or lists based solely on sex.

What Managers Can Do

1. Distinguish on the basis of sex, where sex is a BFOQ.
2. Assign jobs on the basis of differences in capabilities.

Age Discrimination in Employment Act of 1967

(as amended)

Purpose

To promote employment of older persons, to prohibit age discrimination in employment, and to help employers and workers find ways of meeting problems arising from the impact of age on employment

Whom the Act Protects

All persons age 40 or older

What Managers Can't Do

1. Fail or refuse to hire any person or to otherwise discriminate against any person with respect to compensation, terms, conditions, or privileges of employment because of age.
2. Discharge or require retirement of any person because of age.
3. Limit, segregate, or classify employees or applicants for employment in a way that would deprive or tend to deprive a person of employment opportunities or have an adverse effect on the person's employee status on the basis of age.

4. Reduce anyone's wages in order to comply with this Act.
5. Retaliate against any employees or applicants for employment because they made a charge, testified, assisted, or participated in any manner in an action under this title.
6. Print or publish (or have someone else print or publish) any notice or advertisement relating to employment that indicates a preference, limitation, specification, or discrimination based on age.
7. Deny an employee or a spouse over age 65 the same health care coverage offered to employees and their spouses under age 65.
8. Fail to post and keep posted in an obvious place a notice concerning the contents of this law.

What Managers Can Do

1. Discriminate where age is a BFOQ.
2. Observe the terms of a bona fide seniority system or any bona fide employee benefit plan as long as the plan is not a subterfuge; this exception does not excuse the organization's failure to hire someone in this protected group or requiring his or her involuntary retirement because of age.
3. Fire or otherwise discipline someone for good cause.

Penalties for Intentional Violation

1. A court order stopping the organization from conducting unlawful employment practices; ordering affirmative action, which may include but not be limited to reinstating or hiring employees with or without back pay; or providing any other fair relief the court rules is appropriate
2. Court action to force an organization to comply (if necessary)
3. Liquidated damages as well as the penalties in item 1 under "Enforcement"
4. Reasonable attorney fees and other costs

Penalties for Unintentional Violation

1. Appropriate legal and fair relief, including judgments compelling employment, reinstatement or promotion, or unpaid wages

Enforcement

1. Equal Employment Opportunity Commission (EEOC)
2. Attorney General of the United States (AG)

A person may file charges of unintentional discrimination within two years after the alleged unlawful practice took place, and within three years for intentional violations. Notice of the charge will be served afterward within ten days, unless the person filing the claim has filed charges with a state or local agency; then, the person has 300 days in which to file, or else must file within thirty days after the state or local agency finishes its action, whichever is earlier.

If the EEOC is not able to arrange an agreement it finds acceptable within thirty days, it may bring civil action on behalf of the individual through the AG.

[*Note:* The terms and conditions of the ADEA have been extended to cover harassment in the workplace on the basis of age. Not only may the individual defendant be held liable, but the organization can be held liable also if it has not taken reasonable steps to prevent harassment. The organization is particularly liable if it can be shown that its policies or indifference has created a "hostile environment."]

Rehabilitation Act of 1973

Purpose

To protect the constitutional rights and employment opportu- nities of disabled people applying to or working for a federal agency, or a business or an institution under contract or receiving federal funds

Whom/What the Act Protects

Any person who:

1. Has a physical or mental disability or impairment that constitutes or results in a major handicap to employ- ment; *and*
2. That largely limits one or more of the person's major life activities;
3. Can reasonably be expected to benefit from vocational rehabilitation services;
4. Has a record of an impairment; or
5. Is regarded as having an impairment.

This definition is used to cover many different conditions, such as obesity, drug abuse, alcoholism, and facial skin problems common among black men that prevent them from shaving.

What Managers Can't Do

1. Fail or refuse to hire any person or to otherwise discrim- inate against any person with respect to compensation,

terms, conditions, or privileges of employment because he or she is disabled.

2. Discharge any person because he or she is disabled.
3. Limit, segregate, or classify employees or applicants for employment in any way that would deprive or tend to deprive them of employment opportunities or have an adverse effect on their status as an employee.
4. Fail to provide training to a person because he or she is disabled.
5. Retaliate against any employees or applicants for employment because they made a charge, testified, assisted, or participated in any manner protected by this law.
6. Print or publish (or have someone else print or publish) any notice or advertisement relating to employment that may adversely affect people who are disabled.
7. Fail to post and keep posted in an obvious place a notice concerning the contents of this law.

What Managers Can Do

1. Deny employment where the disability or impairment would interfere with the person's ability to perform the duties of the job.
2. Deny employment to any person whose alcohol or other drug abuse would prevent him or her from performing the duties of the job in question or would be a direct threat to property or to the safety of other people.
3. Hire without regard to quotas or preferential treatment.
4. Fire or otherwise discipline someone for good cause.

Penalties for Intentional Violation

1. A court order stopping the organization from conducting unlawful employment practices; ordering affirmative action, which may include but not be limited to reinstating or hiring employees with or without back pay; or any other fair relief the court rules is appropriate. However, the court takes into account the reason-

able costs of any necessary workplace changes to accommodate disabled people and the availability of options for accommodation or other relief in order to achieve a fair and proper solution.
2. Court action to force an organization to comply (if necessary)
3. Reasonable attorney fees and other costs
4. The burden of proof is on the employer

Enforcement

1. Equal Employment Opportunity Commission (EEOC)
2. Attorney General of the United States (AG)

A person may file charges within 180 days after the alleged unlawful practice took place, and notice of the charge will be served within 10 days, unless the person filing the claim has filed charges with a state or local agency; then the person has 300 days in which to file, or else must file within thirty days after the state or local agency finishes its action, whichever is earlier.

If the EEOC is not able to arrange an agreement it finds acceptable within thirty days, it may bring civil action through the AG.

[*Note*: The terms and conditions of the Rehabilitation Act have been extended to cover harassment in the workplace on the basis of disability and to include failure to provide reasonable accommodation. In a case of harassment, the individual defendant can be held liable, but the organization can be held liable also if it has not taken reasonable steps to prevent harassment. The organization is particularly liable if it can be shown that organization policies or indifference has created a "hostile environment."]

[*Note*: The "Americans With Disabilities Act" has been signed by President George Bush. The new law, effective July 24, 1992, extends coverage to the private as well as to the public sector. By 1994, enactment will affect all but the smallest of employers (fourteen or fewer employees) and an estimated 43 million people. More precisely worded and more comprehensive than the Rehabilitation Act, it will also require service companies, e.g., restaurants, to improve their accommodations for disabled people. See the Epilogue for additional discussion.]

Vietnam Era Veterans Readjustment Assistance Act of 1974 Title IV: Veterans, Wives, and Widow Employment Assistance and Preference and Veterans' Reemployment Rights

Purpose

To protect the constitutional rights and employment opportunities of veterans, especially of veterans of the Vietnam era

Whom the Act Protects

1. Any veteran of the Vietnam era, which means anyone who served or will serve in the armed forces for 180 days or more between 1964 and 1991
2. Any member of the Active Reserves or National Guard
3. Any person discharged or released from active duty because of a service-connected disability or who is entitled to compensation under the laws administered by the Veterans Administration

What Managers Can't Do

1. Deny reemployment to a veteran who is still qualified to perform the duties of his or her position, as long as he or she applied for reemployment within ninety days after release from military service and has satisfactorily completed that military service.
2. Deny a veteran his or her benefits, seniority, status, or pay.
3. Deny a disabled veteran reemployment in another position for which he or she is qualified if that person is no longer able to perform the duties of his or her previous position, or deny the person his or her benefits, seniority, status, or pay, or any similar condition of employment.
4. Deny military leave time to any person called to active duty by the armed forces, the Ready Reserve, the National Guard, or the Public Health Service.
5. Deny military leave time to any person fulfilling his or her obligation to the Reserve or National Guard or other component of the armed forces, or who is called upon to take additional training.
6. Deny a member of the Reserve or National Guard or other component of the armed forces seniority, status, or pay as a result of his or her obligations.
7. Deny benefits to any person serving in any component of the military or armed forces except in regard to military leave pay if the person and the employer agree to a partial payment plan.

Penalties for Intentional Violation

1. Court order requiring compliance
2. Compensation for loss of wages or benefits
3. Reasonable attorney fees and other costs
4. The burden of proof is on the employer.

Enforcement

The Office of Veterans' Reemployment Rights in the Department of Labor

[*Note:* The terms and conditions of the Vietnam Era Veterans' Readjustment Act have been extended to cover harassment in the workplace on the basis of military status and to include failure to provide reasonable accommodation. In a case of harassment, the individual defendant can be held liable, but the organization can be held liable also if it has not taken reasonable steps to prevent harassment. The organization is particularly liable if it can be shown that organization policies or indifference has created a "hostile environment."]

National Labor Relations Act, 1935

(as amended)

Purpose

To lessen the causes of labor disputes that interfere with interstate or foreign commerce, to create a National Labor Relations Board (NLRB), and for other purposes

Whom/What the Act Protects

The rights of employees to organize themselves; to form, join, or assist labor organizations; to bargain collectively through their own respresentatives. It also allows all workers, nonunion as well as union, to engage in other concerted activities for the purpose of collective bargaining or other mutual aid or protection. It prevents nonunion employees from being forced or coerced into joining a labor organization or engaging in collective bargaining except where membership in a labor organization is a condition of employment and is created by contract.

What Manages Can't Do ("unfair labor practices by employers")

1. Interfere with, restrain, or coerce employees exercising their rights.

2. Dominate or interfere with the formation or administration of a labor organization or contribute financial or other aid to it; however, managers are required to allow employees to meet with them during working hours without a loss of time or pay to discuss issues of collective interest.
3. Discriminate in hiring or tenure on the basis of union or nonunion membership; managers cannot use the terms or conditions of employment to encourage or discourage membership in a labor organization, except where an agreement exists that requires membership.
4. Fire or otherwise discriminate against an employee for filing charges or giving testimony under this Act.
5. Refuse to bargain collectively with the employees' representative (however, see item 2 under "What Managers Can Do").
6. Enter with employees into any contract, express or implied, that would cause the employer to stop or refrain from handling, using, selling, transporting, or otherwise dealing in any of the products of any other employer or person (Hot Cargo Clause).

What Managers Can Do

1. Freely express viewpoints, arguments, or opinions in writing, print, graphics, or visuals about unions or collective bargaining as long as they do not threaten reprisal or force for forming or joining a collective bargaining unit and do not promise benefits for not forming or joining one.
2. Under Section 9a of the Act, hear employee grievances and adjust them without union representation, as long as the adjustment is consistent with the terms of a contract or agreement in effect and as long as the bargaining representative has been given an opportunity to be present.
3. Reject proposals or requests for concessions.
4. Appeal any ruling of the NLRB in any appropriate circuit court of appeals of the United States.

Penalties

1. Injunction or restraining order stopping an alleged unfair labor practice while in arbitration or adjudication
2. A fine of not more than $5,000 or imprisonment for not
   more than one year or both for interfering with the
   activities of the NLRB or any of its members, agents,
   or representatives
3. Specific remedies on a case-by-case basis ruled on by
   the NLRB and/or the courts

Enforcement

The National Labor Relations Board

Fair Labor Standards Act, 1938

(Wage-Hour Act, as amended)

Purpose

To establish fair labor standards in employment in and affecting interstate commerce, and for other purposes

Whom the Act Protects

All workers, including children and women

What Managers Can't Do

1. Employ children under age 16 ("oppressive labor") and certain categories of children ages 16–18.
2. Pay wages under the minimum hourly rate (in 1990 $3.80; in 1991 it will go up to $4.25 per hour).
3. Use sex as a basis for discriminating in wages, although where wages are based on a factor other than sex, such as a seniority system, members of one gender group may be adversely affected.
4. Lower the wage rate of any employee to comply with this Act.
5. Employ nonexempt workers for more than forty hours a week unless they are paid at least time and a half their "regular rate of pay" for the overtime.

6. Discharge or otherwise discriminate against any employee for filing, instituting, or causing to be instituted a complaint relating to this Act or for testifying or being about to testify in an action protected by this Act.
7. Discharge or otherwise discriminate against any employee for taking part in a collective action with respect to wages or other working conditions.

Exclusions From "Regular Rate of Pay"

1. Gifts, special bonuses, rewards for service
2. Payments made for occasional periods in which no work is performed, travel expenses, or other reimbursable expenses
3. Recognition for service awards
4. Contributions irrevocably made to a trustee or third party in a retirement, pension, or insurance plan
5. Extra compensation paid on a premium rate for:
   a. Overtime after a regular eight-hour day
   b. Overtime on a nonworkday
   c. Work outside normal hours as agreed upon through collective bargaining
6. Compensation through a guaranteed wage plan based on a bona fide individual contract or collective bargaining agreement

Exempt Employees

1. Executives, managers, and first-line supervisors
2. Employees whose jobs require making decisions—using personal judgment, creativity, or innovativeness—but who are not classified as managers
3. Teachers and educational administrators
4. Salespeople and other people working on commission or for tips for service
5. Employees of service organizations in which more than 50 percent of the organization's gross income derives from *intra*state as opposed to *inter*state commerce

Criminal Penalties

For willful violation: Up to $10,000 or imprisonment for up to six months or both

Civil Penalties

1. Unpaid minimum wages or unpaid overtime or both, and an equal amount of liquidated damages
2. Fair relief, including employment, reinstatement, promotion, payment of lost wages, liquidated damages, and reasonable attorney and court fees
3. A court order stopping an unfair labor standards practice (injunctive relief)

Enforcement

The Wage and Hour Division of the Department of Labor

Labor Management Relations Act, 1947

(Taft-Hartley Act)

Purpose

To amend the National Labor Relations Act, providing additional support for mediation in labor disputes that affect interstate commerce, to equalize legal responsibilities of labor organizations and employers, to give the President emergency powers, and for other purposes

What the Act Protects

The nation's general welfare

What It Forbids

1. Unwarranted or sudden lockouts
2. Paying, loaning, or delivering money or other assets by an employer to a union, union official, union welfare fund, or employee involved in a labor dispute
3. Employers and unions making contributions to political candidates

Mediation Process

1. The Federal Mediation Service was created to try to avoid industrial controversy by offering services either

on its own initiative or by request from one or more of the parties involved in the dispute.
2. If the Service's director cannot produce an agreement through conciliation within a reasonable time, he or she will try to get the parties to find other means of settling the dispute without resorting to a strike, a lockout, or other coercion (e.g., submitting the employer's last offer to a secret ballot of the employees).
3. Failure to agree is not a violation of any duty or obligation imposed by this Act.

Duties of Employers and Employees

1. Make every reasonable effort to agree on rates of pay, hours, and working conditions, including notice of changes.
2. Arrange promptly to hold a conference to settle any differences between them.
3. If a conference is not successful, participate fully in meetings called by the Service.

National Emergencies and Presidential Powers

1. The Federal Mediation Service will advise the President of a serious threat to the general welfare of the nation.
2. The President is empowered to direct the Attorney General to petition any appropriate district court to stop a threatened strike or lockout or to end one or the other in progress.
3. If a federal court agrees that a strike or a lockout will adversely affect an entire industry or substantial part of it or would threaten the national health, safety, or security, it can stop the strike or lockout or take other appropriate measures.

Penalties (other than injunctions described above)

1. Fine of $5,000 for an organization making illegal contributions to political candidates
2. Fine of up to $1,000 or one year in prison or both for

officers of any organizations making illegal contributions

Enforcement

1. The Attorney General acting on orders from the President
2. Federal district courts

Labor-Management Reporting and Disclosure Act, 1959

(Labor Reform Act)

Purpose

To prevent labor organizations, employers, or their officers and representatives, including labor relations consultants, from distorting and defeating the policies of the Labor Management Relations Act, 1947, as amended (LMRA)

Whom the Act Protects

Nonsupervisory union and nonunion employees

What Managers Can't Do

Interfere with employees' right to work, organize, choose representatives, bargain collectively, and engage in concerted action for their mutual aid or protection.

What Managers Must Do

Under this Act, employers must file a number of reports with the secretary of labor, including the following reports relevant to our subject matter:

1. Reports of any payments, loans, promises, or other agreements to any labor organization, or to an officer, agent, shop steward, or other representative of a union. The report must list pertinent details concerning the transaction.
2. Reports of any person who attempts to persuade employees in favor of or against unionism.
3. Reports of any agreements with a third party who supplies information about a labor dispute involving the employer, unless that information is used solely for administrative, arbitral, or judicial proceedings; also exempted from reporting is anyone who is not a direct or indirect party to the agreement. Regular officers, supervisors, or employees of an employer who do not receive payment over and above their normal compensation are exempt, as are advisers, consultants, or legal representatives.

Criminal Penalties

Not more than $10,000 or imprisonment for up to five years or both, plus civil remedies in the LMRA

Enforcement

Federal district court

Index

absenteeism, 108
absolute privilege, 114, 123
access laws, 115
accommodation
    of alcoholics and drug addicts, 189–191
    of handicapped, 188–189
acknowledgment, by employee, 217
advertising, *see* want ads
affiliations, application form questions
    on, 35
affirmative action, xvii, 48, 57–58
    U.S. Supreme Court on, 266, 269
age discrimination, xv, 270–272
    in want ads, 14–15
Age Discrimination in Employment Act
    of 1967, 246–247, 290–292
age groups, 271
age harassment, 248
    policy to prevent, 251
agency and employer liability, 145
AIDS, 179, 186–188
    testing for, 125–126
alcoholics, accommodation of, 189–191
alcohol use, 182
Americans With Disabilities Act of 1990,
    178, 274
Anti-Defamation League of B'nai B'rith,
    51
antinepotism policies, 62, 76, 151
arbitrary replacement, 248
arrest records, on job application, 26
audit systems, for appraisal program,
    102–103

background checks, 83–85
beards, 183–184
behavior, unwelcome, 145
benefit plans, xii
    and age discrimination, 249
BFOQ (bona fide occupational qualifica-
    tion), 3–4, 16, 47, 54, 75, 79
    and sex discrimination, 60
bilateral contract, 206
birth date, on job application, 26
breach of contract, xiv
brochures, discriminatory language in,
    23–24
building a file, 110, 166, 221
burden of proof, 5, 56
business trips, companion on, 165

cause of action, 86
childbearing and child care, 40–43
citizenship, proof of, 36
civil rights, xvi, 268–270
Civil Rights Act of 1964, 1, 281–283
Civil Rights Law of 1866, 3, 56
civil rights laws, 44
    and effective management, 3
class, protected, 3, 47, 143
cohabitating unmarried couples, 151
committee, for hiring decisions, 46–47
communication, 255
comparable worth, 7, 62, 74
compensation system, dual, 64–65, 74–75
compensatory damages, 141
condescension, 144

311

conflicts of interest, 151
consent, sexual harassment and, 170–172
consent decree, 57
Constitution, U.S., and privacy, 113
constructive discharge, 208
contagious diseases, 184–186
contemporaneous complaints, 155
contract, 206, 268
   discipline procedures as, 225–227
   and good faith, 267–268
   procedure manual as, 224–225
contractors, independent, 91–92
convictions, information on, 81
counseling, for older workers, 250–251
couples, unmarried, 151
crime convictions, 35

danger, imminent, 53
decision making, in layoffs, 258–259
defamation, xiv, 114–118, 123–125, 134
   and firing, 240–242
   implicit, in self-publication, 140–141
demon's jaws, 98
demotion of employees, 256–257
disabilities, job application form questions on, 35
disability leaves, for maternity, 163–164
disabled people, 178–192, 274
discharge
   alternatives to, 152
   constructive, 208
   in policy manual, 221–222
   retaliatory, xiv
   wrongful, xiv, xvi
discipline, 210–211
   equal application of, 109
   procedures as contract, 225–227
   record keeping for, 250
disclaimers, 207–208, 215–216
discrimination, 4
   intentional, 5
   objective records and, 108–109
   reverse, 48
   see also specific types
diseases, contagious, 184–186
doctrine of respondeat superior, 80, 84
documentation
   legality of, 109–110
   of performance appraisals, 99–103
   retroactive, 96
drug addicts, accommodation of, 189–191
drug testing, 117, 120–121, 126–129
drug use, 182
dual compensation system, 64–65, 74–75

due care, 80
due process, 113, 235

early retirement, 252–254
emotional problems, 82
employee handbooks, 208, 211–214
   disclaimer in, 216
employees
   acknowledgment by, 217
   acknowledgment of warning to, 101–102
   definition of, 91–92
   demotion of, 256–257
   liability for former, 140–141
   rights of, xiii
employer liability, in sexual harassment claims, 155–156
employer's right to know, 114
employment application, *see* job application forms
employment-at-will doctrine, xvi, 205, 209, 214–215
   preserving, 223–224
employment decisions, 44–58
environment, hostile, 144–145
epilepsy, 179
equal employment opportunity, 1–3, 266
Equal Employment Opportunity Commission, 49
   on evidence of age harassment, 248–249
   guidelines from, 4–5
   Guidelines on Sex Discrimination, 42, 146, 154, 171, 288–289
Equal Pay Act, 7, 65, 71, 75
equal pay for equal work, 62–63
equal treatment, in interviewing practices, 41–43
evaluations, *see* performance appraisals
evidence, in court, 24
Executive Order No. 11,246, 284–287
exempt employees, 198–199
explicit contract, 206

Fair Labor Standards Act of 1938, 7, 194, 196, 198–199, 303–305
   limitations on management by, 196
   and management rights, 198–199
fairness, in personnel matters, 152
family vs. career, 273
Federal Employee Polygraph Protection Act, 122
federal government, xviii
Federal Mediation Service, 197

firing, 205–208
  for conduct outside workplace, 132–133
  explanations for, 118–119
  for refusal to submit to drug testing, 128–129
  for sex change operation, 69–70
First Amendment, 51
  and employee rights, 233–235
Freedom of Information Act, 115–116
freedom of religion, 51, 113
fringe benefits, *see* benefit plans

generalization, 39–40
generally accepted accounting principles, 240
goals, job appraisals and, 98–99
good faith, 207, 267–268
government agencies, absolute privilege of, 114–115
government record keeping, 43

halo effect, 98
handicapped people, 179
  accommodation of, 188–189
  beards and, 183–184
  managing, 180–183
harassment, *see specific types*
health questions, 35
high blood pressure, 179
high school diploma, 13
hiring practices, 1–9, 44–56
  by committee, 46–47
  equal opportunity in, 1–3
  and guidelines for spouses, 76–77
  nepotism in, 67–68
  promotion in, 64
  religious beliefs and, 50–52
  subjective criteria in, 45–46, 54–55, 68–69
homosexuality, 70
honesty, 241
hostile environment, 144–145, 172–174

ignorance, ix, 2
immigrants, 266
immigration laws, 36
imminent danger, 53
impaired person, 179
implicit (implied) contract, 206–207
independent contractors, 91–92
in-house publications, discriminatory language in, 23–24
intent, 5, 56
intentional torts, 129

interviewing practices, 25–43
  equal treatment in, 41–43
  for performance evaluation, 102
  questions for, 25, 26, 34, 36–39
investigation, of sexual harassment, 157, 160–161

job application forms
  discrimination and, 7
  protected characteristics in, 26
  safe questions on, 34–36
  sample of, 27–34
job descriptions, 17–22
job history, gaps in, 81
job profiles, 17–22
job-relatedness of interview questions, 36–37
job security, 211, 226, 227
judicial discretion, 24
jury duty, 231

labor issues, xii
labor laws, 193–203
Labor Management Relations Act of 1947, 194, 195, 197–198, 306–308
Labor-Management Reporting and Disclosure Act of 1959, 194–195, 196, 199, 309–310
laws, employee ordered to violate, 231–232, 239–240
lawsuits, xvi–xviii
layoffs
  and age discrimination, 249
  decision making in, 258–259
  vs. transfers, 260–261
leaves, 182
legal rights, 232–233
liability
  agency and employer, 145
  of employer for sexual harassment, 174–176
libel, 115
lie detector tests, 80, 117, 122–123, 132

major life activities, 179
malice, 115, 135–136, 138
  absence of, as protection, 138–140
management
  costs of mistakes by, xv–xvi
  effective, civil rights laws and, 3
  proactive, ix
  and union, 201–203
Management Activities Table, ix
Management by Objectives, 99
management practices, 89–92
maternity leaves, 148–149, 163–164

medical questions for women only, 37, 39
medical screenings, mandatory, 116, 120
mental problems, 82
military service discharge, 81
minimum hourly wage, 196
minorities, 46–47, 266
Mommy Track debate, 272

narratives, in job assessment, 100
National Labor Relations Act of 1935, xii, 193–194, 195, 197, 300–302
negligence, in hiring, 79–92
nepotism, 76
nonunion employees, 193

objective records
    and discrimination, 108–109
    misusing in performance evaluation, 95–96
objectives, business vs. personal, ix
occupational safety and health, xii
"off duty" privacy, 117, 122
offers, acceptance of by older employees, 48–50
office
    right to inventory, 122, 131
    searches of, 117
older employees, 246–263
    guidelines for managing, 250–255
    layoffs vs. transfers, 260–261
    offer acceptance by, 48–50
    salaries of, 249
outrageous conduct, 207

parole, 82–83
partners, selecting on basis of gender, 168–170
pay distinctions, and discrimination, 7
peer review, 103
people management, categories of, viii
performance appraisals, 93, 96–98
    documentation of, 99–103
    goals and, 98–99
    interview for, 102
    personnel decisions based on, 103–105
    potentially defamatory statements in, 136
    and promotion, 106–107
    rating scales for, 100
    subjective criteria in, 94–95
performance standards, and handicapped management, 182
personal objectives of employees, ix
personal relationships, in business, 154

personnel files, 100–101
    confidentiality of, 114
physical force, 174
physical impairment, 178–179, 184–186
policies
    and employment-at-will doctrine, 216–217
    to prevent sex discrimination, 63, 67
policy makers, ix–x
policy manuals, viii
    and employment-at-will doctrine, 215
    performance appraisals in, 93
policy statements, 218–220
    vs. procedures, 220
polygraph tests, 80, 117, 122–123, 132
pranks, 237–238
pre-employment tests, 7
pregnancy, 40–43, 147, 150–151
Pregnancy Discrimination Act of 1978, 53
prehire screening, 79
prejudice, 2
privacy, *see* right to privacy
Privacy Act of 1983, 115
privilege, 114, 136–140
proactive management, ix, 47
probation, 82–83
procedures, 220–221
    and employment-at-will doctrine, 216–217
    and layoff decisions, 224–225
promotion, 174
    as hiring, 55, 64
    pay raises after, 73–74
    rejecting women employees for, 153
    subjectivity in, 104
    from within, 95, 103–104, 107–108
proof of citizenship, 36
protected class, 3, 47
    mistreating, 143
psychiatric treatment, confidentiality of, 133–134
public morals, 231, 238
public policy, xiv, 230–231
    and civil rights, 268–270
    and firing, 230–245
punitive damages, 128, 141
perjury, 232

race discrimination, xv, 273
rating standards, objective, 106
reasonable accommodation, 179, 181
reciprocal review, 103
record keeping, of disciplinary actions, 250
recruiting guide, 17, 18, 20–21

recruiting materials, 23
  sexism in, 60–61, 63–64
recruiting practices, 11–24
red circle wage rates, 72
reference checks, 81, 83–85, 125
reference letters, 119
Rehabilitation Act of 1973, 178, 184–186, 274, 293–296
religion
  and hiring process, 50–52
  job application form, questions on, 26
remedial action, 175
  for sexual harassment, 156
reorganization, age discrimination and, 249, 250, 257–258
reprimands, 210
respect, lack of, as discrimination, 167–168
retaliatory discharge, xiv
retroactive documentation, 96
reverse discrimination, 48, 57–58
right of refusal, 49–50
right to apply for job, 61–62
right to fire, *see* employment-at-will doctrine
right to inventory office, 122, 131
right to privacy, 112, 116–119, 124
  Constitutional amendments on, 113
  and employer rights, 114, 129–131
  and handicapped, 188
  in personnel matters, 152
right-to-work papers, 36

Sabbath, work requirements on, 50–52
safe management, xiii, 275–276
safety problems, xii
salaries, of older workers, 249
screening, prehire, 79
searches and seizures
  in office, 117
  policies on, 121–122
  unreasonable, 113, 125–126
self-publication, 119, 140–141
seniority, and demotion, 256
sex change operation, firing for, 69–70
sex discrimination, xiv, 59–78, 143, 144, 272–273
  avoiding, 63
  forms of, 146–148
  and glass ceiling, 272
  lack of respect as, 167–168
  and men, corporate policy re, 273
  in medical questions, 37, 39
  U.S. Supreme Court and, 169–170
  in wages, 70–72
  in want ads, 14

sexism, 144
sexual conduct, and employment opportunities, 167
sexual harassment, xiv, 143, 144–145
  consent and, 170–172
  forms of, 146–148
  investigation of, 153–156, 157, 160–163
  policy prohibiting, 157, 158–160
  quid pro quo, 144
  remedial action for, 156
  witnesses to, 163
  see also hostile environment
slander, xiv, 115, 135–136
spouses, 151
  hiring guidelines for, 76–77
  maternity benefits for, 149–150
  and work rights, 62
stereotypes, 169
strangers, rights of, 57
subjective criteria, in performance evaluations, 94–95
substantial compliance, 213

Taft-Hartley Act, 194, 306–308
tardiness, 108
termination-at-will doctrine, *see* employment-at-will doctrine
termination practices, *see* firing
tokenism, 144
tort law, 128–129
toxic environments, protecting women from, 52–54
training, 56, 73
  for older workers, 250–251
transfers, vs. layoffs, 260–261

unfair labor practices, 200–201
unilateral contract, 206, 212
  personnel handbook as, 211, 227
unintentional torts, 129
union elections, 202–203
union organizing campaign, 200–201
unreasonable searches and seizures, 113, 125–126
unwelcome behavior, 145
U.S. Department of Transportation, 117
U.S. Supreme Court, xvii–xviii, 41–42, 51, 57, 272
  on affirmative action, 266, 269
  on sex discrimination, 169–170

verbal abuse, 144
Vietnam Era Veterans Readjustment Assistance Act of 1974, 297–299
violence, employer liability for, 85

voluntary data record survey, 42
voting, employee time off for, 231

wage discrimination, 70–72
Wage-Hour Act, 194
waiver of rights, 232–233
  to workers comp, 242–243
want ads, 11–18
  sexism in, 68
  study of, 16
whistleblowing, 233–235
window dressing, 144

women, 266
  career paths of, 272
  in hiring process, 46–47
  medical questions for, 37, 39
  protection of from toxic environments,
    52–54
  rejecting for promotion, 153
  in work force, 59
word-of-mouth hiring, 67–68
work force, composition of, 266
working conditions, 166–167
work-related losses, 243–244
wrongful discharge, xiv, xvi